A Treasury of
Nebraska Pioneer Folklore

Compiled by
ROGER L. WELSCH

Illustrated by
Jack Brodie

UNIVERSITY OF NEBRASKA PRESS · *Lincoln and London*

First Bison Book edition: 1984
Most recent printing indicated by the first digit below:
2   3   4   5   6   7   8   9   10

Welsch, Roger L., comp.
    A treasury of Nebraska pioneer folklore. Compiled by Roger
L. Welsch. Illustrated by Jack Brodie. Lincoln, University of
Nebraska Press [1967, c1966]
    xviii, 391 p. 27 cm.
    Includes unacc. melodies.
    Bibliography: p. 384-387.
    1. Folklore—Nebraska. 2. Nebraska—Social life and customs. I. Title.
GR110.N2W4   398'.09782   66-10876
ISBN 0-8032-0192-3
ISBN 0-8032-9707-6 (pbk.)

To my family

Contents

Introduction

Folklore has existed ever since people have lived in groups, told tales, sung, danced, created artifacts, and had common ways of doing things. The word *folklore*, however, was not coined until 1846—possibly as a result of the interest in "popular antiquities" spurred by the publication, in Germany, of the Grimm brothers' collections of fairy tales, legends, and myths (1815–1835). In the United States the systematic study of folklore dates from the last two decades of the nineteenth century, when Francis J. Child, a professor of literature at Harvard, published his five-volume collection, *English and Scottish Popular Ballads* (1883–1898), and the American Folklore Society was founded, with the *Journal of American Folklore* as its official organ (1888).

Because it tells us something about almost every aspect of the life of the people, the study of folklore takes many forms and contributes to a host of disciplines, among them philology, comparative literature, psychology, history, sociology, anthropology, religion, philosophy, and the fine arts. Not surprisingly, with so many fields of study involved, there is a good deal of disagreement on precisely what folklore is and how it may be defined. But the problems and disputes of scholars will not be considered here. *A Treasury of Nebraska Pioneer Folklore* is intended first and foremost for the general reader—in particular, the people of Nebraska, whose heritage it is—and it is to be enjoyed rather than studied.

My object in this introduction is simply to give a brief account of folkloristic activity in Nebraska, incorporating a few pertinent observations on the nature of folklore, and to describe the sources from which the present collection has been compiled. For the benefit of the reader who wants to skip the introduction and get straight to the text, the following is offered as a

ix

guideline: Legends, tales, beliefs, sayings, proverbs, jokes, songs, dances, games, arts and crafts, customs, dialect and ways of speaking, festivals and celebrations, all may come under the head of folklore, *provided* that those forms expressed in words (oral literature) have been learned by hearsay that is, have been transmitted by word of mouth—and those forms that are expressed in action (games, etc.) have been learned by imitation. In short, folklore materials live in the oral tradition: they are not communicated by the printed page, but are passed on first hand from one person to another and from one generation to the next.

One name stands alone in the history of Nebraska folklore research—that of Louise Pound (1872–1958), professor of English at the University of Nebraska, sometime president of both the Modern Language Association and the American Folklore Society, prolific author of scholarly books and articles, and one of the nation's most honored and distinguished scholars. Interest in folklore in this state began with Louise Pound and all subsequent work in the field has revolved about her; even the recently revived Nebraska Folklore Society relies on people who knew Miss Pound or were inspired by her.* The first publication devoted to Nebraska folklore was her *Folk-Song of Nebraska and the Central West: A Syllabus* (1915), edited and with a preface by Addison E. Sheldon, for many years superintendent of the Nebraska State Historical Society. According to Dr. Sheldon, Miss Pound began the collection of Nebraska folksongs about 1905 at the suggestion of Professor H. M. Belden of the University of Missouri, at that time president of the American Folklore Society.

Although Dr. Sheldon's preface is specifically concerned with folksong, much of what he says applies to all types of folklore material collected in Nebraska, and is therefore worth quoting in part:

* The Nebraska Folklore Society was organized in 1962, thanks largely to the efforts of Louise Pound's colleague and friend of many years, Mamie J. Meredith, assistant professor of English, emeritus, University of Nebraska, author of articles on folklore, and president of the American Name Society. The first officers were: G. Thomas Fairclough, president; Mamie J. Meredith, secretary; Robert N. Manley, treasurer; and Jane Shaffer, recording secretary. Among the charter members were John G. Neihardt and the late Mari Sandoz.

In the early settlement of Nebraska were blended two main stocks of American-born ancestry. The larger came from New England, New York and Pennsylvania, via the states of the old Northwest Territory through Iowa. The lesser came from Virginia and the Carolinas through Kentucky, southern Indiana, southern Illinois and Missouri. The former, in the main, gave Nebraska her constitution, laws, political and business framework. The latter, far beyond its numbers, contributed to the oratory, literature and folklore of the new commonwealth. . . .

The material is, as Miss Pound shows, mostly migrant from Europe, often strangely altered in its journey from the Atlantic coast to the Nebraska prairies. I cannot help thinking that there are yet to be found additional songs of purely American origin: for while the medieval minstrel may never have sung here in ivied castles, there dwelt in each pioneer neighborhood of the American frontier the minstrel successor, generally an odd character, half genius and half jester, who was log cabin and sodhouse entertainer, and made his own contributions of song and story to the stock he had inherited. Many of these, I know, have lived in Nebraska.

Beside the folksong of Nebraska in the English tongue there is another folksong, more varied in its origins. Included in it are the songs of the Nebraska Indians, especially those of the Pawnee tribe; songs of the Canadian voyageurs who were the first white explorers; and folklore of the many European peoples who have found homes here for themselves and their children. . . .

At this point, it may not be amiss to remind the reader that in 1880, at about midpoint in the state's main settlement period, 97,414 of the people in Nebraska—more than 20 per cent—were foreign born, and no less than 168,538 were of foreign stock. [The origin of the foreign born, as shown in the Tenth Census, was as follows: Germany, 31,125; Sweden, 10,164; Ireland, 10,133; Bohemia (Czechoslovakia), 8,858; England and Wales, 8,831; British America, 8,678; Denmark, 4,511; Russia, 3,281; Austria, 2,346; Scotland, 2,230; Norway,

2,010; Switzerland, 1,579; Poland, 1,128; France, 749.] In their promotional campaigns to bring immigrants from the Old World to Nebraska, the Burlington and the Union Pacific railroads encouraged group removals, and many of the state's communities were settled on that basis. These European colonies—in Willa Cather's words, "spread across our bronze prairies like the daubs of color on a painter's palette"—often have retained a cultural and national autonomy that has kept alive many of their folksongs, tales, and customs even up to the present day.

Louise Pound's introductory comments on the sources of her folksong material are relevant to the various types of material collected in the present volume. She writes that "Although in every instance the pieces were recovered in Nebraska, the greater part were not learned in this state but brought here from elsewhere . . . from Indiana, Missouri, Illinois, Wyoming, Iowa, Wisconsin, Colorado, New York, etc. For the most part they were preserved in the memory of some dweller in an outlying region, as on a ranch, or by some villager, or they are current in some isolated community. . . . Not many come from city dwellers, and most of the small group which did were learned in childhood on a farm or in a village."

Similarly Miss Pound's chief test for inclusion of an item—"that it has 'lived in the folk-mouth,' and has persisted for a fair number of years"—obtains for folklore in general. Miss Pound emphasizes that a folklore collection "should register what the people have cared to preserve, regardless of questions of origin, or quality, or technique." Thus, a ballad or song was not omitted because it had been, or still was, well known in print—a point that is reiterated when she discusses children's songs, singing games, and rhymes: "Here again the fact that many of these are accessible in books was not allowed to stand in the way of their admission, provided that those reporting them had not learned them from there."

I have quoted Miss Pound in this connection because many of the items in this book were recovered from newspapers of 1870–1900 period and other printed sources. The Songs of the Farmers' Alliance, for example, almost without exception were printed in newspapers. (Some folklorists would claim that these

songs are outside the area of folklore, not because they have
been in print, but because, by one definition, items of oral tradition are materials that by virtue of their age and the method of
their transmission have undergone changes: and in the Farmers'
Alliance songs variations from one version to another are
trivial. On the other hand, another school of folklorists would
accept them as folksongs for they were born of and sung by
"the folk." The reader interested in the pros and cons of this
matter is referred to John Greenway's *American Folksongs of
Protest*, listed in the bibliography.) An example of another kind
of printed material is the body of writing devoted to the adventures of the mythical Nebraska strong man, Febold Feboldson. As will be seen from the account of Febold's origin (page
163), he was the brain child of an individual rather than of folk
creation. While I myself do not consider Febold a folk hero, his
exploits have been accepted as folklore by a number of authori-
ties, including Louise Pound. In her article, "Nebraska Strong
Men," cited on page 163, she writes that "folklore is folklore,
whatever its origin, and Febold now belongs to folklore. But it
is the lore of the literary class, the lore of educated lovers of lore,
rather than of the subliterary, the less educated strata usually
thought of as the 'folk' of 'folklore.' The same may be true, or
is true, of Paul Bunyan. Lore of Paul is now folklore, but it is
the folklore of the reading class. . . ."

Returning again to *Folk-Song of Nebraska and the Central
West*, the discussion there of modes of diffusion—the ways in
which folklore is transmitted—holds true for folktales, legends,
dances, customs, and all other forms of folklore, as well as for
folksongs. Miss Pound writes:

> How did the songs in this collection win diffusion?
> Chiefly they were learned in childhood or youth in the east,
> the south, the north, or in the Old World, and were then
> brought by migration to the middle west. Here they have
> been kept alive in the memory of pioneers, or emigrants,
> and their descendants. Often one acquaintance taught a
> song to another, a member of the same community; or
> sometimes the words were described from hearing [them]
> and preserved in a manuscript songbook or a scrapbook.

The colored minstrels of the past generation who traveled from one section of the country to another giving entertainments undoubtedly gave currency to a surprising number of songs. . . . Still, other songs, those of a religious or moralizing character, were popularized by Moody and Sankey and other revivalists; and some were floated into general currency at temperance gatherings. Another group of popular songs, humorous, sentimental, narrative, gained geographical distribution by their sale in sheet-music form, or with the words only printed, by itinerant vendors of patent medicines and the like, or at booths established in the wake of circuses and wandering bands of entertainers. And, especially, the songs learned and sung in childhood at the schoolhouse have lingered in the memory, and have been handed on in new communities. But very often the exact mode of diffusion and preservation of some popular song cannot now be established.

A firsthand example of the workings of the oral tradition in Nebraska can be found in *Western Story: The Recollections of Charley O'Kieffe, 1884–1898.* Mr. O'Kieffe, who grew up on a homestead near Rushville, in Sheridan County, describes the community Literary and Debating Society which met every other Friday at the schoolhouse, and says:

Because we had so few books, anything which might be suitable for a number on the Literary program was eagerly sought after and preserved, and when a performer could not pick up a new piece somewhere he would give one he had inherited. . . . Our entire community was without a single piece of printed music—excepting maybe somebody had a copy of Gospel Hymns No. 1, 2, 3, or 4—and this meant that all music, whether vocal or instrumental, had to pass from person to person "live." When a song or poem was brought out west from Indiana or Pennsylvania, it had to be picked up and learned by a local resident before he or she could play it at a gathering. . . . Each time a tune or vocal number passed from one person to another some changes would be made, and many words were dropped or mispronounced as it traveled about from mouth to ear.

Mr. O'Kieffe's comment on what the settlers in his neighborhood used to sing is also useful, for it shows why certain kinds of songs gained currency in pioneer Nebraska. There were, he says, songs of "the sad type—many no doubt being used to express the emotion of new settlers in a country that was none too attractive in its early stages"; there were ballads about outlaws and sensational crimes; "strictly local" songs that "pictured the general atmosphere and condition of our new country"; songs that "expressed the loneliness of the prairies and the average cowboy's hankering to be laid to rest in a less dreary country when his final roundup had come"; and "there was this one, popular during the long dry period that sent so many once-hopeful settlers back east to live with the wife's folks:

> Oh, Nebraska land, dear Nebraska land,
> As on thy highest hill I stand
> And look away across the plain
> Wondering will it ever rain
> Till Gabriel comes with trumpet sound
> And says the rain has passed around."
>
> [*For the full text, see page 48.*]

One of the main purposes in publishing *Folk-Song of Nebraska and the Central West*, according to Dr. Sheldon, was "to reach every section of Nebraska with copies of it, stimulating interest, reviving memories now dormant, and bringing to light the texts of many songs familiar to the hearts but unknown to the books of Nebraska." The syllabus, it was hoped, was "the initial step . . . toward the publication of a complete collection, with the full text, of Nebraska folksongs and their music,—which is the ultimate goal." That goal is yet to be realized. In the more than forty years since the start was made, no collection of Nebraska folksongs has appeared in book form, and only two books dealing with aspects of Nebraska folklore—a collection of articles by Louise Pound and *Nebraska Place-Names* by Lilian Fitzpatrick (see Bibliography)—are currently in print.

The most intensive effort to collect folklore materials in this state was undertaken by the Federal Writers' Project in the latter part of the 1930's. The FWP, it will be recalled, was a division of the Works Progress Administration, created in 1935 under the Emergency Relief Appropriation Act to help combat the depression. During the years it was in operation the FWP produced hundreds of books and pamphlets, including the well-known American Guide Series, one volume of which was *Nebraska: A Guide to the Cornhusker State*, published in June, 1939.

An important phase of the FWP's activities was the collection of folklore, for these materials were fast disappearing as the pioneer generations passed away. Many tales and songs, memories and traditional practices, were recorded under this program. In Nebraska, between May, 1937, and December, 1940, the FWP brought out in mimeographed form and distributed to Nebraska schools a series of thirty pamphlets of folklore materials collected and edited by FWP workers. (Some of this material was reprinted in three 32-page brochures, issued between 1939 and 1941.) The pamphlets were meant to be the chapters of a future book, but when World War II brought an end to unemployment the work of collection stopped and the project was shelved. Occasionally compilers of folklore anthologies—as, for instance, Ben Botkin, who had studied with Louise Pound—borrowed a tale or song from the pamphlets, but the rather crude presentation of the FWP materials and their incompleteness discouraged further publication. The Nebraska pamphlets, moreover, suffered from deficiencies common to the FWP studies. As the eminent folklorist Stith Thompson pointed out in *Anthropology Today* (Chicago: University of Chicago Press, 1953): "In some states these inexperienced [FWP] workers were merely told to go out and collect folklore. They were not properly informed as to what they should collect. . . ." As a result, a good deal of what they brought in had no value to the folklorist and much invaluable material was overlooked.

Since *A Treasury of Nebraska Pioneer Folklore* is largely compiled from the Nebraska Folklore Pamphlets, to some extent it is bound to reflect their weaknesses; however, I hope that my selections contain most of the diamonds and only a little of the gravel. While my original intention had been to rely entirely on the pamphlets, in order to present a more rounded and better balanced volume I have supplemented the FWP items with other Nebraska materials. In Part I, I have added four songs from *Folk-Song of Nebraska and the Central West*; in Part II, a group of tall tales from unpublished FWP materials, a version of an Antoine Barada story collected in Louise Pound's "Nebraska Strong Men," and two selections from George Bird Grinnell's *Pawnee Hero Stories and Folk-Tales*; and in Part III, two articles—"Some Old Nebraska Folk Customs" by Louise Pound and "Nebraska Folk Cures" by Pauline Black.

The headnotes to individual items, as well as section introductions, are in part derived from the notes in the pamphlets, and I have also drawn on the works listed in the bibliography under "Works Cited" and "Other Sources." A complete list of the Nebraska Folklore Pamphlets appears in the bibliography, and I have indicated there from which ones I have taken material. Since this volume is directed primarily to the nonspecialist reader, I have eliminated, or incorporated into the text, the footnotes and other scholarly apparatus in the two Part III articles. The selections from the Nebraska Folklore Pamphlets have been lightly edited, misprints corrected, spelling regularized, and punctuation supplied or altered where it has been deemed necessary to prevent a misreading. In a few of the prose selections, the wording of a sentence has been rearranged for the sake of clarity.

Finally, a word about my principles of selection. In addition to the usual folklore criteria, I was guided by what I thought would have the greatest interest and appeal for the people of the State of Nebraska, and limited by the physical dimensions of this volume. Thus, not all types of folklore are represented (proverbial phrases, riddles, dialect, religious songs, and folk verse are among the omissions) and the collections of songs, dance calls, customs, games, sayings, and so on, are far from being exhaustive (suggesting the wealth of available material, Louise Pound's folksong syllabus lists more than 550 songs, and there are around 50 in the Nebraska Folklore Pamphlets, including 17 which also appear in the syllabus). If this volume, in addition to increasing Nebraskans' awareness of the richness of their folklore heritage, provides some impetus toward a definitive scholarly compilation of Nebraska folklore, it will have amply fulfilled my intentions.

ROGER L. WELSCH

Nebraska Wesleyan University

I. SONGS AND DANCES

NOTE

The source of material quoted or paraphrased in the
section introductions and headnotes is indicated by a
number enclosed in parentheses. To ascertain a source,
see the corresponding number in the Bibliography of
Works Cited, pages 384–385.

Songs of Trail and Prairie

When Nebraska became a territory in 1854, its inhabitants numbered less than three thousand, most of them scattered in small settlements on the Missouri River. In 1867, the year that statehood was achieved, the population was estimated at fifty thousand, with an almost continuous line of settlement south of the Platte from Fairbury to Columbus and along the Platte Valley on the north side of the river from Omaha to Grand Island. There were a few homesteaders on the Elkhorn as far north as Norfolk, and a few along the Missouri from Sioux City to the mouth of the Niobrara. Then came a period of dramatic growth and expansion: by 1900 the frontier line had receded to the northwest corner of the state and the population had increased by more than a million.

Twenty-nine of the thirty songs which follow are those that Nebraska pioneers were singing during the years from 1870 to 1900, the three decades that saw the conquest of the wild land and the transformation of a raw, new country into the abiding place of an organized society. The one exception, "The Kinkaiders' Song," dates from the early years of the twentieth century, when the settlement of the Sandhills region brought the curtain down on the drama of pioneer days.

Ranching and farming dominated the Nebraska scene then as now, and this situation is reflected in the songs, which fall into two broad categories: cowboy songs and farmer songs. Even before they fought with shotguns and Colts, wire-cutters and fire, for the possession of the open range, the cowpoke and the sodbuster had little use for each other. They differed in both temperament and conditions of life. One wore chaps and the other wore overalls; one followed a herd, the other a plow; one ate beans and one ate corn; one was a wanderer, the other

3

stayed put. The cowboy was contemptuous of the stick-in-the-mud farmer, and the farmer saw the cowboy as a no-account hell-raiser, bound to come to a bad end. Yet the songs they sang more clearly indicate their kinship than their differences. Both were pioneers, men of the plains, seekers of freedom; and they shared the pioneer characteristics of courage and forti-tude, ingenuity and optimism. They had common enemies in Nebraska's fearsome weather, prairie fires, predatory animals, Indians. Both enjoyed a good dance. And both—as their songs tell us—longed for a handsome woman and lamented her fickleness, both feared a lonely death on the prairie.

To the nomad cowboy and the settler alike, singing was a func-tional, vital part of everyday life. The cowboy sang in the saddle, not only to pass the time but also to soothe the cattle: to reassure them, to announce his approach, to keep the herd from spooking when the cry of a coyote, the snap of a stick, or the rumble of thunder might startle it into a stampede. For the homesteader, singing was an outlet and a diversion: a means of keeping up his spirits when he was alone and a favorite form of entertainment when he joined his neighbors at a gathering.

The songs collected here were taken from Nebraska Folklore Pamphlets Nos. 1, 11, and 16, unless otherwise indicated. The arrangement is chronological by subject-matter: the first song tells of Joe Bowers who crossed the plains in '49, and the last is the song of the men and women who took up homesteads in northwestern Nebraska after the passage of the Kinkaid Act in 1904. The latter song and "The Little Old Sod Shanty," both adaptations of older songs, are the only two for which Nebraska origin is claimed; the remainder were brought to the state from other parts of the country.

JOE BOWERS

Collected by Louise Pound from Francis Withee of Stella. Withee was a freighter on the Denver–Nebraska City trail in 1862–1863, when supplies brought by steamboat to Nebraska City (see map, site 1) were hauled overland by ox train to the Colorado gold fields. Miss Pound has written that "probably no other American song, with the possible exception of 'Frankie and Johnny,' has had so many origins attributed to it" (20). Its authorship has been credited to (among others) a former ambassador to Japan, Mark Twain, and—a more likely candidate—John A. Stone, a song- writer and minstrel known as "Old Put." The song, which was in existence as early as 1854, reputedly had so many verses that a bull- whacker could sing it all the way from Fort Leavenworth to the Rockies without a repetition. According to Miss Pound, some have thought Joe Bowers a real person from Pike County, Missouri, who was one of that army of gold seekers who crossed the plains during the years 1849–1851, after the gold strike at Sutter's Mill, on the Coloma River in California. Others, however, believe him to be merely a typical figure of the time popularized by the ballad.

> My name it is Joe Bowers,
> I've got a brother Ike;
> I come from old Missouri—
> It's all the way from Pike.
> I'll tell you how I came here,
> And how I came to roam,
> And leave my good old mammy,
> So far away from home.

> There was a gal in our town,
> Her name was Sally Black;
> I asked for her to marry me,
> She said it was a whack.
> Says she to me, "Joe Bowers,
> Before we hitch for life,
> You ought to have a little home
> To keep your little wife."

Says I to her, "Dear Sally!
All for your own dear sake,
I'm off to California
To try to raise a stake."
Says she to me, "Joe Bowers,
You are the man to win;
Here's a kiss to bind the bargain."
And she threw a dozen in.

When I got to this country
I hadn't nary a red.
I had such wolfish feelings
I almost wished I was dead.
But when I thought of Sally,
It made those feelings get,
And raised the hopes of Bowers—
I wish I had 'em yet.

And so I went to mining,
Put in my biggest licks;
Come down upon the boulders
Like a thousand ton of bricks.
I labored late and early,
In rain an' sun an' snow.
I was working for my Sally—
'Twas all the same to Joe.

One day I got a letter,
'Twas from my brother Ike;
It came from old Missouri,
And all the way from Pike.
It was the darndest letter
That ever I did see,
And brought the darndest news
That ever was brought to me.

It said that Sal was false to me—
It made me cuss and swear—
How she'd went and married a butcher,
And the butcher had red hair;

And, whether 'twas gal or boy,
The letter never said,
But that Sally had a baby
And the baby's head was red!

IN THE SUMMER OF '60

Collected by Louise Pound. Although rumors of gold in the Pikes Peak area had been in circulation for years, the strike that sparked the Colorado gold rush did not occur until July 6, 1858, when gold was discovered near the mouth of Dry Creek. As Everett Dick tells us, " The rather modest findings of the prospectors were played up in wildly exaggerated accounts by newspapers along the Missouri River in Nebraska, Kansas, and Missouri, . . . and when spring came a full-fledged gold rush was on. All spring and summer, wagons flaunting the slogan ' Pikes Peak or Bust!' streamed westward to the new Golconda, where many of them promptly turned around and rolled back east, their signs now reading ' Busted!' These disappointed gold seekers felt that they had been misled and exploited by the newspapers and business men of the Missouri River communities, and [their] threats so frightened the inhabitants of Omaha that weapons from the territorial arsenal were issued to the citizenry for their protection" (8). But there was gold at Pikes Peak, and the summer of 1860 saw a second rush, not only of prospectors but of families who hoped to settle permanently in the new "promised land." One of this latter group tells his adventures in the following song.

In the summer of '60 as you very well know
The excitement at Pikes Peak was then all the go;
Many went there with fortunes and spent what they had
And came back flat busted and looking quite sad.

'Twas then I heard farming was a very fine branch,
So I spent most of my money in buying a ranch,
And when I got to it with sorrow and shame,
I found a big miner had jumped my fine claim.

So I bought a revolver and swore I'd lay low
The very next fellow that treated me so;
I then went to Denver and cut quite a dash
And took extra pains to show off my cash.

With a fine span of horses, my wife by my side,
I drove through the streets with my hat on one side;
As we were agoin' past the old "Denver Hall"
Sweet music came out that did charm us all.

Says I, "Let's go in and see what's the muss
For I feel right now like having a fuss."
There were tables strung over the hall,
Some was a-whirling a wheel with a ball.

Some playin' cards and some shakin' dice
And lots of half dollars that looked very nice;
I finally strayed to a table at last
Where all the poor suckers did seem to stick fast.

And there stood a man with cards in his hand,
And these were the words which he did command:
"Now, gents, the winning card is the ace,
I guess you will know it if I show you its face."

One corner turned down, its plain to be seen;
I looked at that feller and thought he was green.
Yes, I looked at that feller and thought he was green;
One corner turned down, 'twas so plain to be seen.

So I bet all my money and lo and behold,
'Twas a tray-spot of clubs and he took all my gold.
Then I went home and crawled into bed
And the divil a word to my wife ever said.

'Twas early next morning I felt for my purse
Biting my lips to keep down a curse;
Yes, 'twas early next morning as the sun did rise
You might have seen with your two blessed eyes,

In an ox wagon, 'twas me and my wife
Goin' down the Platte River for death or for life.

THE DREARY BLACK HILLS

During the summer and fall of 1867, as the Union Pacific construction crews forged westward toward Cheyenne (then Dakota Territory), the population of the town soared from zero on July 4, when the site was designated a railroad terminal, to ten thousand, swollen by that rabble of gamblers, saloonkeepers, prostitutes, and assorted bad men who followed end-of-track from one town to the next. Most of the undesirables moved on with the tracklayers, but some "decided to strike roots and found a permanent Hell" (16). Life was comparatively quiet, however, until boom times came again in the mid-seventies, when Cheyenne became a major supply point for gold seekers traveling to the Black Hills. There are several versions of this song, which describes conditions in Cheyenne and the Hills during the rush.

Kind friends, you must pity my horrible tale,
I am the object of pity, I am look quite stale,
I gave up my trade selling Right's Patent Pills
To go hunting gold in the dreary Black Hills.

Chorus:

Don't go away, stay at home if you can,
Stay away from that city, they call it Cheyenne,
For big Walipe or Comanche Bills
They will lift up your hair on the dreary Black Hills.

I got to Cheyenne, no gold could I find,
I thought of the lunch route I'd left far behind;
Through rain, hell, and snow, frozen plumb to the gills—
They call me the orphan of the dreary Black Hills.

(Chorus)

The roundhouse in Cheyenne is filled every night
With loafers and bummers of most every plight;
On their backs is no clothes, in their pockets no bills,
Each day they keep starting for the dreary Black Hills.

(Chorus)

Kind friend, to conclude, my advice I'll unfold,
Don't go to the Black Hills a-hunting for gold;
Railroad speculators their pockets you'll fill
By taking a trip to those dreary Black Hills.

Final chorus:

Don't go away, stay at home if you can,
Stay away from that city, they call it Cheyenne,
For old Sitting Bull or Comanche Bills
They will take off your scalp on the dreary Black Hills.

I Want to Be a Cowboy

Collected by Louise Pound. From this lively description of a cowboy's life, it's apparent that there were two schools of thought about visiting Cheyenne. The song is adapted from "I Want to Be an Angel."

I want to be a cowboy and with the cowboys stand,
Big spurs upon my bootheels and a lasso in my hand;
My hat broad-brimmed and belted upon my head I'd place,
And wear my chaperajos with elegance and grace.

The first bright beam of sunlight that paints the east with red
Would call me forth to breakfast on bacon, beans, and bread;
And then upon my bronco so festive and so bold
I'd rope the frisky heifer and chase the three year old.

And when my work is over to Cheyenne then I'll head,
Fill up on beer and whisky and paint the damn town red.
I'll gallop through the front streets with many a frightful yell;
I'll rope the staid old heathen and yank them all to hell.

The Gal I Left Behind Me

This song was especially popular as a square-dance tune. Although it concerns a cowboy, the song expresses equally well the feelings of the homesteader who left his sweetheart back east.

I struck the trail in '79,
The herd strung out behind me;
As I jogged along my mind ran back
For the gal I left behind me.

Chorus:

That sweet little gal,
That pretty little gal,
The gal I left behind me.

If ever I get off the trail
And the Indians they don't find me,
I'll make my way straight back again
To the gal I left behind me.

(*Chorus*)

The wind did blow, the rain did flow,
The hail did fall and blind me;
I thought of that gal, that sweet little gal,
That gal I'd left behind me.

(*Chorus*)

She wrote ahead to the place I said,
I was always glad to find it;
She says, "I am true; when you get through,
Ride back and you will find me."

(*Chorus*)

When we sold out, I took the train,
I knew where I would find her;
When I got back, we had a smack,
And that was no goldarned liar.

(*Chorus*)

I'VE GOT NO USE FOR THE WOMEN

Collected from R. E. Carlson, who first heard the song when he was growing up in Madison County. He recalled that it was sung by an elderly Norwegian named Elmer Langass, who "had come to this country when in his early twenties. A common story, which had been in circulation for years, was that he had been a Norwegian prince in the old country, and had come to America on account of royal disapproval over a love affair with a commoner. At any rate, he was always known as 'the Prince,' although the title was probably due to his stiff aristocratic bearing, which always lent an

*atmosphere of mystery to everything he did. He was never seen in
the company of women, although it is doubtful if he hated them, as
the title of his favorite ballad indicated. His favorite haunt was the
drugstore, where he showed a special weakness for banana splits
and two-for-a-nickel cigars. Here, comfortably propped up against
the back of the soda fountain, he used to sing this ballad with gusto
and verve, which, in his Norwegian dialect, gave it an irresistible
drollery"* (1).

> I've got no use for the women,
> A true one may never be found.
> They want a man for his money;
> When it's gone, they'll turn him down.
> They're all alike at the bottom,
> Selfish and grasping for all.
> They'll stick to a man when he's winning
> And laugh in his face at his fall.
>
> My pal was a straight young puncher,
> Honest and upright and square,
> Till he turned to a gunman and gambler,
> But a woman sent him there.
> Swift and sure his gunplay,
> Till his heart in his body lay dead.
> When a rascal insulted her picture,
> He filled him full of lead.
>
> All night in the darkness they trailed him
> Through the mesquite and chaparral,
> And I couldn't but think of the woman,
> When I saw him pitch and fall.
> If she'd been the pal she should've,
> He might have been rearing a son,
> Instead of out there on the prairie,
> To be falling by a Ranger's gun.
>
> The cowboy was fatally wounded;
> His chances for life were too slim.
> Where they were putting his body
> Was all that worried him.

He raised his head to his elbow,
And the blood from his wound flowed red.
He looked at his pals grouped about him
And whispered to them and said:

"Oh, bury me out on the prairie,
Where the coyotes may howl o'er my grave,
And cover me over with boulders,
That some of my bones may be saved.
Wrap me up in my blankets
And bury me deep 'neath the ground,
And cover me over with boulders
Of granite so huge and round."

They buried him out on the prairie,
And the coyotes may howl o'er his grave,
But his soul is at rest with its Giver
From the unkind cut that she gave,
And many a similar puncher,
As he rides by that pile of stones,
Recalls some similar woman
And is glad that it's not his bones.

BURY ME NOT ON THE LONE PRAIRIE

Collected from Mrs. Cecile Larson of Lincoln, whose mother sang it as a lullaby. As Louise Pound and others have pointed out, it appears to have been adapted from an English song, "Ocean Burial," telling of a youth dying at sea who had hoped to be buried in the churchyard on a hillside, mourned by his family and sweetheart (19). But his request—"O bury me not in the deep, deep sea, / Where the billowy shroud will roll over me"—is unheeded. On the Great Plains' vast sea of grass, this song in its adapted form was a favorite with both cowboys and homesteaders.

"Oh! bury me not on the lone prairie."
These words came soft but mournfully
From the pale lips of a youth who lay
On the cold damp ground at the close of day.

He had wasted and pained until over his brow
Death's shades were but gathering now.
He thought of home and loved ones nigh,
As the cowboys gathered 'round for to see him die.

"Oh! bury me not on the lone prairie,
Where the wild coyotes will howl o'er me,
Where the rattlesnakes hiss and the wind blows free.
Oh! bury me not on the lone prairie.

"In fancy I listen to the well-known words,
To the free wild winds and songs of birds;
I've thought of home and the cotton bowers,
And the scenes we loved in childhood hours.

"I've hoped to have been laid when I died
In the churchyard there, 'neath the green hillside;
By the bones of my father let my grave be.
Oh! bury me not on the lone prairie."

They heeded not his dying prayer.
They buried him there on the lone prairie
In a little box just six by three.
His bones now rot on the lone prairie.

THE COWBOY'S DREAM

It has been suggested that "The Cowboy's Dream" is connected with "Ocean Burial" (see p. 13) and "The Unfortunate Rake" (see p. 17) because of similarities in sentiment and meter, but the resemblances cannot be taken as proof, for a number of songs embody these same two features. According to Ross Santee (1), the words were written by Will C. Barnes of Arizona to the tune of "The Sweet Bye and Bye," although the melody of "My Bonnie Lies Over the Ocean" can be used. The song first appeared in an article, "Stampede on the Turkey Track Range," in the August, 1895, Cosmopolitan. It is also known by the titles "Roll On, Little Dogies" and "Cowboy's Meditation."

Last night as I lay on the prai - rie_____ and looked at the stars in the sky,_____ I won - dered if ev - er a cow - boy_____ would drift to that sweet by - and - by._____ The road to that bright, hap-py re - gion_____ is a dim, nar-row trail, so they say;_____ But the broad one that leads to per - di - tion_____ is post - ed and blazed all the way._____

Last night as I lay on the prairie and looked at the stars in the
sky,
I wondered if ever a cowboy would drift to that sweet by-and-
by.
The road to that bright, happy region is a dim, narrow trail, so
they say;
But the broad one that leads to perdition is posted and blazed
all the way.

Refrain:

Roll on, roll on; roll on, little dogies, roll on, roll on.
Roll on, roll on; roll on, little dogies, roll on.

They say there will be a great roundup, and cowboys, like
dogies, will stand,
To be marked by the Riders of Judgment who are posted and
know every brand.

I know there's many a stray cowboy who'll be lost at the great
final sale.
When he might have gone in the green pastures, had he known
of the dim, narrow trail.

(*Refrain*)

I wondered if ever a cowboy stood ready for that Judgment
Day,
And could say to the Boss of the Riders, "I'm ready, come
drive me away."
For they, like the cows that are locoed, stampede at the sight
of a hand,
Are dragged with a rope to the roundup, or get marked with
some crooked man's brand.

(*Refrain*)

And I'm scared that I'll be a stray yearling—a maverick, un-
branded on high—
And get cut in the bunch with the "rusties" when the Boss of
the Riders goes by.
For they tell of another big owner who's ne'er overstocked, so
they say,
But who always makes room for the sinner who drifts from the
straight, narrow way.

(*Refrain*)

THE COWBOY'S LAMENT

*Also known as "Streets of Laredo" and "The Dying Cowboy,"
this famous song is related to "The Unfortunate Rake," an
eighteenth-century English ballad; "The Bad Girl's Lament," a
variant most often found in the southern Appalachians; and—
surprisingly—"Saint James's Infirmary," which belongs to the
deep south. In the version below, known throughout the West, the
scene is shifted to Laredo, Texas, and details altered accordingly.
The "Unfortunate Rake" of the earliest version is an English
soldier dying of a venereal disease; he is wrapped in a sheet soaked
with medicine, as was then a common treatment. When the song
traveled to the United States, the soldier became a cowboy but he*

*remained "wrapped in white linen." Another inconsistent detail,
taken over from the parent text, is the cowboy's request that the
Dead March be played on fife and drum, as it would be for a
soldier.*

As I walked out in the streets of Laredo,
As I walked out in Laredo one day,
I spied a poor cowboy wrapped up in white linen,
Wrapped up in white linen as cold as the clay.

Chorus:

"Oh, beat the drum slowly and play the fife lowly,
Play the Dead March as you carry me along;
Take me down the green valley, there lay the sod o'er me,
For I'm a young cowboy and I know I've done wrong."

"I see by your outfit that you are a cowboy,"
These words he did say as I boldly stepped by.
"Come sit down beside me and hear my sad story;
I was shot in the breast and I know I must die.
(*Chorus*)

"Let sixteen gamblers come handle my coffin,
Let sixteen cowboys come sing me a song;.
Take me to the graveyard and lay the sod o'er me,
For I'm a young cowboy and I know I've done wrong.
(*Chorus*)

"My friends and relations, they live in the Nation;
They know not where their boy has gone.
He first came to Texas and hired to a ranchman;
Oh, I'm a young cowboy and I know I've done wrong.
(*Chorus*)

"Go write a letter to my gray-haired mother,
And carry the same to my sister so dear;
But not a word of this shall you mention
When a crowd gathers 'round you my story to hear.
(*Chorus*)

"Then beat your drum lowly and play your fife slowly,
Beat the Dead March as you carry me along;
We all love our cowboys so young and so handsome,
We all love our cowboys although they've done wrong.

(*Chorus*)

"There is another more dear than a sister,
She'll bitterly weep when she hears I am gone.
There is another who will win her affections,
For I'm a young cowboy and they say I've done wrong.

(*Chorus*)

"Go gather around you a crowd of young cowboys,
And tell them the story of this my sad fate;
Tell one and the other before they go further
To stop their wild roving before 'tis too late.

(*Chorus*)

"Oh, muffle your drums, then play your fifes merrily,
Play the Dead March as you go along.
And fire your guns right over my coffin;
There goes an unfortunate boy to his home.

(*Chorus*)

"It was once in the saddle I used to go dashing,
It was once in the saddle I used to go gay;
First to the dram-house, then to the card-house,
Got shot in the breast, I am dying today.

(*Chorus*)

"Get six jolly cowboys to carry my coffin;
Get six pretty maidens to bear up my pall.
Put bunches of roses all over my coffin,
Put roses to deaden the clods as they fall.

(*Chorus*)

"Then swing your rope slowly and rattle your spurs lowly,
And give a wild whoop as you carry me along;

And in the grave throw me and roll the sod o'er me,
For I'm a young cowboy and I know I've done wrong.

(*Chorus*)

"Go bring me a cup, a cup of cold water,
To cool my parched lips," the cowboy said.
Before I turned, the spirit had left him
And gone to its Giver—the cowboy was dead.

(*Chorus*)

We beat the drum slowly and played the fife lowly,
And bitterly wept as we bore him along;
For we all loved our comrade, so brave, young, and handsome,
We all loved our comrade although he'd done wrong.

(*Chorus*)

When the Work's All Done This Fall

J. Frank Dobie reported the following account of this song's origin, which he received from W. W. Burton of Austin, Texas: "We had in our company during the Civil War . . . a fellow named Marshall Johnson from Waco, who was the greatest hand to make songs and speeches that I have ever known. Poor fellow, he got killed in a stampede one fall early in the seventies, up on the Bosque River, and the well-known cowboy ditty, When Work Is Done This Fall, *was made on the occasion" (9). But D. K. Wilgus cites a counterclaim to authorship by O. J. O'Malley, who apparently composed several other popular cowboy songs and may well have written this one (26).*

A group of jolly cowboys, discussing plans at ease,
Says one, "I'll tell you something, boys, if you will listen,
    please.
I am an old cowpuncher and here I'm dressed in rags,
And I used to be a tough one and take on great big jags.

"But I've got a home, boys, a good one, you all know,
Although I have not seen it since long, long ago.
I'm going back to Dixie once more to see them all.
Yes, I'm going to see my mother when the work's all done this fall.

"After the roundups are over and after the shipping is done,
I am going right straight home, boys, ere all my money is gone.
I have changed my ways, boys, no more will I fall;
And I am going home, boys, when work is done this fall.

"When I left home, boys, my mother for me cried.
She begged me not to go, boys, for me she would have died;
My mother's heart is breaking, breaking for me, that's all,
And with God's help I'll see her when the work's all done this
    fall."

That very night this cowboy went out to stand his guard;
The night was dark and cloudy and storming very hard.
The cattle they got frightened and rushed in wild stampede;
The cowboy tried to head them, riding at full speed.

While riding in the darkness, so loudly he did shout,
Trying his best to head them and turn the herd about.
His saddle horse did stumble and on him did fall;
The poor boy won't see his mother when the work's all done this
    fall.

His body was so mangled, the boys all thought him dead;
They picked him up so gently and laid him on a bed.
He opened up his blue eyes and looking all around,
He motioned to his comrades to sit near him on the ground.

"Boys, send Mother my wages, the wages I have earned,
For I'm afraid, boys, my last steer I have turned.
I'm going to a new range, I hear my Master's call,
And I'll not see my mother when the work's all done this fall.

"Fred, you take my saddle; George, you take my bed;
Bill, you take my pistol after I am dead,
And think of me kindly when you look upon them all,
For I'll not see my mother when the work's all done this fall."

Poor Charlie was buried at sunrise, no tombstone at his head,
Nothing but a little board, and this is what it said:
"Charlie died at daybreak, he died from a fall,
And he'll not see his mother when the work's all done this fall."

THE HORSE-WRANGLER

The old-time cowboy boasted about his profession by complaining how hard it was, but if he was the genuine article he would never consider any other kind of work. Although the speaker in this song grumbles like a true cowboy, he clearly qualifies for the title in no other respect. The expression "he'll take you down" means "he'll hire you," and "augured" means "urged." "Set-fasts" are prominent shoulder blades. Regarding the term "cavvyard," Foster-Harris says: "In Texas the horse herd was called the 'remuda,' but as the cattle industry spread northward, the term 'cavvy' came into use up there. Both terms are from the Spanish. A caballada, *strictly speaking, is a band of saddle horses, but that was a little harder for the American cowboy to say than remuda. So he generally made it just cavvyard or cavvy" (12). This song is also known as "The Tenderfoot."*

I thought one spring____ just for fun I'd see how cow-punch-ing was done, And when the round-ups had be-gun, I tack-led the cat-tle king. Says he, "My fore-man is in town, He's at the pla-za, his name is Brown. If you'll see him, he'll take you down." Says I, "That's just the thing."____

I thought one spring just for fun
I'd see how cowpunching was done,
And when the roundups had begun,
I tackled the cattle king.
Says he, "My foreman is in town,
He's at the plaza, his name is Brown.
If you'll see him, he'll take you down."
Says I, "That's just the thing."

We started for the ranch the next day,
Brown augured me most all the way.
He said that cowpunching was nothing but play,
That it was no work at all—
That all you had to do was ride,
And only drifting with the tide;
The son of a gun, oh, how he lied!
Don't you think he had his gall?

He put me in charge of a cavvyard
And told me not to work too hard,
That all I had to do was guard
The horses from getting away;
I had one hundred and sixty head;
I sometimes wished that I was dead.
When one got away, Brown's head turned red,
And there was the devil to pay.

Sometimes one would make a break,
Across the prairie he would take,
As if running for a stake—
It seemed to them but play;
Sometimes I could not head them at all,
Sometimes my horse would catch a fall
And I'd shoot like a cannon ball
Till the earth came in my way!

They saddled me up an old gray hack
With two set-fasts on his back.
They padded him down with a gunny sack
And used my bedding all.

When I got on, he quit the ground,
Went up in the air and turned around,
And I came down and busted the ground—
I got one hell of a fall.

They took me up and carried me in
And rubbed me down with an old stake pin.
"That's the way they all begin;
You're doing well," says Brown.
"And in the morning—if you don't die—
I'll give you another horse to try."
"Oh, say, can't I walk?" says I.
Says he, "Yes, back to town."

I've traveled up and I've traveled down,
I've traveled this country 'round and 'round,
I've lived in the city and I've lived in town,
But I've got this much to say:
Before you try cowpunching, kiss your wife,
Take a heavy insurance on your life,
Then cut your throat with a barlow knife—
For it's easier done that way.

OLD PAINT

"*Perhaps better than any other cowboy creation,*" *writes Alan Lomax, "this song captures the bigness of the West and the love of the Westerner for his wide horizons*" (16). *The unusual phrase "to throw the Hoolihan" means to bulldog a steer by throwing him over on his head rather than twisting him to his side. A bucking horse which pitches forward is also said to throw the Hoolihan. In "Old Paint" the chorus both precedes and follows the first stanza.*

Chorus:

Good-bye, Old Paint, I'm a-leaving Cheyenne,
Good-bye, Old Paint, I'm a-leaving Cheyenne.

I'm a-leaving Cheyenne, I'm off for Montan',
Good-bye, Old Paint, I'm a-leaving Cheyenne.

(*Chorus*)

Old Paint's a good pony, he paces when he can,
Good-bye, Old Paint, I'm a-leaving Cheyenne.

(*Chorus*)

Go hitch up your hosses and give them some hay,
And seat yourself by me so long as you stay.

(*Chorus*)

My hosses ain't hungry, they won't eat your hay,
My wagon is loaded and rolling away.

(*Chorus*)

My foot's in the stirrup, my bridle's in my hand,
Good morning, young lady, my hosses won't stand.

(*Chorus*)

I'm a-ridin' Old Paint, I'm a-leadin' Old Dan,
Good-bye, Little Annie, I'm off for Cheyenne.

(*Chorus*)

I'm a-ridin' Old Paint, I'm a-leadin' Old Dan,
I'm goin' to Montan' for to throw the Hoolihan.

(*Chorus*)

Old Bill Jones had two daughters and a song:
One went to Denver, the other went wrong.

(*Chorus*)

His wife she died in a poolroom fight,
And still he sings from morning to night.

(*Chorus*)

Oh, when I die, take my saddle from the wall,
Put it on my pony, lead him from the stall.

(*Chorus*)

Tie my bones to his back, turn our faces to the west,
And we'll ride the prairie that we love the best.

(*Chorus*)

GIT ALONG LITTLE DOGIES

This familiar song is derived from "The Old Man Rockin' the Cradle," an Irish ballad about a man left with a fatherless child: "Ayie, my laddie lie easy. | 'Tis my misfortune and none of your own, | That she leaves me here weeping and rocking the cradle, | And nursing a baby that's none of me own."

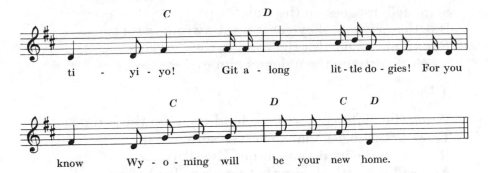

ti - yi - yo!   Git a - long   lit - tle do - gies! For you

know   Wy - o - ming will   be   your   new   home.

As I was a-walking one morning for pleasure
I saw a cowpuncher a-riding along;
His hat was throwed back and his spurs was a-jingling
And as he approached he was singing this song:

Chorus:

Whoopee ti-yi-yo! Git along little dogies!
It's your misfortune and none of my own.
Whoopee ti-yi-yo! Git along little dogies!
For you know Wyoming will be your new home.

Early in the spring, we round up the dogies,
Mark 'em and brand 'em and bob off their tails,
Round up our cayuses, load up the chuck wagon,
Then throw the dogies out on the trail.

(*Chorus*)

Your mothers were raised away down in Texas,
Where the Jimson weed and sandburs grow;
Now we'll fix you up on prickly pear and cholla
And get you ready for the trail to Idaho.

(*Chorus*)

It's whooping and yelling and driving the dogies,
Git along, you little dogies, little dogies, git on!
It's whooping and punching and git along, little dogies,
For you know Wyoming will be your new home.

(*Chorus*)

Some fellows goes up the trail for pleasure,
But that's where they get it most awfully wrong,
For you have no idea the trouble they give us,
As we go driving them dogies along.

(*Chorus*)

When the night comes on we hold them on the bed-ground,
Those little dogies that roll on so slow;
Round up the herd and cut out the strays,
And roll the little dogies that never rolled before.

(*Chorus*)

Oh, you'll be soup for Uncle Sam's Injuns;
"It's beef, heap beef," I hear them cry.
Git along, git along, git along there, little dogies,
You're gonta be beef steers by and by.

(*Chorus*)

THE TEXAS COWBOY

Here's a cowboy who has roamed from Montana to Indian Territory (Oklahoma), and although he seems to favor Nebraska over other states he has visited, to him there is no place like Texas.

Oh, I am a Texas cowboy,
Far away from home.
If ever I get back to Texas,
I never more will roam.

Montana is too cold for me
And the winters are too long;
Before the roundups do begin,
Our money is all gone.

Take this old hen-skin bedding,
Too thin to keep me warm.
I nearly freeze to death, my boys,
Whenever there's a storm.

And take this old tarpoleon,
Too thin to shield my frame.
I got it in Nebraska
A-dealin' a monte game.

Now to win these fancy leggins,
I'll have enough to do;
They cost me twenty dollars
The day that they were new.

I've an outfit on the Musselshell,
But that I'll never see,
Unless I get sent to represent
The Circle or D. T.

I've worked down in Nebraska
Where the grass grows ten feet high,
And the cattle are such rustlers
That they seldom ever die.

I've worked up in the sandhills
And down upon the Platte,
Where the cowboys are good hombres—
They'll never leave you flat.

I've traveled lots of country—
Nebraska's hills of sand,
Down through the Indian Nation,
And up the Rio Grande.

But the badlands of Montana
Are the worst I've ever seen:
The cowboys are all tenderfeet
And the dogies are too lean.

If you want to see some badlands,
Go over on the Dry;
You will bog down in the coulees
Where the mountains reach the sky.

A tenderfoot to lead you,
Who never knows the way.
You are playing in the best of luck
If you eat more than once a day.

Your grub is bread and bacon,
And coffee black as ink;
The water is so full of alkali,
It is hardly fit to drink.

They will wake you in the morning
Before the break of day,
And send you in a circle
A hundred miles away.

All along the Yellowstone
'Tis cold the year around;
You will surely get consumption
By sleeping on the ground.

Work up in Montana
Is six months in the year;
When all your bills are settled,
There's nothing left for beer.

Work down in Texas
Is all the year around;
You will never get consumption
By sleeping on the ground.

Come all you Texas cowboys,
And warning take from me,
And do not go to Montana
To spend your money free.

But stay at home in Texas
Where work lasts the year around,
And you'll never catch consumption
By sleeping on the ground.

TEXAS RANGERS

Said to be the first important ballad of the Far West, "Texas Rangers" became current about the time of the Battle of the Alamo (March 6, 1836) and made a great impression upon the whole country (16).

Come all you Texas Rangers, wherever you may be;
I'll tell you of some troubles that happened unto me.
My name is nothing extra, so it I will not tell—
And here's to all you Rangers, I'm sure I wish you well.

It was at the age of sixteen that I joined the jolly band.
We marched from San Antonio down to the Rio Grande.
Our captain he informed us—perhaps he thought it right—
"Before we reach the station, boys, you'll surely have to fight."

And when the bugle sounded, our captain gave command,
"To arms! To arms!" he shouted, "and by your horses stand!"
I saw the smoke ascending, it seemed to reach the sky;
The first thought that struck me, my time has come to die.

I saw the Indians coming, I heard them give the yell;
My feelings at that moment, no tongue can ever tell.
I saw the glittering lances, their arrows 'round me flew,
And all my strength it left me, and all my courage too.

We fought full nine hours before the strife was o'cr.
The like of dead and wounded I never saw before.
And when the sun was rising and the Indians they had fled,
We loaded up our rifles and counted up our dead.

And all of us were wounded, our noble captain slain,
And the sun was shining sadly across the bloody plain.
Sixteen as brave Rangers as ever roamed the West
Were buried by their comrades with arrows in their breast.

'Twas then I thought of Mother, who to me in tears did say,
"To you they are all strangers, with me you had better stay."
I thought that she was childish, the best she did not know;
My mind was fixed on ranging and I was bound to go.

Perhaps you have a mother, likewise a sister too,
And maybe you have a sweetheart to weep and mourn for you;
If that be your situation, although you'd like to roam,
I'd advise you by experience, you had better stay at home.

I have seen the fruits of rambling, I know its hardships well;
I have crossed the Rocky Mountains, rode down the streets of hell;
I have been in the great Southwest where the wild Apaches roam,
And I tell you from experience, you had better stay at home.

And now my song is ended; I guess I have sung enough.
The life of a Ranger I am sure is very tough.
And here's to all you ladies, I am sure I wish you well.
I am bound to go a-ranging, so ladies, fare you well.

THE RED RIVER VALLEY

According to Carl Sandburg (23), "The Red River Valley" was originally "In the Bright Mohawk Valley." It underwent several changes in the East, moved west, and has enjoyed wide popularity ever since.

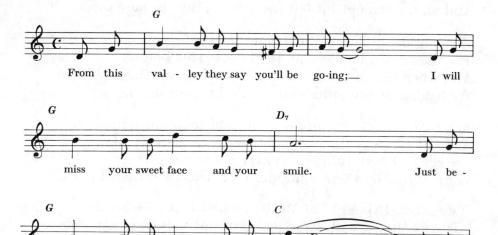

mov - ing your range   for a   while._____   I've been

think - ing a long   time, my   dar - ling,___   Of the

sweet   words you nev - er would   say;   Now a -

las   my fond hopes   have all   van - ished,_____   For they

say   you are go - ing a - way._____   *Chorus:* Then come

sit   by my side   if you   love me;___   Do not

has - ten to bid   me a - dieu.   But re -

From this valley they say you'll be going;
I'll miss your sweet face and your smile.
Just because you are weary and tired,
You are moving your range for a while.
I've been thinking a long time, my darling,
Of the sweet words you never would say;
Now alas my fond hopes have all vanished,
For they say you are going away.

Chorus:

Then come sit by my side if you love me;
Do not hasten to bid me adieu.
But remember the Red River Valley
And the cowboy that loved you so true.

I have promised you darling that never
Shall words from my lips give you pain,
And my life shall be yours forever,
If only you'll love me again.
When you think of the valley you're leaving,
And how lonely and dreary it will be,
Then think too of the fond heart you're breaking
And the pain you are causing me.

(*Chorus*)

GOOD-BYE, YOU OLD DRY LANDERS

Collected by L. C. Wimberly from Pop Adams. The song's implied theme is Nebraska's transition from open range to farms.

"Sizzler-bill" in stanza six is a corruption of "scissorbill," a derogatory slang term which, among other things, meant a know-nothing greenhorn.

A cowboy laid out on the prairie—
Said it was all up with him,
Though he had two pints of good whiskey
And almost a quart full of gin.

His saddle he used for a pillow,
His blankets he used for a bed;
And when he awoke from his slumbers,
These words to himself he said:

"Good-bye, you old dry landers,
You're driving me far from home;
You've set out to plow up the country
Where the slick ears and mavericks roamed.

"No longer we're able to rustle
As in those days gone by."
And he took a drink from his bottle
Of good old eighty-nine rye.

"I was raised on a ranch in Montana,
All I know is to rope an old cow;
I never did work on a sheep ranch
And damned if I'd follow a plow.

"Farewell, you sizzler-bill farmers;
I'm leaving you all at last;
And I hope you succeed in the future
As the cowboys have done in the past."

Sam Bass

Sam Bass was born in Mitchell, Indiana, on July 21, 1851, and was gunned down on his twenty-seventh birthday in Round Rock, Texas. The train robbery referred to in the fourth stanza occurred at Big Springs, Nebraska, on the night of September 18, 1877 (see map, site 2). Joel Collins, Sam Bass, and four other outlaws stopped the Union Pacific's eastbound Number 4 and boarded

*the express car, which was carrying gold from the California fields.
The gang loaded themselves up with sacks of gold coins, but had to
leave $300,000 in gold bullion because the bars were too heavy to
carry. They did, however, take time to rob the passengers—a
mistake, for one of the passengers recognized Collins and the
"wanted" call went out to peace officers. Although Sam was one of
the three who got safely away, there was a bullet with his name on it
awaiting him in Round Rock. Tyler and Terrell, mentioned in
the eighth stanza, are Texas towns.*

Sam Bass was born in Indiana, it was his native home,
And at the age of seventeen, young Sam began to roam.
Sam first came out to Texas, a cowboy for to be—
A kinder-hearted fellow you seldom ever see.

Sam used to deal in race stock, one called the Denton Mare;
He matched her in scrub races and took her to the fair.
Sam used to coin the money, and spent it just as free.
He always drank good whiskey wherever he might be.

Sam left the Collins ranch in the merry month of May
With a herd of Texas cattle, the Black Hills for to see;
Sold out in Custer City and then got on a spree—
A harder set of cowboys you seldom ever see.

On their way back to Texas they robbed the U.P. train,
And then split up in couples and started out again.
Joe Collins and his partner were overtaken soon;
With all their hard-earned money, they had to meet their doom.

Sam made it back to Texas, all right side up with care,
Rode into the town of Denton with all his friends to share.
Sam's life was short in Texas; three robberies did he do,
The passenger and express and U.S. mail cars too.

Now Sam had four companions—all daring, bold, and bad;
They were Richardson and Jackson, Joe Collins, and Old Dad.
Four more bold and daring cowboys the Rangers never knew;
They whipped the Texas Rangers and ran the boys in blue.

Sam had another companion, called "Arkansas" for short,
But Thomas Floyd, the Ranger, cut his career short.
Oh, Tom is a big six-footer and thinks he's mighty fly
But I can tell you his racket—he's a deadbeat on the sly.

Jim Murphy was arrested and then released on bail;
He jumped his bond at Tyler and then took the train for Terrell;
But Mayor Jones had posted Jim and that was all a stall,
'Twas only a plan to capture Sam before the coming fall.

Sam met his fate at Round Rock, July the twenty-first;
They pierced poor Sam with rifle balls and emptied out his
    purse.
Poor Sam he is a corpse and six foot under clay,
And Jackson's in the bushes, trying to get away.

Jim had borrowed Sam's good gold and didn't want to pay;
The only shot he saw was to give poor Sam away.
He sold out Sam and Barnes and left their friends to mourn—
Oh, what a scorching Jim will get when Gabriel blows his horn.

And so he sold out Sam and Barnes and left their friends to
    mourn—
Oh, what a scorching Jim will get when Gabriel blows his horn.
Perhaps he's gone to heaven, there's none of us can say,
But if I'm right in my surmise, he's gone the other way.

JESSE JAMES

Although Missouri, as his native state—he was born at Center-
ville (now Kearney) on September 5, 1847—staked primary claim
on Jesse James, he belonged to the entire West. Nebraska settlers
considered him a compatriot and fellow crusader against the
oppression of the railroads, and it is possible that Jesse was
planning to spend his years of "retirement" on a Nebraska farm.
One of his biographers, Carl Breihan, reprints a letter signed
"Tho. Howard"—alleged to be an alias for Jesse James—
addressed to J. D. Calhoun of Lincoln and inquiring about "160
acres of land for sale in Franklin Co Neb" (4). The letter is dated
March 2, 1882, exactly one month before Jesse's death at the hands
of Robert Ford.

Jesse James was a lad that killed many a man;
He robbed the Danville train.
But that dirty little coward that shot Mister Howard
Has laid poor Jesse in his grave.

Chorus:

Poor Jesse had a wife to mourn for his life,
Three children, they were brave.
But that dirty little coward that shot Mister Howard
Has laid poor Jesse in his grave.

It was Robert Ford, that dirty little coward,
I wonder how he does feel,
For he ate of Jesse's bread and he slept in Jesse's bed,
Then laid poor Jesse in his grave.

(*Chorus*)

Jesse was a man, a friend to the poor,
He never would see a man suffer pain;
And with his brother Frank he robbed the Chicago bank,
And stopped the Glendale train.

(*Chorus*)

It was his brother Frank that robbed the Gallatin bank,
And carried the money from the town;
It was in this very place that they had a little race
For they shot Captain Sheets to the ground.

(*Chorus*)

They went to a crossing not very far from there,
And there they did the same;
With the agent on his knees, he delivered up the keys
To the outlaws, Frank and Jesse James.

(*Chorus*)

It was on Wednesday night, the moon was shining bright,
They robbed the Glendale train;
The people they did say, for many miles away,
It was robbed by Frank and Jesse James.

(*Chorus*)

It was on Saturday night, Jesse was at home,
Talking with his family brave.
Robert Ford came along like a thief in the night
And laid poor Jesse in his grave.

(*Chorus*)

The people held their breath when they heard of Jesse's death,
And wondered how he ever came to die.

It was one of the gang called little Robert Ford;
He shot poor Jesse on the sly.

(*Chorus*)

Jesse went to his rest with his hand on his breast;
The devil will be upon his knee.
He was born one day in the county of Clay
And came from a solitary race.

(*Chorus*)

This song was made by Billy Gashade
As soon as the news did arrive;
He said there was no man with the law in his hand
Who could take Jesse James when alive.

(*Chorus*)

COLE YOUNGER

One of the notorious Younger brothers, Thomas Coleman Younger was born July 15, 1844, in Cass County, Missouri, and fought for the Confederacy with Quantrill's raiders before teaming up with his brothers and Frank and Jesse James to ride the outlaw trail. Their career of crime culminated in the Northfield, Minnesota, bank robbery on the afternoon of September 7, 1876, in which Cole and Jim and Bob Younger were badly wounded and captured. Sentenced to life imprisonment in the state prison at Stillwater, Cole served twenty-five years. Surprisingly enough, he lived out his allotted three score and ten; he died in bed in 1916 at the age of seventy-two.

I am one of a band of highwaymen, Cole Younger is my name;
My crimes and depredations have brought my friends to shame;
The robbing of the Northfield bank, the same I can't deny,
For now I am a prisoner, in the Stillwater jail I lie.

'Tis of a bold, high robbery, a story to you I'll tell,
Of a California miner who unto us befell;
We robbed him of his money and bid him go his way,
For which I will be sorry until my dying day.

And then we started homeward, when brother Bob did say:
"Now, Cole, we will buy fast horses and on them ride away.
We will ride to avenge our father's death and try to win the
    prize;
We will fight those anti-guerrillas until the day we die."

And then we rode towards Texas, that good old Lone Star State,
But on Nebraska's prairies the James Boys we did meet.
With knives, guns, and revolvers, we all sat down to play,
A-drinking of good whiskey to pass the time away.

A Union Pacific railway train was the next we did surprise,
And the crimes done by our bloody hands bring tears into my
    eyes.
The engineer and fireman killed, the conductor escaped alive,
And now their bones lie moldering beneath Nebraska's skics.

Then we saddled horses, northwestward we did go,
To the Godforsaken country called Min-ne-so-te-o;
I had my eye on the Northfield bank when brother Bob did say,
"Now, Cole, if you undertake the job, you will surely curse the
    day."

But I stationed out my pickets and up to the bank did go,
And there upon the counter I struck my fatal blow.
"Just hand us over your money and make no further dclay,
We are the famous Younger brothers, we spare no time to pray."

OLD DAD MORTON

*Collected by L. C. Wimberly from Pop Adams. Concerning the
origin of this song, which is also known as " The Criderville [or
Cryderville] Jail," John A. Lomax cites a letter from a Fort
Worth physician who says it "was composed by Sam Houston, a
white desperado and horse stealer, while he was in jail in Austin,
Texas, in 1880. He was sentenced to twenty-five years in Hunts-
ville. . . . The tune is cynical but lively" (17). Lomax also gives a
version by a writer named C. E. Scoggins who "learned it from
Dad Levins, of Omaha, who learned it sixty years ago as a small*

*boy sitting on the sidewalk outside the jail in Cryderville—
Kentucky, I think; or maybe it's West Virginia; I've never looked
it up." No town of this name is listed for any state in recent
atlases and postal directories.*

Old Dad Morton has got us in jail,
  'Tis hard.
Old Dad Morton has got us in jail,
Both Father and Mother refused us bail,
  'Tis hard.
With the doors all locked and barred,
With a big log chain bound down to the floor,
Damn their fool souls, what could they do more?
  'Tis hard times in the Criderville jail,
  'Tis hard times, I say.

They'll keep us here for a year or two,
  'Tis hard.
They'll keep us here for a year or two,
For makin' a barrel of mountain dew,
  'Tis hard.
With the doors all locked and barred,
With a big log chain bound down to the floor,
Damn their souls, what could they do more?
  'Tis hard times in the Criderville jail,
  'Tis hard times, I say.

Old Judge Tanner will read us the law,
  'Tis hard.
Old Judge Tanner will read us the law,
The damnedest old fool that ever you saw,
  'Tis hard.
With the doors all locked and barred,
With a big log chain bound down to the floor,
Damn their fool souls, what could they do more?
  'Tis hard times in the Criderville jail,
  'Tis hard times, I say.

THE LITTLE OLD SOD SHANTY

This adaptation of W. S. Hays's " The Little Old Log Cabin in the Lane" (1871) may be the work of a Nebraskan, Emery Miller. At any rate, friends of Mr. Miller said that he wrote it while holding down a Nebraska claim.

board roof lets the howl - ing bliz - zards in,___

— And I hear the hun - gry coy - ote as he

slinks up through the grass 'Round that lit - tle old sod

shan - ty on my claim.___

I am looking rather seedy now while holding down my claim,
And my victuals are not always of the best;
And the mice play shyly 'round me as I nestle down to rest
In my little old sod shanty on my claim.

Chorus:

The hinges are of leather and the windows have no glass,
While the board roof lets the howling blizzards in,
And I hear the hungry coyote as he slinks up through the grass
'Round that little old sod shanty on my claim.

Yet I rather like the novelty of living in this way,
Though my bill of fare is always rather tame;
But I'm happy as a clam on the land of Uncle Sam,
In the little old sod shanty on my claim.

(Chorus)

But when I left my eastern home, a bachelor so gay,
To try and win my way to wealth and fame,
I little thought that I'd come down to burning twisted hay
In the little old sod shanty on my claim.

(*Chorus*)

My clothes are plastered o'er with dough, I'm looking like a
  fright,
And everything is scattered 'round the room.
But I wouldn't give the freedom that I have out in the West
For the table of the eastern man's old home.

(*Chorus*)

Still, I wish that some kindhearted girl would pity on me take,
And relieve me from the mess that I am in;
The angel, how I'd bless her if this her home she'd make
In the little old sod shanty on my claim.

(*Chorus*)

And we would make our fortune on the prairies of the West,
Just as happy as two lovers we'd remain;
We'd forget the trials and troubles we endured at the first
In the little old sod shanty on my claim.

(*Chorus*)

And if fate should bless us with now and then an heir
To cheer our hearts with honest pride of fame,
Oh, then we'd be contented for the toil that we had spent
In that little old sod shanty on our claim.

(*Chorus*)

When time enough had lapsed and all those little brats
To noble man- and womanhood had grown,
It wouldn't seem half so lonely as 'round us we should look
And we'd see the old sod shanty on our claim.

(*Chorus*)

Nebraska Variant Verses

Collected by L. C. Wimberly from Kate Deems in Keith County, in 1903.

A bumper crop of corn we raised in 1892;
To dress our wife in silk we thought was plain;
But we sold our corn for thirteen cents, three cents beside a
  share,
So the wife stayed in the shanty on the claim.

(*Chorus*)

Our hogs they died of cholera, our chickens had the pip;
The baby swallowed buttons like a chain;
Our wife was married thirteen years before she saw a dime
When we lived in that sod shanty on the claim.

(*Chorus*)

Yet for all the hardships we went through, we never gave up
  hope,
But plugged the harder till we made it gain,
For love was close beside us in all our ups and downs
In that little old sod shanty on the claim.

(*Chorus*)

STARVING TO DEATH ON A GOVERNMENT CLAIM

*Collected by Louise Pound. Also known as " The Lane County
Bachelor," this song was extremely popular with the pioneers. It is
sung to the tune of " The Irish Washerwoman."*

Frank Baker's my name, and a bachelor I am.
I'm keeping old batch on an elegant plan,
You'll find me out west in the county of Lane
A-starving to death on a government claim.

My house is constructed of natural soil,
The walls are erected according to Hoyle,
The roof has no pitch, but is level and plain,
And I never get wet till it happens to rain.

Hurrah for Lane County, the land of the free,
The home of the grasshopper, bedbug, and flea,
I'll holler its praises, and sing of its fame,
While starving to death on a government claim.

How happy I am as I crawl into my bed,
The rattlesnakes rattling a tune at my head,
While the gay little centipede, so void of all fear,
Crawls over my neck, and into my ear.
And the gay little bedbug so cheerful and bright,
He keeps me a-going two-thirds of the night.

My clothes are all ragged, my language is rough,
My bread is case-hardened, both solid and tough,
The dough is scattered all over the room,
And the floor would get scared at the sight of a broom.

The dishes are scattered all over the bed,
All covered with sorghum and government bread;
Still I have a good time and I live at my ease
On common sop sorghum an' bacon an' cheese.

How happy I am on my government claim,
I've nothing to lose, I've nothing to gain,
I've nothing to eat and I've nothing to wear,
And nothing from nothing is honest and fair.

Oh, here I am safe, so here I will stay,
My money's all gone, and I can't get away.
There's nothing to make a man hard and profane
Like starving to death on a government claim.

Now come on to Lane County, there's room for you all,
Where the wind never ceases and the rains never fall.
Come join in our chorus to sing for its fame,
You sinners that're stuck on your government claim.

Now hurrah for Lane County, where the blizzards arise,
The wind never ceases and the moon never rise,
Where the sun never sets, but it always remains
Till it burns us all out on our government claims.

Now don't get discouraged, you poor hungry men,
You're all just as free as the pig in the pen.
Just stick to your homestead and battle the fleas,
And look to your Maker to send you a breeze.

Hurrah for Lane County, the land of the West,
Where the farmers and laborers are ever at rest;
There's nothing to do but to stick and remain,
And starve like a dog on a government claim.

Now, all you poor sinners, I hope you will stay,
And chew the hard rag till you're toothless and gray,
But as for myself I'll no longer remain
To starve like a dog on a government claim.

Farewell to Lane County, farewell to the West,
I'll travel back east to the girl I love best;
I'll stop at Missouri and get me a wife,
Then live on corn dodgers the rest of my life.

NEBRASKA LAND

Collected by L. C. Wimberly from Cyrus Korben of Chase County, Nebraska. It can be sung to the tune of either "Maryland, My Maryland" or "Beulah Land." When the latter tune is used, the chorus is changed to "Nebraska land, sweet Nebraska land," and the lines "Till Gabriel blows his trumpet sound | And says the rain's just gone around" are added. Settlers in the Dakotas, Kansas, and Saskatchewan knew this song as, respectively, "Dakota Land," "Kansas Land," and "Saskatchewan."

We've reached the land of desert sweet
Where nothing grows for man to eat.
The wind does blow with blist'ring heat
O'er the plains so hard to beat.

Chorus:

Nebraska land, Nebraska land,
As on thy desert soil I stand
And look away across the plains,
I wonder why it never rains.

There is no wheat, there is no oats,
Not even corn to feed our shoats.
Our chickens are so thin and poor,
They come and peck crumbs off the floor.

(*Chorus*)

Our horses are of bronco breed;
They nothing have on which to feed.
We do not live, we only stay;
We're all too poor to get away.

(*Chorus*)

BILL STAFFORD

Collected by L. C. Wimberly from a Chase County settler who would sing it in a lusty voice after he had gotten himself comfortably settled by taking off his wooden leg and downing half a bottle of whiskey (1). Sometimes a long narrative about conditions in Arkansas and the custom there of using pelts for currency is recited between verses, but in the Nebraska version only the fourth line of the third stanza is spoken rather than sung. The first line of the second stanza, missing in the original material, has been supplied.

My name is Bill Stafford; I was born in Buffalo town.
For nine long years and over I've traveled this wide world
    'round.
I saw both woe and mis'ry, but few good days I saw,
But I never knew what mis'ry was till I landed in Arkansas.

['Twas in the year of '82, in the merry month of June.]
I landed in Arkansas one sultry afternoon.
Up stepped a walking skeleton with a long and lantern jaw;
He invited me to his hotel—'twas the best in Arkansas.

"I'll give you fifty cents a day, your wash and board and all,
"And you'll find yourself a different man when you leave old
    Arkansas."
Six months I worked and toiled for this old whiskey bloat.
[*Spoken*] Jeff Harold was his name.
Six feet seven in his boots and lean as any crane.

His bread it was corn dodgers, his beef I could not chaw,
And you bet I was a different man when I left old Arkansas,
And if ever I see that land again, I'll give you to my paw.
It'll be through a telescope from here to Arkansas.

BUT THE MORTGAGE WORKED THE HARDEST

During the hard times of the 1890's, this song, attributed to Will Carleton (1), was quite popular in Nebraska. Although there was no financial relief for their problems, farmers at least could relieve their feelings by singing about them.

We worked through spring and winter,
Through summer and through fall,
But the mortgage worked the hardest—
And the steadiest of them all.
It worked on nights and Sundays;
It worked each holiday;
It settled down among us—
And never went away.

Whatever we kept from it
Seemed almost as a theft.
It watched us every minute;
It ruled us right and left.
The rust and blight were with us—
Sometimes, and sometimes not.
But the dark-browed, scowling mortgage
Was forever on the spot.

The weevil and cutworm,
They went as well as came;
The mortgage stayed forever,
Eating hearty all the same.
It nailed up every window,
Stood guard at every door,
And happiness and sunshine
Made their home with us no more.

Till with failing crops and sickness
We got stalled upon the grade,
And there came a dark day on us
When the interest wasn't paid;
And there came a sharp foreclosure,
And I kind o' lost my hold,
And grew weary and discouraged,
And the farm was cheaply sold.

The children left and scattered
When they hardly yet were grown;
My wife she pined and perished,
And I found myself alone.
What she died of was a "mystery,"
The doctors never knew;
But I knew she died of mortgage—
Just as well as I wanted to.

If to trace the hidden arrow
Was within the doctor's art,
They'd ha' found a mortgage lying
On that woman's broken heart.
Worm or beetle, drouth or tempest,
On a farmer's land may fall,
But for first-class ruination,
Trust a mortgage 'gainst them all.

HARD TIMES

Collected by L. C. Wimberly from Miss Ruby Beaty of Wilcox, Nebraska. Here we have a reasonably complete inventory of the pioneer community's scoundrels, real and imagined.

Come listen awhile and I'll sing you a song,
Concerning the times—it will not be long—
When everybody is striving to buy,
And cheating each other, I cannot tell why.
　　And it's hard, hard times.

From father to mother, from sister to brother,
From cousin to cousin, they're cheating each other;
Since cheating has grown to be the fashion,
I believe to my soul it will ruin the nation.
    And it's hard, hard times.

Now there is the talker, by talking he eats,
And so does the butcher, by killing his meats;
He'll toss the steel yards and weigh it right down,
And swear it's just right if it lacks forty pounds.
    And it's hard, hard times.

And there is the merchant, as honest we're told—
Whatever he sells you, my friend, you are sold.
Believe what I tell you and don't be surprised
If you find yourself cheated half out of your eyes.
    And it's hard, hard times.

And there is the lawyer, you plainly will see,
He'll plead your case for a very large fee;
He'll law you and tell you the wrong side is right,
And make you believe that a black horse is white.
    And it's hard, hard times.

And there is the doctor, I like to forgot—
I believe to my soul he's the worst of the lot!
He'll tell you he'll cure you for half you possess,
And when you are buried, he'll take all the rest.
    And it's hard, hard times.

And there's the old bachelor, all hated with scorn—
He's like an old garment all tattered and torn.
The girls and the widows all toss him a sigh
And think it's quite right—and so do I.
    And it's hard, hard times.

And there's the young widow, coquettish and shy,
With a smile on her lips and a tear in her eye;
But when she gets married, she'll cut quite a dash—
She'll give him the reins, and she'll handle the cash.
    And it's hard, hard times.

And there's the young lady, I liked to have missed—
I believe to my soul she'd like to be kissed.
She'll tell you she loves you with all pretense,
And ask you to call again sometime hence.
   And it's hard, hard times.

And there's the young man, the worst of the whole,
He will tell you he loves you with all of his soul.
He will tell you he loves you, for you he will die,
And when he's away, he will swear it's a lie.
   And it's hard, hard times.

In Kansas

Collected by L. C. Wimberly from a "tobacco-chewing Keith County woman. Her hatred of Kansas was intense . . . because her second husband had come from there, so she always recited this ballad of disparagement with unusual passion and color" (1). *It comes from an Irish famine song, "The Praties, They Grow Small."*

Oh, they chaw tobacco thin
   In Kansas.
They chaw tobacco thin
   In Kansas.
They chaw tobacco thin
And they spit it on their chin
And they lap it up agin
   In Kansas.

Oh, they churn the butter well
   In Kansas.
They churn the butter well
   In Kansas.
They churn the butter well
And the buttermilk they sell
And they get as lean as hell
   In Kansas.

Oh, potatoes they grow small
   In Kansas.
Potatoes they grow small
   In Kansas.
Oh, potatoes they grow small
And they dig 'em in the fall
And they eat 'em hides and all
   In Kansas.

Oh, they say that drink's a sin
   In Kansas.
They say that drink's a sin
   In Kansas.
They say that drink's a sin,
So they guzzle all they kin,
And they throw it up agin
   In Kansas.

Come all who want to roam
   To Kansas.
Come all who want to roam
   To Kansas.
Come all who want to roam
And seek yourself a home
And be happy with your doom
   In Kansas.

KANSAS BOYS

Collected from Edwin Ford Piper, a distinguished poet and educator, who first heard the song when he was a boy in Nemaha County, not too many miles from the Kansas border. A variant, "Cheyenne Boys," appears in Louise Pound's Folk-Song of Nebraska and the Central West.

Come, all young girls, pay attention to my noise;
Don't fall in love with the Kansas boys,
For if you do, your portion it will be,
Johnnycake and antelope is all you'll see.

They'll take you out on the jet-black hill,
Take you there so much against your will,
Leave you there to perish on the plains,
For that is the way with the Kansas range.

Some live in a cabin with a huge log wall,
Nary a window in it at all,
Sandstone chimney and a puncheon floor,
Clapboard roof and a button door.

When they get hungry and go to make bread,
They kindle a fire as high as your head,
Rake around the ashes and in they throw;
The name they give it is "doughboy's dough."

When they go to milk, they milk in a gourd,
Heave it in a corner, and cover with a board;
Some get plenty and some get none,
That is the way with the Kansas run.

When they go to meeting, the clothes that they wear
Is an old brown coat all picked and bare,
An old white hat more rim than crown,
A pair of cotton socks they wore the week around.

When they go to farming, you needn't be alarmed;
In February they plant their corn;
The way they tend it, I'll tell you now,
With a Texas pony and a grasshopper plow.

When they go a-fishin', they take along a worm,
Put it on a hook just to see it squirm;
The first thing they say when they get a bite
Is "I caught a fish as big as Johnny White."

When they go a-courting, they take along a chair;
The first thing they say is, "Has your daddy killed a bear?"
The second thing they say, when they sit down,
Is "Madam, your johnnycake is baking brown."

The Kinkaider's Song

Collected by Louise Pound. This song belongs to northwest Nebraska, the region of the Sandhills and high tablelands, which remained a frontier area during the first decade of the twentieth century. The Kinkaid Act, signed by President Theodore Roosevelt on April 28, 1904, permitted enlarged homestead holdings in thirty-seven counties. The author of the act was Moses P. Kinkaid, congressman from 1902 until his death in 1922. The words, by Edwin Ford Piper, are to be sung to the tune of "Maryland, My Maryland."

You ask what place I like the best,
The sand hills, oh the old sand hills;
The place Kinkaiders make their home
   And prairie chickens freely roam.

Chorus (for first and second verses):

In all Nebraska's wide domain
'Tis the place we long to see again;
The sand hills are the very best,
She is queen of all the rest.

The corn we raise is our delight,
The melons, too, are out of sight.
Potatoes grown are extra fine
And can't be beat in any clime.

The peaceful cows in pastures dream
And furnish us with golden cream,
So I shall keep my Kinkaid home
And never far away shall roam.

Chorus (third verse):

Then let us all with hearts sincere
Thank him for what has brought us here,
And for the homestead law he made,
This noble Moses P. Kinkaid.

Songs of the Farmers' Alliance

The hard times of the late 1880's and of the 1890's brought with them the revival of militant agrarianism and a spirit of revolt which found an effective voice in the Farmers' Alliance party. The Alliance was founded in Illinois in 1879 and was first established in Nebraska in 1880, with the formation of an Alliance in Gage County. The State Alliance was formed in Lincoln the following year. At first membership was meager, but in 1886 more than two hundred local Alliances were chartered in Nebraska, and in 1887 the State Alliance was re-organized as a secret society. In its declaration of principles the Farmers' Alliance was pledged to work for "the education of the agricultural classes in the science of economical government in a strictly non-partisan spirit," but the times and the political situation were such that even if it had wanted to, the organization could not have stayed out of politics.

The developments from 1888 on are summarized in the introductions to Nebraska Folklore Pamphlets No. 18 and No. 20, from which the songs included here were selected.

The Farmers' Alliance party was formally organized in Lincoln, Nebraska, January 5–6, 1888, when delegates from twenty-five counties met in Lincoln. This organization—later absorbed by the nation-wide Populist Party—was an attempt on the part of the farmers of the state to secure, through political means, higher prices for their farm products (hogs and cattle at this time sold for two cents a pound, corn for ten cents a bushel); lower freight rates (it took one bushel of wheat to send another bushel to market); and protection against unfair farm foreclosures.

57

All these grievances had been caused or aggravated by rampant speculation, drouth, and financial panic.

A third party, in those turbulent times, seemed to be the only answer to these problems, since nearly every farmer in the state was dissatisfied with the two major political parties, both of which seemed to favor the large monopolies and Eastern bankers. This attitude was well expressed in a song called "The Hayseed." [For the song text, see page 67.]

Throughout Nebraska from 1885 to 1905, crusading farmers gathered at hundreds of political rallies, barbecues, and picnics to hear orators from among their own people, many of whom had never spoken to a crowd before, discuss the pressing questions of the day. To reach these meetings it was necessary for many farmers to drive in clumsy lumber wagons for long distances. Seemingly endless parades of farm wagons were arranged to impress the spectators. . . . In order to add excitement to these parades and create diversion between speeches at the rallies, songs were sung. Glee Clubs were organized, the most popular of which, the Cat Creek Glee Club of Custer County, became so popular that it sang at the National Populist Convention held in Omaha in 1892.

But for the most part the farmers and their sympathizers did their own singing. They especially liked parodies of familiar verse or ballads, arranged so that they could easily be sung to old familiar tunes . . . .

Pamphlet No. 20 continues:

. . . The present collection continues the recital of the farmers' grievances against the railroads . . . and the banking and political interests allied with them. Throughout the 1890's high freight and interest rates, coupled with ruinously low prices for farm products, monopoly, and speculation, were dispossessing the farmer and arousing him to a reform campaign that produced a lively body of verse and song. In this as in the previous collection, parodies of old favorites—"Bring Back My Bonnie to Me," "Old Dan Tucker," and "John Brown"—brought the songs close to folk sources.

All the following selections appeared in the *Farmers' Alliance* (originally called the *Alliance* and later known by a variety of titles, such as the *Alliance-Independent, Independent, Nebraska-Independent,* and the *Wealth-Makers*), the official organ of the State Alliance, published weekly in Lincoln. Jay Burrows, chairman of the State Executive Committee, moved to Lincoln from Filley to take over its editorship in 1887—the same year he was elected president of the National Alliance—and made it into a dynamic and influential outlet.

The arrangement of the songs is roughly chronological. Date of publication in the *Farmers' Alliance* is given when it is known; the approximate dates of the other songs have been determined by topical references.

ALLIANCE SONG

Written by C. E. Vaughan. Collected from the Farmers' Alliance, October 4, 1890. By the middle of 1890 the Nebraska Farmers' Alliance had more than fifty thousand members. Songs like this one, which was sung to the tune of "Marching Along," suggest the tense, revivalistic nature of their campaign meetings.

The farmers are gathering from near and from far,
The Alliance is sounding the call for the war.
The battle is raging, it will be fearful and long,
We'll gird on our armor and be marching along.
The battle is raging, it will be fearful and long.
Men are before us that would lead us astray,
But let us not follow or turn from the way;
The password our strength, be this ever our song,
We'll join the Alliance and go marching along.
We've 'listed for life and will camp on the field;
With faith in the Alliance we never will yield.
United we stand, both trusty and strong,
We will pull together and be marching along.
Through hardships and trials our gold we must bring,
For here we contend against monopolies' ring;
But one thing is certain, we cannot go wrong,
If we pull all together while marching along.

Chorus:

Marching along, we are marching along,
Stand by each other while marching along.
The battle is raging, 'twill be fearful and strong,
Then pull all together while marching along.

MARCHING FOR FREEDOM

Written by Mrs. J. T. Kellie to the tune of "Marching Through Georgia." Collected from the Farmers' Alliance, August 23, 1890. John H. Powers, whom the song celebrates, was elected president of the Alliance in 1889. A Civil War veteran who lived in a sod house on his homestead in Thayer County, he was the Independent candidate for governor in 1890 and lost to the Republican candidate, James E. Boyd, by the narrow margin of 1,144 votes.

The farmers of Nebraska now are in a fearful plight,
For years they have been worse than slaves; it is a woeful sight
To see the way they have been robbed by banks and railroads'
    might—
But now they are marching for freedom.

Chorus:

Hurrah for Powers, a farmer true and grand;
Hurrah! For Powers we pledge our heart and hand—
And ne'er again shall lawyer or banker rule our land—
For we are marching for freedom.

Oh, never more to party rule the farmer's knee shall bow,
To work his own salvation out he takes a solemn vow;
He'll vote for home and justice, for wife and baby now,
For we are marching for freedom.

(Chorus)

No banks shall corner the exchange provided by the State,
No speculators shall get rich on wealth that we create,
No railroad e'er again shall tax three-fourths our crops for
    freight,
For we are marching for freedom.

(Chorus)

THE DONKEY'S SONG

*Written by Mrs. J. T. Kellie to the tune of "When Johnny
Comes Marching Home." Collected from the* Farmers' Alliance,
*September 6, 1890. Among the anti-Alliance figures mentioned are
Church Howe of Nemaha County, who introduced a resolution in
the legislature that "the so-called Farmers' Alliance, being a
private and non-representative body, has no right or title to speak
in behalf of the farmers of the state . . ."; George W. Holdrege,
general manager of the Burlington Railroad's Lines West; and
Thomas Benton, president of the Western Exchange Fire and
Marine Insurance Company, representative of the railroads, and
moneylender (at the usual exorbitant interest rate). The song's first
three lines are spoken rather than sung. "Yonc huh, yonc huh"
imitates the bray of a donkey.*

As I close to the railroad camp passed the other day,
I much delighted was to hear the long-eared donkey's bray,
It sure was Howe's and Holdrege's voice and this they seemed
    to say:

Oh, Thomas Benton is his name,
    Yonc huh, yonc huh,
That is well known to railroad fame,
    Yonc huh, yonc huh,
Lease traitor to the railroads turned,
But to his sorrow soon he learned,
We had our way
When Tommy was on the board.

When Tommy gets on the board again,
    Yonc huh, yonc huh,
When Tommy gets on the board again,
    Yonc huh, yonc huh,
Us poor railroads will have to show—
For by the past we surely know
We'll have our own way
When Tommy is on the board.

Oh, Tommy, we are not afraid—
    Yonc huh, yonc huh,
We keep in mind the bargain made,
    Yonc huh, yonc huh,
To hide the check of brass he stole
He gave a mortgage on his soul,
Which gives us our way
When Tommy is on the board.

When we steal half the farmer's grain,
    Yonc huh, yonc huh,
Shrewd Tommy, he does not explain,
    Yonc huh, yonc huh,
But coolly looks each office o'er
And finds place for one brother more;
Yes, we've our own way
When Tommy is on the board.

Who Has Managed

Written by Mrs. J. T. Kellie to the tune of "Twenty Years Ago." Collected from the Farmers' Alliance, September 6, 1890. The incident referred to in the second verse may have occurred in either 1868 or 1869 ("some twenty years ago") when a large band of Sioux occupied the Republican River valley. In the spring of 1869 General Eugene A. Carr led an expedition against the Sioux, which culminated in the Battle of Summit Springs on July 11. This was the last significant Indian battle on the central plains.

I've traveled through the state, dear Tom,
We long have loved so well,
And what's the matter with things here
I want to have you tell.
The working class are very poor—
I've looked them o'er and o'er—
Say, who has managed this great state
For twenty years or more?

You mind well where the Cottonwood
Flows down towards the Blue,
Where we one time went after wood,
Hid from the bloody Sioux.
Near where the Mayflower schoolhouse stands
They chased the buffalo,
While we up near the bridge were hid
Some twenty years ago.

Soon schooners filled with hardy men
Came o'er the barren plain,
And where last year was prairie grass
Were fields of golden grain.
Snug houses were built and orchards made;
Ah! all we ever knew.
To gain homes, what plots were laid
Some twenty years ago?

Of all the men who helped to change
This land from desert plain,
But very few are left to know;
The others have again

Been driven as we once drove
Red men and buffalo—
Robbed of the homes for which they toiled
Some twenty years ago.

The men who settled up these plains
When they were in their prime
Are gray-haired now—hard toil has made
Them old before their time;
With splendid crops of stock and grain,
They're poorer than before.
Say, who has managed this great state
For twenty years or more

The Negroes of the South, dear Tom,
Before the cruel war,
Were better sheltered, better fed,
And better clothes they wore;
Yet slaves through all the years ne'er worked
So hard on earth before.
Say, who has managed this great state
For twenty years or more

The only ones who've prospered here—
It made my blood to boil—
Were bankers, lawyers, railroad men,
Or men who never toil.
Why should they now own all the wealth—
I've pondered o'er and o'er.
Say, who has managed this great state
For twenty years or more?

THE INDEPENDENT BROOM

Written by Mrs. J. T. Kellie to the tune of " The Star-Spangled Banner." Collected from the Farmers' Alliance, *September 6, 1890. Frequently the man of a pioneering family came west ahead of his wife and children to get settled and the crops planted before they joined him—hence the reference in the first verse to "bachelor's hall." The second verse assails "the free pass bribery system"—*

the railroads' practice of issuing free passes to every elected official from dogcatcher to governor. Some of the emotion aroused by the words of the song may have been dampened by the fact that it is virtually unsingable.

Oh, say did you ever in years long gone by,
When you bachelor's hall were so lonesomely keeping,
To sweep with an old lopsided broom try?
If so, you when done surely felt like weeping.
To clean up a room you will own, I presume,
In twenty-four years one should have a new broom.
The dust it will raise may be stifling and great,
But the broom Independent will clean up the state.

On the floor thickly strewn all over the state
Are sown in confusion the railroad free passes.
The new broom will soon sweep them in piles that are great,
And the proceeds we'll use for the good of the masses.
Bring to light soon, it must, laws now hidden by dust,
Brighten up constitution now covered with rust,
Yes, it will soon have everything in shipshape—
The new broom Independent that's sweeping the state.

And thus was it ever when freemen did strive
To clean up rubbish laws which create the rich classes.
To let freedom's light in so people might thrive,
Brush the dust from the laws made to protect the masses.
Then the beauty is seen of the broom new and clean,
You must surely admire the broom that I mean;
'Tis the broom Independent, new, honest, and straight,
With which brave sons of toil are now sweeping the state.

DEAR PRAIRIE HOME

Written by Mrs. J. T. Kellie to the tune of "Nellie Gray."
Collected from the Farmers' Alliance, *September 27, 1890. After a summer which had dried up their crops, the farmers spent the energy which would have gone into harvesting in politicking. A Populist picnic in Lincoln on September 1 was attended by 20,000 people; at a meeting on September 23, at Wymore, more than a thousand farmers' wagons were in the parade; and 1,600*

wagons were counted in a parade at Hastings on the same day. Since the threat of mortgage foreclosure darkened many a household at this time, songs like "Dear Prairie Home" were sung with heartfelt feeling.

There's a dear old homestead on Nebraska's fertile plain
Where I toiled my manhood's strength away;
All that labor now is lost to me, but it is Shylock's gain,
For that dear old home he claims today.

Chorus:

Oh, my dear prairie home! Never more in years to come
Can I call what I made by toil my own;
The railroads and banks combined, the lawyers paid to find
Out a way to rob me of my home.

When first I took that prairie home, my heart was free and light,
And I sang as I turned the prairie sod;
My hair that then was thick and brown today is thin and white,
And I've lost all faith in man or God.

(*Chorus*)

It was many years ago that I first saw through this scheme,
And I struggled from their meshes to get free;
But my neighbors all around me then were in a party dream,
And they voted to rob my home from me.

(*Chorus*)

Now their homes are gone as well as mine, and they're awake at
    last,
And they see now the great injustice done;
While some few their homes may save, yet the greater part,
    alas!
Must be homeless for all time to come.

(*Chorus*)

We must now the robbers pay for a chance to till the soil,
And when God calls us over the great range,
All Heaven will be owned, I s'pose, by men who never toil,
So doubt if we notice the exchange.

(*Chorus*)

THE HAYSEED

Written by Arthur Kellog to the tune of "Save a Poor Sinner Like Me." Collected from the Farmers' Alliance, *October 4, 1890.*

I was once a tool of oppression,
And as green as a sucker could be;
And monopolies banded together
To beat a poor hayseed like me.

The railroads and old party bosses
Together did sweetly agree;
And they thought there would be little trouble
In working a hayseed like me.

But now I've roused up a little,
And their greed and corruption I see;
And the ticket we vote next November
Will be made up of hayseeds like me.

THE PAUPER'S COWHIDES

Written by Mrs. J. T. Kellie to the tune of "Kingdom Coming." Collected from the Farmers' Alliance, *October 4, 1890. Bartlett Richards, mentioned in the first line, was a rancher and president of the Nebraska Land and Feeding Company which operated the Spade, Bar C, and Overton ranches—a spread of more than a half-million acres in Cherry, Sheridan, and Box Butte counties. In 1905 Richards and William G. Comstock pleaded guilty to the charge of having illegally fenced 212,000 acres of government land.*

Say, Richards, have you seen the paupers,
With a mortgage on their lands,
Going to Congress with their cowhides
And honest, horny hands?
They saw the schemers each year stealing
Their hard-earned crops away,
And their sod houses they are leaving
To right their wrongs today.

Chorus:

To Congress now, ho! ho!
The cowhide boots will run.
This must be the hayseed jubilo,
And the pauper's kingdom come.

Money-changers say that by no paupers
Their demands shall be denied;
They scorn them now as long ago
Scorned a pauper crucified.
They judge men by the wealth they've stolen
And the patent boots they wear.
Say drones of earth alone can rule us,
That no cowboy rule they'll bear.

(*Chorus*)

They used to tan the skins of paupers
Down in the eastern land,
But Richards' patent turns them out
With skins already tanned.
But the bankers' power will soon be broken;
Their gold will lose its sway.
When the cowhide boots get into Congress,
They'll bring a better day.

(*Chorus*)

WE'LL MEET YOU BY AND BY

Collected by Louise Pound. The most popular singing group to perform at Alliance-Populist meetings, according to Addison E. Sheldon, was Custer County's Cat Creek Glee Club: S. R. Brown, Harvey Brown, S. Brown, and Thomas Emrich. "The club possessed fresh voices, ready wit, and soon became general favorites at all the early Farmers' Alliance and Populist gatherings. They sang during the campaigns of 1890 to 1896 and appeared at the National Populist Convention held at Omaha in 1892. . . . ['We'll Meet You By and By' was] one of the most characteristic of their songs and the one which never failed to evoke wild enthusiasm" (19).

W. V. Allen, mentioned in the first verse, was Populist United

*States senator from Nebraska for six years (1893–1899); O. M.
Kem was elected Populist congressman from the third district in
1890 and re-elected in 1892 and 1894. W. M. Taylor, referred to
in the third verse from the end, was elected to the legislature on the
Farmers' Alliance ticket in 1890. "He fled the state in the winter
of 1891 when the legislature was in session and the maximum railroad rate bill was pending. His vote was needed to pass the bill
and it was generally believed that he was paid several thousand
dollars to 'sell out' and leave the state"* (19).

> I have heard W. V. Allen preach
> And I've heard O. M. Kem tell,
> There may be a place like Paradise,
> But there's no such a place as ——
> Hallelujah; and we'll meet you by and by,
> Hallelujah; and we'll meet you by and by.
>
> Oh, the campaign is a-coming,
> The fact you all know well,
> The Republicans will do the best they can,
> But you bet we'll give 'em ——
> Hallelujah; and we'll meet you by and by.
>
> English capitalists are a-taking this country,
> The fact you all know well,
> And the fifth of next November
> You can bet we'll give 'em ——
> Hallelujah; and we'll meet you by and by.
>
> Come all you Republicans
> From valley, hill, and dell,
> You'll have to change your evil ways
> Or else you're gone to ——
> Hallelujah; and we'll meet you by and by.
>
> Come all you Democrats,
> You who have votes to sell,
> You'll have to join the Republicans
> Or else you're gone to ——
> Hallelujah; and we'll meet you by and by.

Come all you Prohibitionists,
You who love whiskey well,
You'll have to join the Democrats
Or else you're gone to ——
Hallelujah; and we'll meet you by and by.

Oh, the contest now is a-coming,
The fact you all know well,
Monopolies will do the best they can,
But you bet we'll give 'em ——
Hallelujah; and we'll meet you by and by.

All you northern and southern soldiers,
All you who do mean well,
You'll have to leave the two old parties
Or else you're gone to ——
Hallelujah; and we'll meet you by and by.

O. M. Kem, he is no Taylor,
He has no votes to sell,
But the very next man who sells us out,
Had better be in ——
Hallelujah; and we'll meet you by and by.

Oh say now, Billy Bryan,
The fact you all know well,
You'll have to leave the Democrats
Or else you're gone to ——
Hallelujah; and we'll meet you by and by.

I've sung you now my story,
And I hope I've sung it well,—
But before I sing any more to you
I'll see you all in ——
Hallelujah,—and I'll meet you by and by.

THE ROSEWATER *BEE*

Written by John King of Rock Creek Precinct, Saunders County. Collected from the Farmers' Alliance, *February 14, 1891.*

The Omaha Bee *was established in 1871 by Edward Rosewater, who edited it. A man of fiery temper, Rosewater once (in 1873) took out after another editor, who had written a vitriolic article about him, with a rawhide whip. He was a Republican National Committeeman, and the* Bee *reflected his politics. It argued that the farmer's only hope was to remain loyal to the party. Farmers' Alliance papers, with typical touchiness, viciously attacked Rosewater and the* Bee. *Jay Burrows, mentioned in the first stanza of the song, published the* Farmers' Alliance *(see page 59). Charles Gere, mentioned in the third stanza, founded the* Nebraska State Journal *at Lincoln in 1867, and was its publisher and editor until 1904.*

> The Rosewater *Bee* is a dandy,
> I can't help but watch as he flies;
> He is steering straight for your brain, boys,
> And his sting it is loaded with lies.
> He is ruled by political shysters
> And governed by combines, you see,
> But while you read Burrows' paper
> You'll never get stung by the *Bee*.
>
> This delicate *Bee* is a beauty,
> The finest that eyes ever seen;
> It hives with the Democrat party,
> Intending to hatch a new queen.
> But now the Alliance comes along, boys,
> And sure as corruption's alive,
> With a ticket that's called Independent,
> We'll stir them all up in their hive.
>
> We'll rap on their hive till they swarm, boys,
> We'll stand by and bid them adieu,
> To the bottomless pit of corruption
> Fitted up to receive such a crew.
> Good-bye to the *Bee* and Rosewater,
> *World-Herald*, the *Journal*, and Gere;
> Get out of our sight to the Devil,
> Don't come back for ten thousand years.

A SONG OF THE TIMES

Written by Mrs. J. T. Kellie to the tune of "John Brown." In the spring of 1894 Jacob S. Coxey led a march of unemployed men to Washington, D.C., to petition federal aid. "Coxey's Army" had dwindled to 336 marchers when it reached the capital on May 1; it was soon dispersed and Coxey himself was arrested for trespassing on the Capitol grounds. His plan for rescuing the nation from the depression that followed the Panic of 1893 included the printing of 500 million dollars in legal tender notes to finance a program of road construction and local improvements.

There's a deep and growing murmur
Going up through all the land
From millions who are suffering
Beneath oppression's hand
No charity, but justice
Do the working poor demand;
And justice they will gain.

Chorus:

Rally, rally, all ye voters,
Rally, rally, all ye voters,
Rally, rally, all ye voters,
And vote for home and right.

There's an army at the Capitol,
A valiant band of peace,
And many more are marching on
Its numbers to increase;
They voice the people's sentiment,
That evil laws shall cease
And equity shall reign.

(*Chorus*)

They may sneer at General Coxey
And may call his plans unwise,
May style him a fanatic,
And his followers despise;

Yet Coxey's cause is righteous
And above the wrong 'twill rise—
The Lord hath spoken it.

(*Chorus*)

Though prison walls may hold awhile
The champions of the poor,
The principles they advocate
Will only spread the more;
And soon the people will declare
That Shylock's reign is o'er,
For light is spreading fast.

(*Chorus*)

The hirelings of the plutocrats,
Whose legislative might
Would rob the people of their homes
And every free man's right,
Are doomed to see their sun go down
In everlasting night;
For they'll be voted out.

(*Chorus*)

TARIFF ON THE BRAIN

To be sung to the tune of "Brennan on the Moor." The high protective tariff of the 1890's allowed manufacturers and other representatives of Big Business to control the American market. The farmer, as a result, had to pay high prices for manufactured goods, especially those imported from Europe, while receiving low prices for his own products. The "scheme to throttle labor" refers to the Pullman Strike of 1894. The strike, called on June 21 by Eugene V. Debs of the American Railway Union, had tied up every Middle Western railroad by the end of the month. When violence broke out in July, President Cleveland sent federal troops to Chicago to restore order and safeguard the mail, over the protest of Illinois Governor John P. Altgeld. The reference to "goldbugs" is an allusion to the free-silver controversy (see page 74 f.) which, with the protective tariff, was to be the major campaign issue in 1896.

Come all you honest people,
Whoever you may be,
And help the honest workingmen
Resist monopoly.
'Tis headed by the brokers—
They deal in bonds and stocks;
They cite us to the tariff
While they're getting in their knocks.

Chorus:

Tariff on the brain! Tariff on the brain!
Look out for politicians
Who have tariff on the brain.

The goldbugs, knowing Grover
To their scheming would agree,
They put him in the White House,
Their agent there to be.
They robbed us of our silver
And grabbed up all our gold—
They cite us to the tariff
And leave us in the cold.

(*Chorus*)

They've a scheme to throttle labor
And monopolize the land,
To make of us a servile herd
While they are rich and grand.
Their schemes cause want and hunger,
And they may get foiled perhaps;
Or will our fair Columbia
By their greediness collapse?

(*Chorus*)

WE WANT NONE OF THEE

Written by Nellie Saunders to the tune of "My Bonnie Lies Over the Ocean." The song concerns the 1896 presidential campaign in which the Republicans, whose nominee was William McKinley, upheld the single gold standard, while the Democrats, led by

William Jennings Bryan, favored the free and unlimited coinage of silver at the 16 to 1 ratio. The opening stanzas allude to the gold-bond issue of 1895: in order to bolster the dwindling gold reserve, President Cleveland arranged for the issue of $65,000,000 in gold bonds, half of which were to be purchased abroad. British investors were quick to respond, hence the "Johnny Bull" references. A banking syndicate headed by J. P. Morgan and August Belmont placed the loan, netting a $7,000,000 profit, which explains the reference to Wall Street. Mark Hanna, mentioned in stanza three, masterminded the nomination of his fellow Ohioan, McKinley, and raised the then unprecedented sum of $3,500,000 for campaign funds. Bryan, who was only thirty-six when he ran for the presidency the first time, was known as the "Boy Orator of the Platte."

> Old Johnny Bull's over the ocean,
> Old Johnny Bull's over the sea;
> He wants to dictate to our people,
> But, Johnny, we want none of thee.
>
> Ah, there! Stay there! Lombard and
> Wall Street, we want none of thee.
> Ah, there! Stay there! Johnny, stay
> Over the sea.
>
> Our millionaires seem to be troubled;
> They're opening their coffers, you see,
> And are loading Mark Hanna with boodle,
> But the people are bound to be free.
>
> Ah, there! Stay there! Protection and
> Goldbugs, we want none of thee.
> Ah, there! Stay there! Old goldbugs,
> From you we'll be free.
>
> McKinley lives over at Canton;
> He's backed up by the East, don't you see?
> But the people will say in November,
> Oh, Billee, we want none of thee.

Ah, there! Stay there! McKinley and
Chestnuts, from you we'll be free.
Ah, there! Stay there! Old goldbugs,
You can't "befuddle" me.

Our hero, he comes from Nebraska,
He's "the orator boy of the Platte";
He's offering relief to the poor man,
And I tell you we're voting for that.

Ah, there! Stay there! Bryan's the
Man that will make silver free.
Ah, there! Stay there! We're bound
To elect him, you see.

THAT PROSPERITY WAVE

*Written by L. P. Cummins. The election of 1896 ended in a
victory for McKinley, but seldom has there been a closer or more
exciting presidential race; a change of 14,001 votes distributed in
the proper states would have given Bryan a majority of three
electoral votes. When the prosperity promised by the victors failed
to materialize, members of the Farmers' Alliance expressed their
feelings about "Mack" (McKinley) and Mark Hanna in such
songs as this one.*

We rise now to put the main question:
Just how we should act and behave
When we're completely submerged by the waters
Of that prosperity wave.

It was printed and spread o'er the country,
Told the freeman, the white and black slave,
That McKinley's triumphant election
Would our country both honor and save.

So wide was to be its diffusion,
All our shores with a blessing 'twould leave.
Now the people have a right to demand it,
And this right they never will waive.

Yes, and Mack, it is claimed, was elected
(To be sure a plaguy close shave).
Just the same we hoped (not expected)
A ride on a newly made wave.

But the banks, it seems, are still breaking,
And depositors are all on the rave,
While many of the "honest" bankers
Are seeking the suicide's grave.

And money is a mighty sight scarcer—
"Indade, sor, we really belave—"
And business throughout the whole country
Continues to totter and cave.

Their "confidence barl" is all busted,
It's no longer convex and concave;
About all that's now left of the humbug
Are the hoops, the bung, and a stave.

Mark Hanna, like robber and pirate—
The heinous old villain and knave—
He lied like the devil in Sheol,
McKinley to bolster and save.

From utter defeat and disaster,
He promised, he pled, and he gave
Many millions of ill-gotten money
To hire, corrupt, and deprave

The voters, the rabble, and suckers
And whoever might happen to crave
A bowl or a spoonful of old party soup—
Old Hanna's more devilish than brave.

So now the poor dupes are all looking
As it were in the gloom of a cave
For a sign of expected salvation,
But they see not a sign of the "wave."

The Patches on My Pants

To be sung to "Auld Lang Syne." The anonymous—and hungry—author of these lines had backed a Republican winner (Harrison over Cleveland in 1888) and a Democratic loser (Bryan in 1896) and traces his present plight to the former occasion.

Of all the years since I began
To mix in politics,
The one that tries my inner man
Is 1896.
And as this aching void I feel
I cast a wistful glance
And count them all from hip to heel—
The patches on my pants.

My mind runs back to '88—
When first I tried them on
I walked with proud and joyous gait
To vote for Harrison.
Had I prophetic eyes to see
They'd swim with tears, perchance,
To find that vote brought out on me
Those patches on my pants.

Campaign Song

To be sung to the tune of "Old Dan Tucker." In 1900 the Democratic National Convention, meeting in Kansas City, again selected William Jennings Bryan as the party's presidential candidate. He was nominated by David B. Hill, former United States senator from New York, and the delegates chose former Vice-President Adlai E. Stevenson of Illinois as his running mate. Opposing them on the Republican ticket were "Mack and Teddy" —McKinley, running for his second term, and Theodore Roosevelt of Rough Rider fame. Although Bryan was supported by the fusion Populists, he was again defeated.

Voters, come and hear my ditty,
What was done at Kansas City:
David Hill, the New York lion,
Nominated Billy Bryan.

Chorus:

Get out of the way, you Grand Old Party,
Get out of the way, you Grand Old Party,
Get out of the way, you Grand Old Party,
You're so old, you're getting warty.

For running mate there was a pull,
But 'twas no use, the woods were full;
And then and there to still the noise
They gave the job to Illinois.

(*Chorus*)

Still your boss is Mark A. Hanner,
He looks just like a stockyard's tanner.
In the ring our hats we're shying,
Whoop! Hurrah! for Billy Bryan.

(*Chorus*)

Keep the banners ever flying;
Follow always Billy Bryan.
Onward now and all keep steady,
'Cause we're after Mack and Teddy.

(*Chorus*)

Square Dances

*There was dancing, lots of dancing. We went
miles to attend a good square dance. . . . Every
caller had his own version of the way a dance
should be called, and of course his way was the
right way. I'd call for "Swing like thunder"
and boy! they'd swing like thunder, too. They'd
land that gal clean in "old Arkansaw."*

Frank Grady, a pioneer Nebraska dance-caller

Of the social diversions open to the pioneers, dancing was far
and away the most popular. Everett Dick, Nebraska's chron-
icler of life on the sod-house frontier, speaks of dances as "the
universal indoor amusement. . . . They were held on every
holiday, when a new ferry boat was brought into service, in
celebration of the election of successful candidates, when a new
bridge was built, when a couple was married, on the occasion of
the first trip of each steamboat of the season, and on any other
occasion for which an excuse could be found. They were held in
homes, barns, stores, restaurants, courthouses, hotel dining
rooms, and even on the prairie" (7).

Among the dances the quadrille, better known as the square
dance, was a general favorite in all frontier communities, for it
was peculiarly well adapted to the conditions of frontier life.
Not only could it be danced anywhere but it could be danced
by any number from eight to a thousand; music could be supplied by any instrument—"dances were known to have been
held with only the hum of a Jew's harp for music" (7), although
usually a fiddler presided—and the dances themselves, boisterous and energetic, suited the pioneer taste.

80

The following description of a square dance in the 1890's has been preserved in Nebraska Folklore Pamphlet No. 22, one of three devoted to pioneer dance calls. The informant, John Hartje, used to hold dances in his machine shed twelve miles south of Lincoln.

A stream of buggies, carriages, spring wagons, and horseback riders would begin arriving at [Hartje's] farmyard as soon as the shadows of early evening had begun to fall. Later, after sundown, shadowy figures, laughing and bantering in the dusk, converged upon the machine shed, whose entrance was lit up by a huge iron lamp. Inside the building a dozen kerosene lanterns shed a pale glow over rustic walls and benches. The girls and women wore long checkered gingham dresses with wide skirts and tight waists. Their hair was long, combed into coils and fastened with many pins and sidecombs. Some had long, thick braids hanging to the waist, tied with colored ribbons. Now and then "topped" shoes were revealed when skirts were daringly whisked aside. The men, old and young, wore every possible kind of dress, from tight fitting pants and high collars to overalls. . . .

Mr. Hartje says that after the preliminary sideplay was over, W. G. "Scovie" Seidell of Lincoln, one of the state's most popular dance callers, would take his place beside the orchestra, which, in addition to Scovie's violin, generally consisted of parlor organ, cello, guitar, and mandolin. Here, seated on a raised platform, he would call: "Choose your partners, choose your partners, and be ready to go! Choose your partners!" With shuffling of feet and ready laughter, couple after couple fell into position for the dance, which nearly always began with the Grand March, according to the following call:

Fall in by couples and once around the hall,
Then down the center, one by one . . . .*

The quadrilles, which are sets of four couples, have now been formed. Scovie nods to his orchestra and they begin

* For the complete call, see page 100.

to play a popular tune of the day, such as "Leather Breeches" or "Old Zip Coon," as Scovie calls:

"Now salute your partner,
Opposite lady, too.
Join hands and circle to the left.
Promenade back."

Scovie's voice, clear and sharp, rises louder and louder above the music and the shuffle of the dancers' feet as he continues:

"First four forward and back,
Forward again and right and left.
Forward and back.
Right and left home."

The dance is on as the caller improvises one dance call after another, in time with the music, while every move of the dancers is gracefully executed in perfect unison.

In earlier times, writes Everett Dick, "on the rawer frontier the dances were, if anything, even less formal and more hilarious. The dance was a true leveler in which staid matrons, grave gentlemen of mature years, and little children all mingled. Women brought their babies and tried hard, but often without results, to quiet them . . . [but] in spite of the cries of wakeful babes the dance went gloriously forward." The exuberant character of these gatherings is suggested in Mr. Dick's report of an early settler who "went to a place about ten in the morning and found the family just arising. The ceiling bore marked evidence of a dance the previous evening; there were marks on it made by male dancers. It was the custom for a gentleman to swing his lady around and kick the ceiling, then swing her around and kick the ceiling again, keeping perfect time to the music." Because of the surplus of men on the frontier—they outnumbered women three to one—a little girl of ten and a grandmother of eighty were no less eligible than the neighborhood belle to join in the fun. Frequently, however, to make up the sets it was necessary for men to take the part of women. In such cases, a man tied a handkerchief around his arm to denote that he was temporarily a member of the fair sex (7). Whenever possible the dances were held in a dwelling with a board floor— Charley O'Kieffe, who grew up in Sheridan County, lived in a soddy that could boast this refinement, and "because of our fine floor our home became the mecca for square dancers" (18) —but when they had to, the dancers could make do with a dirt floor, stopping every so often to "water down" the dirt to abate the dust (1).

Besides the dances derived from the quadrille, there were reels and other descendants of the contra-dance which, like the quadrille, came to America from England and France. (Such terms as *sashay*, *doe-si-doe*, and *promenade* and the steps that go with them are French additions to English country dances.) In America, a caller—usually the fiddler or the band leader— was added, so that dancers no longer danced memorized figures but to the caller's direction. Thanks to this innovation the square dance became an imaginative, vital improvisation instead of petrifying into a formalized pattern, as it did in Europe (6).

Because the call is a blueprint of the dance itself, the square dance is especially valuable to the folklorist: so long as the words of the call exist, the dance is preserved. The calls presented here were collected from native Nebraska dance callers who sang them and in some instances created them. The arrangement is alphabetical.

ALL THE MEN LEFT (I)

Collected from Fillmore Greenfield of Lincoln, whose father, Albert Greenfield, called dances for fifty years.

> All the men left with the old left hand.
> Why in the world don't you right and left grand?
> Mind what I say, don't go away.
> The old man's gone, and we'll all chaw hay!

ALL THE MEN LEFT (II)

Collected from Charles Weaver of Hastings, who called dances in the area around Friend and Hastings. Many of his calls were handed down to him by his father, who, in turn, had learned them from his father.

All the men left with the left-hand partner to a left-hand round.
Right hand to your partner and right and left around the ring.
Meet your partner and grand promenade.
Everybody swing.
Three couples form arches and first couple play croquet.
Swing your partner.
All the men left, grand right and left.
Promenade eight until you get straight.
(*Repeat*)

All join hands and circle left.
It's a right and left and promenade all.
When you get straight, swing your partner.
All join hands and circle to the left.
Promenade back single file,
Lady in the lead, Indian style.
Then swing that girl behind you.
Repeat four times until you come to your own partner.
All the men left with the left-hand partner to a left-hand round.
Right hand to your partner and right and left around the ring.
Meet your partner and grand promenade.
(*Repeat.*)

Balance and swing, all the men left,
Grand right and left.
Promenade eight until you get straight.
First couple out to the couple on the right.
Two gents whirl with the elbow whirl.
Now whirl your opposite partner.
Now four hands round.
The ladies doe and the gents solo.
On to the next.
Two gents whirl with the elbow whirl,
And then whirl your opposite partner.
Four hands round.
Ladies doe and gents solo.
(*Repeat for third and fourth couples.*)

Balance your weight and swing.
All the men left and grand right and left.
Promenade eight until you get straight.
First couple out to the right.
Four hands round.
Two ladies whirl, two gents whirl, all four whirl.
Ladies doe and gents solo.
(*Repeat for third and fourth couples.*)

Balance and swing, all the men left,
Grand right and left.
Promenade eight till you get straight.
First couple out to the couple on the right.
Four hands round.
Swing with the butterfly swing.
Join your hands and go it again.
Ladies doe and gents solo.
On to the next.
(*Repeat.*)

BALANCE EIGHT

Collected from H. C. Whittington of Lincoln, who called dances in Malcolm in the 1880's and 1890's. Mr. Whittington recalled an occasion when a young minister walked into the schoolhouse where he was calling a dance, and "at first thought the dance crowd was a rousing good congregation that had become enthusiastic over a sermon. As soon as he discovered his mistake he prepared to leave but was persuaded by the women to remain and join in one of the sets. Later in the week, when he conducted a religious service in the same building, the entire dance group came to hear him preach. He, because of his open mind, was the most popular minister in the community" (1).

> Promenade.
> First couple lead to the couple on the right.
> Right and left through and right and left six.
> And in between side couple and forward six.
> Balance home and balance eight.
> Swing on the corner like swingin' on a gate.
> All the men left with your old left hand.
> Right-hand your partner with a right and left grand.
> Meet your pard and promenade home.
> (*Repeat for second, third, and fourth couples.*)

BALANCE FOUR

Collected from George Nye of Lincoln, who played the fiddle and called dances for more than thirty years. To be danced to the tune of "Joy of the Dance."

> First four right and left.
> Balance four.
> Turn partners, ladies change.
> Half promenade, right and left back.
> Sides the same.
> (*Repeat four times.*)

BALANCE HOME

Collected from Charles Weaver of Hastings, who said that the call sometimes had to be altered to suit the size of the dance floor.

The dancers form a straight line down the hall one couple wide.
First and third couples out to right and four hands round.
A right and left four and a right and left eight across the hall.
Balance home and swing your partner.

Second and fourth repeat but not across the hall.
Balance home and swing your partner.
First and third couples out to right and four hands round.
Right and left four and right and left eight and across the hall.
Balance you home and swing your partner.

BIRDIE IN THE CAGE

Collected from J. J. Senn of Lincoln, who began dancing in square dance sets when he was ten, and became a popular caller in Wheeler County. To be danced to the tune of " Buffalo Gals."

Honor your partners, right and left.
All join hands and circle to the left.
Break and swing and all promenade.
The first lady swing the right-hand gent with the right-hand
    round,
Partner by the left as you come around.
Birdie in the cage and seven hands round.
The lady hop out and the gent hop in.
Join your hands and go it again.
Now the gent swing out with an all the men left.
Right-hand your partners and go right and left.
Meet your partner and all promenade.
(*Repeat for second, third, and fourth couples.*)

BUFFALO GALS

Collected from Claude C. " Pat " Haggarty of Lincoln, who began calling dances in Nebraska in the early 1880's. " Buffalo Gals " was his favorite call, and he felt that it was especially suited to small country dances.

    Balance all, swing all.
    Join hands and circle left and promenade around.
    First one little girl run around the outside,
    And around the outside,
    And around the outside.
    And one little girl run around the outside,
    And pass your partner and swing all around.

And two little girls run around the outside.
And two little girls run around the outside,
And around the outside,
And around the outside.
And pass your partner and swing all around.

And three little girls run around the outside,
Around the outside,
Around the outside.
And three little girls run around the outside,
And pass your partner and swing 'em all around.

And four little girls run around the outside,
Around the outside,
Around the outside.
And four little girls run around the outside,
And pass your partner and balance home.

Everybody dance!
All the men left, grand right and left,
And hurry up, boys, and pat her on the head.
If she don't like biscuits, feed her corn bread.
Keep a-goin'; don't wait till you get straight,
Promenade home.

First one little boy run around the outside,
Around the outside,
Around the outside.
And one little boy run around the outside,
Pass your partner and swing 'em all around.

Two little boys run around the outside,
Around the outside,
Around the outside.
Two little boys run around the outside,
Pass your partner and swing 'em all around.

Three little boys run around the outside.
Four little boys run around the outside.
Balance home, everybody dance.
All the men left, right to your partner, and go right and
    left.
Meet your partner,
Promenade the ring as you are.

BUTTERFLY WHIRL

Collected from Claude C. Haggarty, who said that this intriguing figure was popular in the 1880's.

First couple lead to the right and four hands round.
And break and swing with a butterfly whirl, four hands round.
And ladies doe and gents you know,
And chicken in the bread pan, pickin' out dough.

CAST OFF SIX

Collected from Claude C. Haggarty. He believed that this is one of the oldest dances in the state.

First couple down the center and divide the ring,
Lady to the right and the gent to the left,
And when you come around, swing.
And all four swing down the center and cast off four,
Lady to the right and gent to the left,
And when you come around, swing.
And all four swing, same couple down the center,
And cast off two,
And when you come around, balance home and everybody
    swing.
All the men left and right to your partner
And grand right and left.
And hurry up boys and pat her on the head.
If she don't like biscuits, feed her corn bread.
And when you meet your partner, promenade home.
(*Repeat for second, third, and fourth couples.*)

CECILIAN CIRCLE

Collected from Jesse A. Pound of Lincoln, who came to Nebraska in 1870 and began calling dances in 1886 at the age of seventeen. At one dance he called at Lincoln's old City Auditorium, there were eighty-three sets—six hundred and sixty-four people—on the floor at one time. Lemon juice, he said, was the only thing that kept his voice from cracking during the twenty dances, which lasted until three o'clock in the morning. According to Mr. Pound, "Cecilian Circle" was a great favorite in the 1870's, and had raised the dust from many a sodhouse dirt floor.

> Everybody in the hall join hands.
> Balance and swing.
> All the men left, grand right and left.
> Promenade where you are.
> Balance and swing again, grand right and left.
> Promenade again.
> (*Repeat as many times as desired.*)

CHANGE HALF AROUND

Collected from Patrick Oliver of Lincoln, who drove a horse car in the 1890's and remembered calling square dances when the only music was a man whistling.

> First couple balance and swing.
> Change opposite partners and swing half around.
> Change again and swing half around.
> Right and left through, on to the next,
> And change half around.
> All the men left, grand right and left,
> Promenade home.
> (*Repeat for second, third, and fourth couples.*)

CHASE THE SQUIRREL

Collected from John A. Bauer, who said the call was being used as early as 1864. Mr. Bauer was born near Murdock, Cass County, in 1857 and started calling square dances at the old Metz Hall in Omaha in 1878.

Honor your partner, the lady on the left.
Join hands and circle to the left.
Break and swing.
All the men left, grand right and left.
Meet your partners and promenade back.

First couple out to the right, four hands right.
Right and left, right and left back.
Two ladies change, change right back.
(*Repeat three more times.*)

CHEATER SWING

Collected from Claude C. Haggarty. The ladies may, if they wish, refuse to swing with their partners, hence the name "Cheater Swing." If a lady refused, however, it was a coquettish rather than serious gesture.

First lady lead out to the right,
Cheat or swing or do as you like.
Now the one that curls his hair,
Now the one that looks so cute,
And now the belle of the ballroom.
(*Repeat for second, third, and fourth couples.*)

First gent lead out to the right,
And cheat or swing or do as you like.
Now the gal that smiles so cute,
Now the gal with the golden slippers,
Balance home and swing the one you love the best.
All the men left, and around you go,
And hurry up, boys.
Meet your partners and promenade.
(*Repeat for second, third, and fourth couples.*)

CHICKEN IN THE BREAD PAN (I)

Collected from George Nye. The title is a square-dance cliché which occurs in a host of calls. To be danced to the tune of "Skip to My Lou."

Chicken in the bread pan, pickin' up dough,
Chicken in the bread pan, pickin' up dough,
Chicken in the bread pan, pickin' up dough,
Skip to my Lou, my darling.

Little more dough and on you go,
Little more dough and on you go,
Little more dough and on you go,
Skip to my Lou, my darling.

Ma hit Dad with her old shoe,
Ma hit Dad with her old shoe,
Ma hit Dad with her old shoe,
Skip to my Lou, my darling.

Skip a little further, this will never do,
Skip a little further, this will never do,
Skip a little further, this will never do,
Skip to my Lou, my darling.

CHICKEN IN THE BREAD PAN (II)

Collected from Claude C. Haggarty, who believed it was one of the oldest calls in the state. Despite the title, it is clearly a different call from that above.

Honor your ladies and all join hands and circle to your left.
Break and swing and promenade back.
First couple balance and swing and lead to the right, off the ring.
Round the couple with the lady in the lead,
Gent step through and around that couple with the gent in the lead,
And the lady step through and four hands around.
And the ladies doe and gents you know and doe-si-doe,
And the gents meow and chicken in the bread pan, pickin' out dough.
Balance your partner and swing on the corner, the corner swing,
And now your own and don't be late,
Like swinging on a gate.

And all the men left, grand right and left.
Hurry up, boys!
If she don't like biscuits, feed her slapjacks.
Mect your partner and promenade home.
(*Repeat for second, third, and fourth couples.*)

CIRCLE THROUGH

Collected from Claude C. Haggarty. To be danced to the tune of "Ragtime Annie."

First couple lead to the right and four hands around.
Birdie in the cage and three hands around.
Join hands and circle three.
Lady swing out and gent swing in.
Honey in the comb and three hands around,
And circle three.
Gent fly out and three hands around.
Ladies doe and gents you know,
Doe-si-doe and gents just so,
Chicken in the bread pan, pickin' out dough.
Take that lady and lead to the next,
And four hands around.
Lady in the center and three go around.
Birdie fly out and birdie fly in,
And three go around.
Gent fly out and four hands around.
Ladies doe and gents you know
With a little more dough,
Chicken in the bread pan, pickin' out dough.
On to the next and honey in the comb,
And three hands around.
Birdie fly out and birdie fly in,
And circle three.
Balance home and swing your partner home.
Grand right and left, pat her on the head.
If she don't like your biscuits, feed her slapjacks.
Promenade when you get straight.
(*Repeat for second, third, and fourth couples.*)

CIRCLE TWO-STEP

Collected from John A. Bauer. The caller of this unusually complete two-step opens the dance by having the partners two-step once around.

Promenade all.
Ladies step forward, gents step back.
Everybody two-step.

All the men left, right and left.
Everybody two-step.
Ladies to the inside, gents to the outside in a circle.
Circle around.

Everybody two-step.
Gents to the inside, ladies to the outside,
Circle around reverse.
Everybody two-step.

Promenade with your partner.
Ladies to the north, gents to the south,
Forward and back.
Forward and right and left through,
Forward and two-step.

CORNER SWING

Collected from Claude C. Haggarty. To be danced to the tune of "Old Lady Pickin' Chickens."

First couple balance and swing,
And down the center and divide the ring,
Lady to right and gent to the left,
And when you come around,
Swing on the corner and promenade the ring.
Down the center and divide the ring,
Lady to right and gent to the left,
And when you come around,
Swing the corner, corner swing,
And take that lady and promenade the ring.

And roll them again,
And same couple down center and divide the ring,
Lady to the right and gent to the left,
And when you come around,
Swing on the corner.
And take that lady and roll them again,
And down the center and divide the ring,
Lady to the right and gent to the left,
And when you come around,
Balance home and swing your pard home,
And everybody swing.
(*Repeat for second, third, and fourth couples.*)

CROSS OVER

Collected from George Nye. To be danced to the tune of "New Century."

> First four forward, ladies cross over.
> Sides forward and ladies cross over.
> Grand right and left.
> Quarter round, meet partners.
> Promenade to place.
> (*Repeat four times.*)

CROSS OVER FOUR

Collected from George Nye. To be danced to the tune of "Silver Slipper Hornpipe."

> First four forward and back, cross over four.
> Chase to the right and left, promenade and turn.
> Cross back and partners separate.
> All forward and back, turn partners to place.
> (*Repeat four times.*)

CUT A FIGURE EIGHT (I)

Collected from M. B. Packard of Lincoln, who was in the happy situation of combining the professions of auctioneer and dance

caller. He said that because of its intricacy, "Cut a Figure Eight"
—which he referred to as his "marathon call"—was suitable only
for couples who "possess a great deal of physical endurance."

Balance all and swing.
All the men left, grand right and left.
Meet your partner and promenade all.
First lady swing with the right-hand gent,
The right-hand gent, the right-hand gent,
Partner by the left as you come around.
Lady in the center and seven hands around.
The lady swing out and the gent swing in.
Join your paddies and go it again.
Balance all and swing partners home.
All the men left and promenade eight.
(*Repeat for second couple, adding the following:*)
Balance home, turn 'em around.
With all the men left and a left all the men,
Right-hand your partner, balance all and swing.
All the men left and a left all the men,
Right-hand your partner and right and left grand.
First couple and third couple forward and back.
Forward again and balance four in a line.
It's break in the center and swing half around.
Cut a figure eight with a lady in the lead.
Break in the center and cut a figure eight with the gent in the
    lead.
Four hands round, lady doe and gents solo,
Chicken in the bread pan, pickin' up dough.
A little more dough and on you go.
Break with the right and swing with the left,
And cut a figure eight as you go around.
And right and left grand with a double elbow,
Once and a half and then let 'er go.
Promenade eight when you get straight.
(*Repeat for third couple, then repeat again for fourth couple, adding*
the following:)
Promenade eight when you get straight,
You know where and I don't care.

Cut a Figure Eight (ii)

Collected from M. B. Packard, who arranged it for those who think the preceding call is too long.

Turn 'em all eight with an all the men left and a left all the men.
Right-hand your partner and right and left grand.
Meet your partner and promenade home.
(*Repeat for second, third, and fourth couples.*)

Cut a Figure Eight (iii)

Collected from John A. Bauer, who stated in a 1939 interview that this call was at least seventy-five years old and that it was identified with Nebraska square dances in " Poor Man's Holler," Cass County, in the early 1870's.

> First lady and opposite gent give right hands across.
> Join your partners, balance four in line.
> Break in the center, swing half around.
> Cut a figure eight with the lady in the lead.
> Break in the center, swing half around.
> Cut a figure eight with a gent in the lead.
> (*Repeat three more times.*)

Variant

Collected from Claude C. Haggarty. To be danced to the tune of " Eighth of January."

First lady and opposite gent give right hands across.
Balance four in line, swing half around and cut a figure eight,
With the lady in the lead and the lady lead around.
Break to the center and swing half around and cut a figure eight,
With the gent in the lead and the gent lead around.
Balance home and everybody swing,
All the men left and promenade the ring.
(*Repeat for second, third, and fourth couples.*)

CUTTIN' THE MUSTARD

Collected from Patrick Oliver.

First couple lead out to the right of the ring.
Four hands half, right and left through, right and left four.
Right and left six, right and left back.
Four hands half.
Ladies doe-si-doe, gents the same.
Break and swing opposite partner, then your own.
And on to the next, four hands half.
(*Repeat three more times.*)

DOLLAR DANCE

Collected from Fillmore Greenfield, who used it as one of his novelty calls. "Twenty-five cents" means "swing the lady in front of you," "fifty cents" means "change and swing your own partner," "seventy-five cents" means "swing your opposite partner," and "big, round dollar" means "change and swing your own partner."

First couple balance and swing.
Lead out to the right of the ring.
Change and swing your twenty-five cents.
Now your fifty cents.
Now your seventy-five cents.
Now the big, round dollar.
Four hands half, right and left through.
Right and left back, on to the next.
(*Repeat three more times.*)

DOUBLE SASHAY

Collected from William Carson of Lincoln, who called many dances in Holt County during the 1880's and 1890's. In those days, said Mr. Carson, space for dancing was limited, so, in order to accommodate overflow crowds, sets were called to the floor by numbers. For example, the couples who had numbers one to sixteen would make up the first dance, seventeen to thirty-two the second, and so on. In this way, everyone had an opportunity to dance. In "Double Sashay" the caller can mix the couples after the dance has begun by making partners out of the first and third couples, second and fourth, third and first, fourth and second.

> First and opposite couples forward and back.
> Forward again and cross, cross right back.
> Two ladies change, change right back.
> Double sashay.
> Half promenade, half right and left.
> Balance all, all the men left, grand right and left.
> Promenade home.
> (*Repeat for other two couples.*)

FORM A STAR

Collected from Patrick Oliver.

> Four gents to center of the bar and back.
> Four ladies to the center and right hands across.
> Swing half around, back by the left.
> Pass your partner once and swing.
> Pass your partner twice and swing.
> Pass your partner three times and swing.
> Clear around and swing your partner.
> Balance home.

THE GIRL I LEFT BEHIND ME (I)

Collected from Elmer Dellett, who played the fiddle and called at dances in Seward, Custer, and Buffalo counties. His repertoire was so rich that he "could play all night and never play the same piece twice."

> First two couples lead up to the right,
> Pass right through, balance two,
> And swing with the girl behind you.
> Four times around and promenade eight.
> (*Repeat four times for each two couples.*)

THE GIRL I LEFT BEHIND ME (II)

Collected from M. B. Packard.

> Balance all and swing,
> All the men left and all promenade.

Lead to the first couple and balance there so nicely.
Pass right through and balance two,
And swing that girl behind you.
Pass right back in the same old track,
And swing that girl behind you,
That pretty little girl, that pretty little girl,
The one you left behind you.
And on to the next and balance there so nicely.
It's pass right through and balance two,
And swing that one behind you,
That pretty little girl, that pretty little girl,
The one you left behind you.
Pass right back in the same old track,
And swing that one behind you.

THE GIRL I LEFT BEHIND ME (III)
Collected from John A. Bauer.

> First couple out to the couple on the right,
> Balance two and pass right through,
> Swing that lady you left behind you.
> Balance two and pass right through,
> Swing that lady you left behind.
> (*Repeat three more times.*)

GRAND MARCH
Collected from W. G. "Scovie" Seidell of Lincoln, one of the most popular callers in the state. "Grand March" was usually his opening call.

> Fall in by couples and once around the hall,
> Then down the center, one by one,
> Then around and meet.
> Down the center in couples,
> One couple to the right, one to the left,
> Around the hall again.
> Meet in fours, down center by fours,
> First four to the right, second four to the left.
> Around by fours and meet center in eights,
> Down center by eights.

GRAPEVINE TWIST (I)

Collected from Claude C. Haggarty. The figures formed by the dancers imitate the encircling, entwining design of the grapevine.

> First couple lead to the right and four hands around.
> Grand right and left four and promenade four.
> And four and two and six hands around.
> Grand right and left six and break to the head
> With a grapevine twist.
> (*Repeat for second, third, and fourth couples.*)

GRAPEVINE TWIST (II)

Collected from J. J. Senn.

> All jump up and when you come down,
> Turn that pretty one round and around.
> All the men left, grand right and left,
> Meet your partner and all promenade.
> First couple lead to the right and four hands round.
> Four to six and six hands round.
> Six to eight and eight hands round.
> The first gent break with the grapevine swing.
> All the men left, grand right and left,
> Meet your partner and all promenade.
> (*Repeat for second, third, and fourth couples.*)

GRAPEVINE TWIST (III)

Collected from Fillmore Greenfield. To be danced in 6/8 time.

> Balance to your places and all swing.
> All the men left and promenade.
> Join your hands and circle to the left.
> First couple break with the grapevine twist.
> (*Repeat for second, third, and fourth couples.*)

HEAD SWING AND FOOT SWING TOO

Collected from J. J. Senn.

> Honor your partners right and left.
> All join hands and circle to the left.

Break and swing and promenade home.
First couple balance and swing.
Down the center and divide the ring,
Lady to the right and gent to the left,
Head swing and foot swing too.
Down the center and cast off four,
Just that many and not any more,
Head swing and foot swing too.
Down the center and cast off two,
Just the same as you used to do,
Big ones swing and little ones too.
All the men left, grand right and left,
Meet your partners and promenade home.
(*Repeat for second, third, and fourth couples.*)

HOME

Collected from Fillmore Greenfield.

Two ladies change in front of the rest.
Change your way back.
Half promenade,
Then right and left home.
Four hands half.
Doe-si-doe,
Balance home and swing.
(*Repeat three more times.*)

HONEST JOHN

Collected from Fillmore Greenfield. At the words "how do you do," the couple make a low bow.

Balance to your places and all swing.
All the men left and promenade.
First couple lead out to the right,
Hold right hands.
Sashay by and how do you do.
Sashay back, that was pretty well done.
Right and left through, right and left back,
And on to the next.
(*Repeat for second, third, and fourth couples.*)

Variant 1

Collected from William Carson.

> Sashay back and honor John.
> Sashay back, salute your honor.
> Right and left through, right and left back.
> Two ladies change, change right back.
> Balance to the next.
> (*Repeat three more times.*)

Variant 2

Collected from M. B. Packard.

> Balance all and swing.
> All the men left, grand right and left,
> Meet your partner and promenade eight.
> First couple balance and swing.
> Lead to the right and balance four.
> Sashay by and make a bow,
> Sashay back, another one now.
> Right and left through, and right and left back.
> Lead to the next and balance four.
> (*Repeat for second, third, and fourth couples, then repeat
> the entire dance again.*)

HONEY COMB

*Collected from Claude C. Haggarty, who called it his "honey
call."*

> First lady lead to the right,
> And right-hand gent with right-hand round,
> Offset gent with right-hand round.
> Now left-hand gent with right around,
> And now your own with right around.
> Birdie in the cage and seven hands around,
> And all join hands.
> Hit 'er down eight when you come around.

Lady swing out and honey in the comb,
And seven round.
And join hands and hit 'er down again.
Balance home, swing your partner.
All the men left, grand right and left,
And hurry up, boys, pat 'er on the head.
If she don't like biscuits, feed 'er slapjacks,
If she don't like slapjacks, feed 'er corn bread.
Then meet your partner and promenade ring.
(*Repeat for second, third, and fourth couples.*)

HONEY COMB REEL
Collected from George Nye.

Grand right and left, forward all.
Chase by couples across.
Half right and left to places.
Balance all, turn partner.
First four forward and back.
First couple cross over inside, back on outside.
Salute corner and turn.
Sides separate, join hands with first four.
Forward eight.
Forward, turn opposite lady to place.
Turn partner, all forward.
Salute and return to place.

HONEYSUCKLE VINE HORNPIPE
Collected from George Nye.

First couple lead to the right, balance four.
Gents take two ladies, balance to the next,
Turn five hands around.
Take three ladies, balance to the next,
Turn six hands around.
All join hands, circle to the right.
(*Repeat for each couple.*)

INDIAN FILE DANCE
Collected from John A. Bauer.

> All the men left,
> Right-hand your partner,
> Grand right and left.
> Meet your partner,
> Promenade back.
> First couple out to the couple on the right,
> Four hands half.
> Join the opposite couple,
> Six hands around.
> Six to two and eight hands around.
> Break and swing.
> Promenade single file, Indian style.
> Stop and swing them every little while.

IRISH WASHERWOMAN
Collected from James M. White of Lincoln, who played the fiddle at Nebraska dances for some forty years.

> First couple balance right in the middle,
> And make your left foot keep time to the fiddle.
> Lady swing in and gent swing out,
> Join your hands and circle about.
> The lady swing out and the gent swing in,
> Hold your holds and circle again.
> All the men left, grand right and left,
> Meet your partner, promenade home.

LADIES BOW AND GENTS BOW UNDER
Collected from Fillmore Greenfield. This dance is so violent that it was not permitted in most halls, though there was no law against it. When the gents swing the ladies " like thunder" sometimes their feet are lifted off the floor, and if a couple's hold is broken the lady

may go sailing against a wall or window. This was said to have happened to a woman in Eagle, Nebraska, who wound up with a broken leg.

First couple lead out to the right.
With the eight hands high, ladies bow and gents bow under.
Hug 'em tight and swing like thunder.
(*Repeat for second, third, and fourth couples.*)

LADY ROUND LADY AND GENTS SOLO

Collected from Claude C. Haggarty. To be danced to the tune of "Mississippi Sawyer."

First couple lead to the right of the ring,
Lady round lady and gent don't go.
Four hands around.
Ladies doe and gents you know with a little more dough,
And chicken in the bread pan, pickin' up dough.
On to the next.
And lady round lady and gents solo,
Lady round gent and gent don't go.
Four hands around.
Lady doe and gents you know,
Doe-si-doe and a little more dough.
On to the next.
And lady round lady and gents solo,
Lady round gent and gent don't go.
And four hands round.
Ladies doe and gents you know.
Take your lady and gents solo,
Lady round gent and gent don't go.
Balance home and everybody swing.
All the men left and around you go,
And hurry up, boys, pat her on the head.
If she don't like flapjacks, feed her corn bread.
Promenade when you get straight.
(*Repeat for second, third, and fourth couples.*)

THE LANCERS

Collected from John Hartje of Lincoln, who heard it called by W. G. Seidell.

> First four forward and back.
> Forward again, turn opposite partner.
> Back to your place.
> Swing on the corner and back to your place,
> And swing your partner.
> (*Repeat three more times.*)
>
> First four forward and back.
> Forward again and salute.
> Back to your place.
> Ladies change, change right back.
> (*Repeat three more times.*)
>
> Head couple lead to the right and salute.
> Lead to the left and salute.
> Back to your place and all salute.
> (*Repeat three more times.*)
>
> Right hand to your partner,
> And grand right and left.
> First couple face out,
> Sashay forward, sashay back.
> Lady to the right, gent to the left,
> Forward and back.
> Swing your partner to your place.
> (*Repeat three more times.*)

LIFE ON THE OCEAN WAVES (1)

Collected from William Carson.

> Salute your opposite partner,
> Now your own true love.
> Swing your opposite partner,
> Now your own true love.
> Promenade around the hall with the polka waltz.
> Balance to the next.
> (*Repeat three more times.*)

LIFE ON THE OCEAN WAVES (II)
  Collected from J. J. Senn.

Honor your partners, right and left.
All join hands and circle to the left.
Break and swing and promenade home.
Four ladies to the center and pass right through.
Swing with your opposite partner, just as you ought to do.
Honor to that partner and the corner the same.
Swing that corner partner and all promenade.
(*Repeat last four lines three more times.*)

Swing on the corner and now your own.
All the men left, grand right and left.
Meet your partner and all promenade.
Four gents to the center and pass right through.
Swing with your opposite partner, just as you ought to do.
Honor to that partner and the corner the same.
Swing that corner partner and all promenade.
(*Repeat last four lines three more times.*)

Variant

Collected from G. C. Carter. This is an old call which may have originated in Nebraska, but probably was brought into the state. It was particularly popular with older dancers.

All four ladies to the center and pass right through.
Swing your opposite partner as you had ought to do.
Honor your corner partner, your partner the same.
Swing corner partner and all promenade.
(*Repeat three more times.*)

All four gents to the center and pass right through.
Swing your opposite partner as you had ought to do.
Honor your corner partner, your partner the same.
Swing corner partner and all promenade.
(*Repeat three more times.*)

Life on the Ocean Waves (III)
Collected from Fillmore Greenfield.

Balance to your places and all swing.
All the men left and promenade.
First gent and opposite lady hold hands right across.
Swing with your right, back with your left.
Balance all four in a line, be sure to take your time.
Break in the center and turn half around.
And cut a figure eight with the lady in the lead.
Break in the center and the gent in the lead.
(*Repeat three more times.*)

Little Brown Jug
Collected from G. C. Carter of Lincoln, who said this was his favorite call.

First and second on the floor,
Swing your partner and balance four.
On the corner, all alone,
Now return and swing your own.
(*Repeat for first and third couples, then first and fourth, second and third, second and fourth, second and first, third and fourth, third and first, third and second, fourth and first, fourth and second, and fourth and third.*)

The Miller
Collected from George Nye.

There was a little miller lived by the mill.
The wheel turned around with a right good will.
One hand in the hopper and the other in the sack,
Ladies step forward and gents fall back.
(*Repeat.*)

My Gal Is Pretty

Collected from Claude C. Haggarty, who said the call has been used in Nebraska since the 1870's. To be danced to the tune of "Billie in the Low Ground."

First couple lead out to the right of the ring,
Four hands around.
You swing my gal and I'll swing yours,
My gal is pretty and so is yours.
You swing your gal and I'll swing mine,
Four hands around.
Ladies doe and gents you know,
Doe-si-doe and a little more dough,
Chicken in the bread pan, pickin' out dough.
Take that lady and lead to the next,
And four hands around.
You swing my gal and I'll swing yours,
My gal is pretty and so is yours.
You swing yours and I'll swing mine,
Four hands around.
And ladies doe and gents you know, doe-si-doe,
Chicken in the bread pan, pickin' out dough.
On to the next and four hands round.
You swing my gal and I'll swing yours,
Your gal is pretty and so is mine.
You swing yours and I'll swing mine,
Balance home and everybody dance.
Swing corner lady and now pass one,
And don't be too late.
All the men left, right to your partner and grand right and left.
Pat her on the head.
If she don't like biscuits, feed her slapjacks.
Promenade home.
(*Repeat for second, third, and fourth couples.*)

Position and Call to Start a Tucker

Collected from Fillmore Greenfield. "Old Dan Tucker" is a man without a partner who stands in the center of the square, or set, which is made up of four couples. When the caller signals a change of partners, such as "grand right and left," Tucker tries to get a partner. If he succeeds, the displaced man must take Tucker's place in the center and seek another partner.

> Form a circle, Tucker to the center.
> Grand right and left, everybody dance.

OLD DAN TUCKER

Collected from George Nye.

> Old Dan Tucker, he's in town,
> Swingin' the ladies all around.
> First to the right and then to the left,
> And then to the one you love the best.

POLKA CALL

Collected from John A. Bauer, who said that it was used in Cass County in the 1880's.

> Join hands and circle to the left.
> Meet your partner and promenade back.
> All the men left, grand right and left.
> Promenade to place.
> First lady out to the right.
> Three by three with a polka step.
> Three hands around, lead to the next.
> And solo gent, three by three and six hands around.
> (*Repeat three more times.*)
>
> Join your hands and circle to the left.
> Meet your partner and promenade back.
> All the men left.
> Right-hand your partner, meet your partner.
> Turn right back with a double elbow.
> Keep a-hookin' on.
> First couple swing, lady in the center.
> Seven hands up and around.
> You did so nice, now do it again.

Swing her out and swing her in.
Seven hands up and around again.
(*Repeat three more times.*)

Polka Swing

Collected from Claude C. Haggarty.

First couple lead to the right and four hands around.
And leave that lady and on to the next
And three hands around.
Gents follow up and three hands around.
Three by six and a polka swing.
All the men left, grand right and left.
Meet your partner, promenade home.

Pop Goes the Weasel

Collected from William Carson. At the call of "pop goes the weasel," which the fiddler emphasized by plucking the strings of his instrument, the ladies joined hands to form an arch and the gents passed under it.

First lady out to the couple on the right,
The monkey chased the weasel.
Circle three times and half around,
Pop goes the weasel.
It's on to the next, the gent solo,
The monkey chased the weasel.
Circle three times and half around,
Pop goes the weasel.
(*Repeat for second, third, and fourth couples.*)

Variant

Collected from Elmer Dellett. "Balliente" may be a corruption of the French balloner, "to flare out." Thus the ladies would doe-si-doe in a wide circle.

First gent lead up to the right,
Three hands around and pass right through.
Pop goes the weasel.
(*Repeat three more times.*)

Ladies doe-si-doe balliente.
First two lead to the couple on the right, halfway round.
Doe-si-doe balliente.
Break and swing, half right and pass right through.
Doe-si-doe balliente.
(*Repeat three more times.*)

PROMENADE

*Collected from G. C. Carter. A lilting cadence makes the dance
seem shorter and less strenuous than it really is.*

Circle four in the middle of the floor.
Ladies doe and the gents you know.
Break by the left and then by the right
And on you go.

First couple balance and swing down the center
And around the ring.
Lady goes gee and gent goes haw.
Corner balance, corner whirl.
Promenade that corner girl.

The same little guy with another little girl,
Down the center and around the world.
Lady goes gee and the gent goes haw.
Corner balance, corner whirl.
Promenade that corner girl.

And the same little guy with another little girl,
Down the center and around the world.
Lady goes gee and the gent goes haw.
Corner balance, corner whirl.
Promenade that corner girl.

And the same little gent with another little girl,
Down the center and around the world.
Lady goes gee and the gent goes haw.
Corner balance, corner whirl.
Promenade that corner girl.
(*Repeat for second, third, and fourth couples.*)

PUT ON STYLE

Collected from Patrick Oliver.

> First couple balance and swing.
> Lead out to the right of the ring.
> Right-hand your partner.
> Sashay by and honor your partner.
> Sashay back and put on style.
> Right and left through, right and left back.
> Lead to the next.
> (*Repeat for second, third, and fourth couples.*)

QUADRILLE (I)

Collected from John Hartje. Mr. Hartje was not a caller himself, but he remembered this as one of several calls used at dances on his farm near Roca.

> First four forward and back.
> Forward again and right and left.
> Forward and back.
> Ladies change, change right back.
> Half promenade.
> Balance all and swing.
> All the men left, grand right and left
> Till you meet your partner.
> (*Repeat for side couples.*)

> Balance all and swing your partner.
> First couple round the outside.
> In the center and six hands around.
> To your place and swing your partner.
> (*Repeat for second, third, and fourth couples.*)

> Balance all and swing.
> First couple face out.
> Sashay right, sashay left.
> Ladies to the right, gents to the left.
> Forward and back, forward again,
> And swing your partner to your place.
> (*Repeat for second, third, and fourth couples.*)

Variant

Collected from W. G. Seidell.

Honor your partner, opposite lady too.
Join hands and circle to the left.
Promenade back.
First four forward and back,
Forward again and right and left.
Forward and back, right and left home.
Ladies change, change right back.
Half promenade, right and left back.
Balance all, swing your partner.
All the men left, grand right and left.
All promenade.
(*Repeat.*)

Slide four forward and back,
Forward again and right and left,
Right and left back.
Balance and swing your partner.
Meet your partner and promenade.
All four ladies lead to the right and swing,
And to the next swing.
Home and swing your partner.
All the men left, grand right and left.
All the four gents lead to the right and swing.
(*Repeat until all the couples "come home."*)

QUADRILLE (II)
Collected from Charles Weaver.

All the men left with a left-hand partner to a left-hand round.
Right hand to your partner and right and left around the ring.
Meet your partner and grand promenade.
Everybody swing.
First couple out to the right and three hands around.
Lady promenades, open the door, and circle four.
Ladies doe and gents solo.

Then on to the next and then to the third,
Right on home and grand promenade.
(*Repeat for second, third, and fourth couples.*)

All the men left with the left-hand partner to a left-hand round.
Right hand to your partner and left around the ring.
Meet your partner and grand promenade.
Everybody swing.
First couple out to right and left through.
Swing in the center and outside.
And a right and left back.
Four hands around.
Ladies doe and gents solo.
All the men left.
(*Repeat for second, third, and fourth couples.*)

All the men left with the left-hand to a left-hand round.
Right hand to your partner and right and left around the ring.
Meet your partner and grand promenade.
Everybody swing.
First lady out to couple on the right.
Right-hand gent with a right-hand round,
Now your partner with a left-hand round.
The opposite gent with a right-hand round,
Now your partner with a left-hand round.
Left-hand gent with a right-hand round.
Then your partner with a left-hand round.
Birdie in the center and seven hands round.
Birdie hops out and crow hops in.
Join your hands and do it again.
(*Repeat, adding the following:*)

All the men left with the left-hand partner to a left-hand round.
Right hand to your partner and right and left around the ring.
Meet your partner and grand promenade,
You know where and I don't care.

All the men left with the left-hand partner to a left-hand round.
Right hand to your partner and right and left round the ring.

Meet your partner and grand promenade.
Everybody swing.
All four ladies to center and back to the bar.
All four gents to center and form a star.
Give the right hand across, left hand back, and don't get lost.
Pass your partner first and swing.
Then swing your partner.
(*Repeat with gents to the center.*)

All join hands and circle to the left.
A right and left and grand promenade.
First couple balance and swing.
Promenade around the outside ring.
Right and left through the couple you meet.
Side four the same.
Right and left back and the two ladies change.
Change right back and half promenade.
Right and left home and swing your partner.

QUADRILLE (III)
   Collected from George Nye.

> Salute your partner.
> Then lady on your left.
> Grand right and left.
> Half right and left.
> Balance and promenade.
> Ladies choice.
> Grand promenade.

QUADRILLE (IV)
   Collected from Charles Cole of Doniphan, who called dances for many years around the state.

All the men left and a grand promenade right and left.
Promenade till you meet your own.
First couple down center and cast off six.
Swing at the head and swing at the foot.

Down center and cast off four,
Lady to the right and gent to the left.
Swing her once more.
Down the center and cast off two,
Lady to the right and gent go through.
Everybody swing.
All the men left.
(*Repeat for each couple.*)

QUADRILLE (V)

Collected from Charles Cole.

All the men right and left and a grand promenade
Until you meet your own.
All four gents out to right of the ring.
When they get there, they balance and swing.
Always remember the call,
A right and a left and promenade all.
(*Repeat for the ladies.*)

First couple out to the right,
Birdie in the cage and three hands round.
Birdie in the cage and five hands round.
Birdie in the cage and seven hands round.
Birdie fall out and crow fall in.
All join hands and circle again.
Swing 'em on the corner like you would on a gate.
Now your own.
All the men left.
(*Repeat.*)

QUADRILLE (VI)

Collected from John A. Bauer. To be danced to the tune of
"*Turkey in the Straw.*"

All join hands and circle to the left.
Break and swing and promenade back.
First couple out to the right,
Four hands around.

Right and left with the opposite couple.
Right and left back.
Two ladies change,
Change right back with a half promenade.
Lead to the next.
(*Repeat for second, third, and fourth couples.*)

Variant

Collected from John A. Bauer. To be danced to the tune of "Buffalo Gals" in quick time.

All join hands and circle to the left.
Break and swing and promenade back.
First couple balance and first couple swing.
Promenade the outside ring.
Right and left with the couple you meet,
Opposite couples the same.
Swing your opposite partner.
Now your own, if you're not too late.
Hurry up, George, get a move on.
All the men left, grand right and left.
Promenade all.
(*Repeat three more times.*)

JOHNSON QUADRILLE

Collected from Jesse A. Pound. The music for the first two changes should be played in 2/4 time; that of the third change is best played in jig time.

First four forward and back.
Forward again.
Right and left through, right and left back.
Balance on the corner and swing, grand right and left.
(*Repeat for side couples, then repeat the entire call again.*)

First couple to the right.
Four hands around, right and left six.
Lead to the next.

Four hands around and doe-si-doe.
Break to the right and swing to the left,
And lead to the next, four hands around.
Right and left six, balance home.

All forward to the center and back.
All the men left, grand right and left
First couple to the right, change partners and swing.
Take that lady and lead to the next, four hands around.
Lead to the next, four hands around.
Cheat or swing.
Balance home.

POLKA DOT QUADRILLE
Collected from Charles Weaver.

All the men left with the left-hand partner to a left-hand round.
Right hand to your partner and right and left around the ring.
Meet your partner and grand promenade.
Balance and swing.
First couple out to the right and four hands around.
Ladies doe and gents solo.
It's lady on to the next and three hands around.
Open up the door and circle five.
That's three in the kitchen and five in the hall.
And the way you go with a polka dot all.
Balance home and swing your partner.
(*Repeat.*)

All the men left with the left-hand partner to a left-hand round.
Right hand to your partner and right and left around the ring.
Meet your partner and grand promenade.
Everybody swing.
First couple balance and swing,
Down the center and divide the ring,
Lady go right and gent go left.
Swing at the head and swing at the foot.
Down the center and cast off four.
Swing the same as you did before.

Down the center and cast off two.
Now everybody swing your partner.
(*Repeat.*)

All join hands and left around the ring.
Balance and swing.
First lady, opposite gent give right hand across,
Left hand back and don't get lost.
Forward up four in line,
Break in center and swing half round.
Cut a figure eight with lady in the lead.
Break in center and swing half round.
Cut a figure eight with gent in the lead.
Center four and four hands round.
Ladies doe and gents solo.
(*Repeat.*)

Honor your partners right and left.
Join your patties and circle left.
First couple break and circle to right with a post-auger twist.
Break and swing.
All the men left with the left-hand partner to a left-hand round.
Right hand to your partner and right and left around the ring.
Meet your partner and grand promenade.
Now on to the next.
(*Repeat.*)

Join hands and circle left.
Everybody swing.
First couple out to the right, four hands around.
Leave that lady and on to the next with three hands round.
Take that lady and on to the next with four hands round.
Leave that couple and balance home.
Forward up six and fall back six.
Forward up six and cross over.
Two gents doe-si-doe.
Two gents to the right and four hands round.
Ladies doe and gents solo.
Balance home.
(*Repeat.*)

All the men left with the left-hand partner to a left-hand round.
Right hand to your partner and right and left around the ring.
Meet your partner and grand promenade.
Everybody swing.
First couple out to the right.
Lady round the lady and gents solo.
Lady round the gent and the gent don't go.
Four hands up and around you go.
Ladies doe and gents solo.
(*Repeat.*)

Left-hand circle and a right and left around the ring.
Meet your partner and promenade.
First couple out to couple on the right, four hands round.
Peek-a-boo four, peek-a-boo six.
On to the next and four hands round.
Doe-si lady and solo gent.
Then on to the next and four hands round.
Peek-a-boo four, peek-a-boo six.
Balance home and swing your partner.
(*Repeat.*)

Ring Around the Rosie
Collected from J. J. Senn.

Honors right, honors left.
Join hands and circle to the left.
Break and swing and promenade home.
Four ladies lead out to the right of the ring.
When you get there, you may balance and swing.
And when you have swung, remember the call:
All the men left and promenade all.
(*Repeat last four lines three more times.*)

Swing on the corner,
Then swing your girl.
All the men left, grand right and left.
Meet your partner and promenade home.
Four gents lead out to the right of the ring.

When you get there, you may balance and swing.
And when you have swung, remember the call:
All the men left and promenade all.
(*Repeat last four lines three more times.*)

ROUND SQUARE DANCE
Collected from Fillmore Greenfield.

>Join hands and circle to the left.
>Break, swing, and promenade a ring.
>First couple balance and swing.
>Promenade outside the ring.
>Right and left through the couple you meet.
>
>Side four the same.
>Two ladies change, change away back.
>Half promenade.
>Right and left home.
>Balance home and swing through.
>All the men left,
>Meet your partner and promenade.
>(*Repeat three more times.*)

SAILIN' BY
Collected from J. J. Senn.

>Honor your partners, right and left.
>All join hands and circle to the left.
>Break and swing and promenade home.
>First couple balance and swing,
>Promenade the outside ring.
>Right and left with the couple you meet,
>And the side fours the same.
>Right and left back and two ladies change.
>Change right back with a half promenade.
>Half right and left to your place in the set.
>Swing them all eight and all the men left.
>Grand right and left.
>Meet your partner and promenade home.
>(*Repeat for second, third, and fourth couples.*)

SASHAY ACROSS

Collected from H. C. Whittington.

> All join hands and circle to the left.
> Break and swing and promenade back.
> First couple lead to the couple on the right.
> Sashay across and honor four.
> Sashay back and right and left and lead to the next.
> Break and swing, swing on the corner.
> All the men left, grand right and left.
> Meet your partner and promenade home.
> (*Repeat for second, third, and fourth couples.*)

SASHAY THROUGH

Collected from G. C. Carter.

> First couple balance and swing,
> Promenade the outside ring.
> Sashay through with couple you meet.
> Side four the same.
> Sashay back.
> Two ladies change, change right back
> With a half promenade.
> Four hands half.
> Ladies doe and the gents you know,
> Right and left through
> And home you go.
> Turn 'em all eight.
> All the men left.
> All promenade.
> (*Repeat for second, third, and fourth couples.*)

SEVEN HANDS AROUND

Collected from Jesse A. Pound, who learned it in California. He did not think the call was used in Nebraska until the 1890's, although it was said to have originated before 1839.

Honors right and left.
All the men left, grand right and left.
First lady swing right-hand gent with the right hand.
Rough partner with the left and the left hand around.
Lady swing out and gents swing in.
Join your hands and circle again.
All the men left, grand right and left.
Promenade home.
(*Repeat three more times.*)

SHORT DANCE

Collected from H. C. Whittington.

> Swing your opposite all alone.
> And now the one you call your own.
> Four hands half and right and left.
> And lead to the next.
> (*Repeat for second, third, and fourth couples.*)

SINGING CALL (1)

Collected from Charles Cole. Singing calls were actually sung, in contrast to the others, which were either shouted or chanted.

> All the men left and right and promenade all.
> First lady out to the right,
> Swing that guy with the great big feet.
> Now the one that looks so neat.
> Now the one with the little mustache.
> Now go home and swing your hash.
> All the men left.
> (*Repeat.*)

> First couple out to the right,
> Ladies bow and gents go under.
> Hold 'em tight and swing like thunder.
> All the men left and back home.
> (*Repeat.*)

First couple out to right,
Form a star with a right-hand round.
With the left hand back,
You swing your opposite, then your own.
(*Repeat.*)

First couple round the outside ring,
A right and left to the couple you meet.
Side four the same.
Half promenade, promenade right back.
Two ladies change, change right back.
All the men left and grand parade.
Promenade till you get straight.
(*Repeat.*)

Balance and swing.
First lady out to the right to swing the Indian.
Then the squaw.
Then the little papoose from Arkansas.
All the men left.
(*Repeat.*)

All the men left.
First couple out to the right of the ring,
Lady round lady and gent don't go.
Four hands half.
Two ladies change, change right back.
Swing your opposite, then your own.
All the men left.
(*Repeat.*)

SINGING CALL (II)
Collected from Til McGowan of Lincoln.

Teet 'em up and down, turn 'em all around.
All the men left as you come around.
Right to your pard and right on around.
Hand over hand, right and left grand.
Walk along, John, with your leather breeches on.

If you ever get 'em off, you'll never get 'em on.
Meet your partner and promenade.
Promenade home.

First couple balance and swing,
Lead right out to the right of the ring.
Round that couple with the lady in the lead,
Gent fall through and take the lead.
Lead her off to Arkansas to eat corn bread and possum jaw.
Lady fall through and four hands around,
Four hands up and round you go.
Ladies doe-si-doe and gents you know,
Two little boys, rollin' the dough.
One more change and on you go.

Second couple out and two around,
Two gents fall through.
Chase the possum, chase the coon,
Chase the pretty girl round the room.
Ladies fall through and four hands half.
Ladies doe-si-doe and round,
Pat 'em on the head.
If you can't get biscuits, get corn bread.
Meet your pard with the elbow hook.
I see you and you see me,
Elbow hook and you I see.
Keep hookin' on.
Kill the cow and skin the calf,
Keep hookin' on for an hour and a half.
Meet your partner and promenade home.
You're half done.

SQUARE-DANCE CALL

Collected from Mr. Spellmeyer of Sumner, for whom no first name is given. He called dances in Nebraska for more than twenty years.

All four gents to center and back to the bar.
All four ladies to center and form a star.

With right hands cross, left hands back, and don't get lost.
Pass your partner one and swing.
(*Repeat for partners two and three and original partner.*)
All the men left, right and left.
Meet your partner and promenade.

All four ladies to center and back to the bar.
All four gents to center and form a star.
With right hands cross, left hands back, and don't get lost.
Pass your partner one and swing.
(*Repeat for partners two and three and original partner.*)
All the men left, right and left.
Meet your partner and promenade.

STAR DANCE

Collected from Claude C. Haggarty.

> First four gents to center and back.
> Ladies to the center and form a star,
> With the right hand across and back to the left.
> Circle once and swing on the quarter way round.
> (*Repeat.*)

SWING AUNT SALLY

Collected from Fillmore Greenfield.

> First gent lead out to the right.
> Swing the girl with the crooked nose,
> And on to the next.
> Swing the one with the great big shoes.
> Now the one with the great big feet.
> Now the one that looks so neat.
> (*Repeat three more times.*)

SWING 'EM ALL RIGHT

Collected from M. B. Packard.

> All jump up and when you come down,
> Turn that pretty one round and round.
> All the men left, grand right and left.

Meet your partner and promenade.
First couple balance and swing,
Lead to the right and four hands halfway round.
Now right and left four and right and left six.
Right and left back and lead to the next and four hands half.
Ladies doe-si-doe, the gents you know.
Break by the right, swing partner by the left,
And balance to the next and four hands half.
Right and left four and right and left six.
Right and left back and balance home.
Swing 'em all eight and all the men left, grand right and left.
Meet your partner and all promenade.
(*Repeat for second, third, and fourth couples.*)

SWING 'EM BY THE HEELS

Collected from Charles Weaver. Because its violent swinging posed a threat to life and limb, this call was outlawed in Nebraska.

All the men left with the left-hand partner to a left-hand round.
Right hand to your partner and right and left around the ring.
Meet your partner and grand promenade,
And everybody swing.
First couple out to the right and four hands across,
The ladies bow-wow and the gents yow-yow.
Pick 'em up and swing like thunder,
Then on to the next.
(*Repeat.*)

All the men left with the left-hand partner to a left-hand round.
Right hand to your partner and right and left around the ring.
Meet your partner and grand promenade,
Everybody swing.
First couple out to the right,
Lady round the lady, gent around the gent,
Lady round the gent and gent around the lady.
Four hands up and round you go.
Ladies doe and gents solo.
On to the next till you get home,
Then balance and swing your partner.
(*Repeat.*)

SWINGING ON THE GATE
Collected from H. C. Whittington.

> Side four forward and first four divide.
> All to your places and straighten up your faces.
> First four forward and sides divide.
> Change in the center and swing on the side.
> Same four forward and sides divide.
> Change in the center and swing on the side.
> Break and swing.
> Swing on the corner like swingin' on a gate.
> All the men left with your old left hand.
> Right-hand your partner and right and left grand.
> Meet your partner and promenade back.
> (*Repeat for side couples.*)

SWING OLD ADAM
Collected from Fillmore Greenfield. The music should be in 6/8 time.

> Balance to your places and all swing.
> All the men left and promenade.
> First gent lead out to the right.
> Swing old Adam and now swing Eve.
> Don't forget old Adam before you leave.
> (*Repeat three more times, then repeat the entire pattern for the second, third, and fourth gents. Repeat the same series for the four ladies.*)

SWING THE GIRL BEHIND YOU
Collected from Mr. Spellmeyer.

All join hands and circle to the left.
All the men left around and whirl with a grand right and left.
First couple balance and swing out to the right of the ring.
Balance two, pass right through, and swing that girl behind you.
Pass right back in the same old track and swing that girl behind
   you.
Four hands half, right and left through, and on to the next.

Balance two and pass right through and swing that girl behind
you.
Pass right back in the same old track and swing that girl behind
you.
Four hands half, right and left through, and on to the next.
Balance two, pass right through, and swing that girl behind you.
Four hands half, right and left through,
And swing all eight and around the world with a grand right
and left.

Second couple balance and swing out to the right of the ring.
Balance two and pass right through and swing the girl behind
you.
Four hands half, right and left through, and on to the next.
And balance two and pass right through and swing the girl
behind you.
Pass right back in the same old track and swing the girl behind
you.
Four hands half, right and left through, and on to the next.
Balance two and pass right through and swing that girl behind
you.
Pass right back in the same old track and swing that girl behind
you.
Four hands half, right and left through, home you go.
Swing all eight, all the men left around the world.
With a grand right and left, meet your partner and all
promenade.
(*Repeat for third couple.*)

Fourth couple balance and swing out to the right of the ring.
Balance two and pass right through and swing the girl behind
you.
Pass right back in the same old track and swing the girl behind
you.
Four hands half, right and left through, on to the next.
Balance two, pass right through, and swing the girl behind you.
Pass right back in the same old track and swing that girl behind
you.

Four hands half, right and left through,
Home you go and swing all eight,
Now on the corner if you're not too late,
Like an old hen swinging on a barn-door gate.
Hand a man, Joe; if they don't like biscuits, feed 'em on dough.
Meet your partner and all promenade,
You know where and I don't care.

TRAVEL ON AND TRAVEL ON

Collected from Fillmore Greenfield. Each gent swings the ladies a total of sixty-four times—enough to make him want to rest for a while.

> First couple lead out to the right and swing.
> Swing the ladies and travel on.
> Swing the next and the next.
> (*First man swings each lady four times. He then repeats this procedure four times. Repeat the pattern for the second, third, and fourth couples.*)

UNTITLED CALL

Collected from Robert Rustermeier of Lincoln, who knew one hundred and twenty-five calls, and called dances in many rural communities. Mr. Rustermeier was able to dance and call at the same time. In the first change, at "ballinette" (see p. 112) the ladies would dance a wide pattern, with the gents counterdancing.

First couple balance out to the couple on the right with the half-
 circle turn.
Ladies ballinette and gents counterdance.
On to the next.
(*Repeat for second, third, and fourth couples.*)

First couple balance out to the couple on the right,
Lady round the lady, gent round the gent.
The lady round the gent, four half around, balance on through.
On to the next.
(*Repeat for second, third, and fourth couples.*)

First couple balance to the couple on the right,
Right and left, circle six, then circle eight.
Round once on the left eight.
Cast off four little gents.
On to the left eight.
Promenade to your seats, you know where.
(*Repeat for second, third, and fourth couples.*)

First couple forward up to the center and back,
Lady to the right, gent to the left.
Forward up to the center and cut off four,
Two on the side, with the lady to the right and the gent to the
left.
Forward up and retreat back.
Cast off six, three on a side.
Return balance and swing.
(*Repeat for second, third, and fourth couples.*)

VIRGINIA REEL (I)
*Collected from H. C. Filley, former chairman of the Department
of Rural Education at the University of Nebraska College of
Agriculture, who sponsored square dancing on the campus.*

Meet in the center.
Swing round, right hands.
Swing round, left hands.
Swing round, both hands.
Doe-si-doe.

Meet in center, right hands across.
Meet in a promenade down the center.
Swing partner with right hand.
Swing first of partner's line with left hand.
Swing partner, right hand.
Swing second of partner's line with left hand.
Swing partner, right hand.
(*Continue call until end of partner's line is reached.*)

Leaders skip down center to places at head of line.
Around the outside, lines following.
Leaders join hands and form a bridge under which the others
  pass.
(*The head couple is now at the foot; continue call until head couple
returns to original position.*)

VIRGINIA REEL (II)
  *Collected from Jesse A. Pound, who said it was popular among
the settlers during the 1870's and 1880's.*

>   Head lady, foot gent, forward and back.
>   Side the same.
>   Head lady, foot gent, right hand around.
>   Side the same.
>   Head lady, foot gent, doe-si-doe.
>   Side the same.
>   Head couple down the center and back,
>   Swing once and a half at the head.
>   And opposites down the line and up the center.
>   Ladies to the right and gents to the left,
>   Form needle's eye and balance.
>   Pass through.
>   (*The head couple is now at the foot; repeat call for each
>   couple on the floor.*)

WALTZ QUADRILLE (I)
  *Collected from Til McGowan. As the title implies, the music
here is a waltz.*

>   First couple down center and there you divide,
>   Ladies to the left, gents around the outside.
>   Bow to your partner, don't be afraid.
>   Swing on the corner and waltz promenade.

Variant 1

Collected from M. B. Packard. The interspersed singing verses add variety to the dance and make it more enjoyable for the caller.

First couple down the center and there you divide,
Lady to the right and gent to the left.
And honor your partner and don't be afraid
To swing corner lady with a waltz promenade.

(*Waltz while the caller sings the following verse:*)
Peek-a-boo, you rascal you,
I see you hiding there.
Peek-a-boo, you rascal you,
Come out from behind that chair.

(*Repeat call with first couple while the caller sings:*)
Oh where, oh where has my little dog gone?
Oh where, oh where can he be?
With his ears cut short and his tail cut long,
Oh where, oh where can he be?

(*Repeat call again, after which the waltz verse is sung:*)
Bring back, bring back,
Bring back my Bonnie to me.
Bring back, bring back,
Bring back my Bonnie to me.

(*Repeat call once more, then sing:*)
I wish I had someone to love me,
And someone to call me their own, etc.

(*Repeat call for second, third, and fourth couples and then sing:*)
It's come to my arms, Nora darling.
Bid your friend and old sweetheart good-bye.
Before tomorrow morning,
You will leave that joyful home
To go roaming with your Barney McCoy.

(*Repeat call and follow with:*)
Times have changed since those days,
Soaring up in G,
While others ride a hog train,
But they all feel just like me.
They would part with all they get,
Could they have but one twirl
And have a waltz with their best girl
On the sidewalks of New York.

(*Repeat call with fourth couple and sing:*)
After the ball is over,
After the dancers have gone,
Many a heart is breaking,
If you could read them o'er.
Many a hope has vanished,
Many a romance done.
Sad are the hearts that are broken,
After the ball.

Variant 2

Collected from J. J. Senn.

First couple down center and there you divide,
Lady to the right and gent other side.
Honor your partner and don't be afraid,
And swing corner lady and waltz promenade.
(*First couple repeats the call three more times; then repeat
for each couple.*)

Waltz Quadrille (ii)

Collected from Charles Cole.

All join hands and circle left.
All the men right and left,
Promenade eight till you get straight.
First couple down center and there you divide,
Lady to the right and gent to the side.

Don't be bashful and don't be afraid,
Swing on the corner in a waltz promenade.
(*Repeat.*)

You Swing Mine and I'll Swing Yours
Collected from H. C. Whittington.

> You swing mine while I swing yours.
> All balance and swing.
> Promenade, first couple to the right.
> You swing mine while I swing yours.
> Mine's as pretty as yours.
> You swing mine and I'll swing yours,
> Your hands half and right and left,
> And lead to the next.
> I'll swing mine while you swing yours.
> You swing mine and I'll swing yours.
> (*Repeat for second, third, and fourth couples.*)

II. TALES

White Man's Tales

The frontier, whether by Turner's famous definition or by any other, is a land of storytellers, and in this respect remains frontier in nature until the last original settler is gone.

Mari Sandoz

When Sir Richard Burton, the explorer and translator of the *Arabian Nights' Entertainment*, crossed the Nebraska plains in 1860, he noted in his journal that the imagination of the western man "is inflamed by scenery and climate, difficulty and danger; . . . I have been gravely told of a herd of bison which arrested the course of the Platte River, causing its waters, like those of the Red Sea, to stand up, wall fashion, whilst the animals were crossing." Certainly it is true that the frontiersmen and pioneers relished nothing more than spinning tall tales for the benefit of credulous visiting firemen and tenderfeet from the East. But such tales also found an appreciative local audience. The early settlers loved a good story—or a good lie—for its own sake; perhaps even more important, by exaggerating the hardships they endured and the calamities that befell them, they were able, paradoxically enough, to cut them down to size.

While some of the selections included here appear to be simple reminiscences, the majority are clearly from the oral tradition—that is, some are history and some are folklore—with the tall tale predominating. For the reader who is interested in parallels with folktales from other regions in this country and abroad, motif analyses of these stories and the Indian tales that follow are given in the Appendix.

THE STUMP SUCKER

Collected from Grant Dehart of Lincoln, who came to Nebraska with his parents in 1879 and lived first in a sod house south of Central City. When he was interviewed in 1940, Mr. Dehart was more than eighty years old. The interviewer noted that he liked particularly "to relate his and his father's horse-trading experiences in an age and section of the country where trading horses was a game of wits as well as an exchange of chattels" (1).

A neighboring horse trader who lived ten miles from our place pulled into the yard one morning, driving what seemed to be a fair to middling good work team. The off horse, however, aroused my suspicions although he was a big-boned gray who was as sleek and well fleshed as a ripened watermelon. In fact, he was too sleek. If he had acted sick I would have thought he was bloated. But some horses look that way for no particular reason. Father, of course, was circling around him in his best professional manner, but then he did that to every horse he saw. Anyway, Swapper apparently wasn't bent on a trade. His coming looked like a sociable drop-in that so many folks were in the habit of doing in those days. Besides, he said he was on his way on an important errand elsewhere.

But father, who was becoming interested in the gray, didn't listen to Swapper's talk about leaving. There was something about the gray that had captured his eye. I suppose it was his sleek appearance—the same sleek appearance that had aroused my suspicions.

So, knowing of father's interest, I wasn't surprised when he went into the barn and brought out an eight-year-old bay mare he had traded for a few months before. She was a good piece of horseflesh except for her bad habit of riding the singletree [letting the other horse do all the pulling] when doing team work.

Swapper, as soon as father began showing her off, forgot all about the hurry he had said he was in. Instead he sat down and slowly filled his pipe with corncake.

"I tell you, Dehart," said Swapper, now leisurely puffing away on his briar, "I'm not hankering to part with Gray Bill. He's too good a hoss. But, as a personal favor, I might be

willing to trade for your mare if you will throw in a little boot—
say $15."

This offer started father and Swapper off into a typical horse-
trader's argument, with Swapper trying to keep his original
price where he had placed it and father attempting to cut it
down to what he regarded as a more reasonable figure.

They finally struck a compromise of $7.50 and it looked like
a trade. I noticed that father was now in such a hurry to finish
the deal he neglected to ask some of the usual trader's questions
about hidden defects. His only one was when he asked, "Your
gray ain't wind-broke, is he?"

Swapper, in an insulted tone, answered, "Look here, Dehart,
you'll find that hoss has more wind than any hoss you ever had."

Well, this answer settled the deal. They made the swap. Our
bay was harnessed and hitched in jig time. Father led Gray Bill
off to the side while Swapper got into his buggy, gathered up
the lines and then, after mumbling something about being in a
hurry, went away rather suddenlike. His actions still seemed
queer to me, but I didn't say anything.

Father, after Swapper had left, took Gray Bill into the barn
and tied him in a stall that had a straight pole running across.
It was now eleven-thirty. The horse trade had taken most of the
morning, so I didn't see how Swapper could have been in a hurry
after spending so much time with us. Father however, thought
he had done a good morning's work; but I reserved my conclu-
sions. Gray Bill still seemed too perfect. He was so sleek that he
looked more like a shiny, over-sized toy horse than the real
thing.

About half an hour later we all sat down to dinner, but only
had time to pass the food around before an infernal racket
started in the barn. It sounded like a dozen bellows and a
hundred frogs all blowing and croaking in unison. It went "ooph
ker chug, ooph ker chug," and then for variety reversed itself
to "chug ker ooph, chug ker ooph." Hell had certainly broken
loose in the barn.

Ma was the first to jump up. She yelled, "Pa, that's your new
horse! You and your smart horse swapping has gotten us a
stump sucker!"

Sure enough, when we got to the barn we found Gray Bill

with his jaws clamped on the pole that ran across the manger, making the most unearthly noises I have ever heard. He was sucking wind like a cow pulling her foot out of the mud.

It was a sight to see and I couldn't help but laugh. "Yep, you've got a wind sucker there for fair."

Father was raving mad. "That skunk, Swapper, knew about this."

"Well, didn't he tell you Gray Bill had more wind than any horse around here?" I asked.

The horse was blowed up like a balloon and still going strong. I thought he'd bust, but he didn't. That was why he looked so fat and sleek when Swapper drove him in. The old rascal had stopped the horse at a post and let him suck wind just before he came to our house.

We thought we could bring him out of his wind-sucking habit by keeping him away from wooden fences or poles, but that was a difficult thing to do. Then too, he wouldn't eat much, so as soon as his "wind pressure" went down he looked like a walking skeleton. I doubt if he ate more than half a dozen mouthfuls of hay a day—just enough to keep from falling over.

The first thing father did the next Sunday morning was to drive over to Swapper's place with the stump sucker. To his surprise Swapper was unusually lenient for being a horse trader. He offered to exchange the bay mare for Gray Bill provided he could keep the $7.50. Father was glad to get out of the deal this easy.

Later we learned that Swapper had traded his stump sucker to nearly every newcomer in the county. Swapper always got him back, keeping, of course, the money that had been involved in the transactions.

TRADING BY MOONLIGHT
Collected from Grant Dehart.

A few years after father's horse trade with Swapper I got a job in a water mill near Central City. When working there I made a horse trade with Swapper for what looked like a fair saddle horse whose name was Baldy. This horse was a smooth, bald-faced bay whose only apparent fault was that he had ornery eyes. I thought I could handle him if he got nasty, so his mean expression didn't bother me. It looked like a good deal.

But it didn't require a long time to find out he was just as ornery as he looked. He behaved fine at first, was so gentle that he could have been a ladies' horse. But our honeymoon was soon over with. One evening, when I was leaving Central City after visiting friends, I found myself sitting on Main Street in a puddle of water with a bunch of loafers whooping and laughing around me.

The horse, who I soon began to suspect was the devil himself, didn't run away. Instead he stood still and actually looked amused as I started to get up. I managed to ride him home that night without being thrown a second time, but only because I didn't let him take me by surprise.

The next morning I fixed up a bucking stick, which is a crotched stick that is fastened to the belly band and runs up to the bridle-bit rings. This arrangement kept him from getting his head down so he could buck.

I was now anxious to get rid of Old Baldy before everyone in the neighborhood caught on that he was a bucker. So, with this in mind, I rode him one night to a party given a few miles south of the mill, where I hoped to meet someone who would be interested in a trade. I took off the bucking stick when I got near the place and tied him at the pasture gate, which was located some distance from the house. This was done to keep too many people from seeing and asking questions about him. The less advertising you do with a bad horse you wish to sell, the better off you are.

Lem Troost, who was a newcomer to the neighborhood, showed up at the party a little later and we got to discussing this and that. Finally we got on the subject of horses.

Lem said, "I sure got a bang-up smooth four-year-old filly out there." That remark of Lem's got me interested, so I began bragging up the bald-faced bucking boy Swapper had pawned off on me. Pretty soon we wandered into the yard to compare horses.

There was a good moon, which made Baldy look sleek and racy. Even his eyes had a gentle look. Lem immediately fell in love with my horse and wanted to ride him; but I was scared he would get hurt, and at the same time I didn't want to say anything about Baldy's bad habit of bucking.

Finally I gave in to Lem's request; but before I let him mount, I wheeled Baldy around so he would start off in the opposite direction from where he was standing. I had found he wouldn't buck when I did this, if he wasn't ridden for too great a distance. I also told Lem my horse was used to me but might resent a stranger riding him at night. This was a hint for him to be on his guard. Len mounted while I held my breath for fear he would be thrown off. But nothing happened. Baldy behaved like an angel, which made Lem fall more in love with him than ever.

Lem, after his ride, took me to a side of the barn where his horse was hitched. She wasn't as big as Baldy but looked good. I rode her around the yard in order to get the feel of her. The only thing I regretted was that there were too many rigs around to put her through a fast pace, which is the best way to test a horse.

We traded even, without any boot. Lem seemed anxious to get away after we had exchanged the saddles on our new horses. I would have noticed this more and become suspicious if I hadn't been of the same mind. The party, which was still in progress, was forgotten by both of us.

Lem was the first to leave. I wondered what would happen to him on his way home if Baldy began bucking, but I didn't actually worry because Lem was a good rider who wouldn't get hurt *much* if Baldy decided to give him a spill.

After Lem had left I started for home on my filly, and was delighted. I put her into a trot and then a gallop. We were breezing along at a good clip, feeling extra good, when for what seemed no reason at all she stumbled and went down. At first I thought it was an accident, but a little later it happened again —twice in one mile. I got skinned up that time, so went easy the rest of the way. I knew now that Lem had put over about the same thing on me that I had on him.

The next morning I found out what was the trouble with my new horse, although it took another bad fall to do it. She had a crooked foot which worked all right at a slow trot but when she went into a gallop the foot turned in, causing her to hit it with her other foot. She went down every time she did it.

Lem found out about his side of the trade the next morning when Baldy pitched him into the road. He didn't hang on to Baldy long after that had happened. This time he traded for a one-eyed, old pelter who had the heaves. Lem and I laughed over the way we thought we had outsmarted each other. We figured we had broken even, so remained friends—only we didn't trade any more horses.

A THRESHING HOAX
Collected from Grant Dehart.

Another fellow and I had a threshing outfit in the late '80's with which we threshed grain for the farmers in our part of Merrick and Hamilton counties [the Central City area]. Since most of the grain ripened at the same time, we were kept busy attempting to cover as much territory with our machine in as short a space of time as possible. Then also there was a number of threshing outfits in the same county. This, as was to be expected, created a great deal of rivalry between the different crews. This rivalry didn't always end with friendly banter neither. Skulduggery, sometimes of an injurious nature, was indulged in, but I will tell more about that later.

Breakdowns were another thorn in our side: for us because they created delay when we should be making money, for the farmers because idle threshing help was just as notorious for their eating capacities as when they were working. Then there was always rain to contend with, not only because wet weather prevented threshing, but also because the dirt roads of this period were often no better than tracks that became impassable for the heavy steam engines which furnished power to the threshing machines.

We had been pretty successful in the season of '88. That is, luck was with us as long as we worked our immediate neighborhood. But when we moved into new territory trouble began. First, our engineer turned out to be more of a mule nurse than he was a steam engineer. He managed to keep steam up, but he did it without babying the engine. Consequently, it was being slowly pounded to pieces.

It happened that the Burlington strike was on at this time,

so many train engineers were drifting around looking for work. One of these was a man named McGurk, who, when he heard we were having trouble with our engine, walked ten miles from Aurora to see what the trouble was. He didn't say much at first, just loafed around and looked the outfit over. Then, after a day or so, he hit me for a job by saying he could operate the engine the way it should be run. The moment I found out he wasn't another loafer but a trained railroad engineer, I set him to work.

The engine, under his treatment, immediately picked up in speed and tempo. It even gave more power with a smaller amount of coal. Then, in the evening, after it became too dark to thresh, he adjusted the rings and tightened the loose piston which had been causing most of the trouble. McGurk was a tough guy who wouldn't let anyone near the engine. He didn't even like it when I, its owner, hung around the machine too much, but I didn't mind his attitude because he kept the engine polished and running like clockwork.

Farmers in the '80's, as they still do today, didn't pay cash to the crew that helped with the threshing. This help was paid by returning work in kind. It was not unusual, by this method, for the same farmer to follow the threshing machine to a dozen or more farms. Some of these farmers, especially the young ones, had the tendency to have a smart-alecky, know-it-all attitude toward the man who ran the steam engine. Perhaps it was because of his position, since he, like a war lord, was the one who had the power to make the wheels go around.

But McGurk, who no doubt knew about the ribbing that was going on about him, didn't say a word to anyone. He just stuck close to the engine, which he was always oiling and polishing when he didn't have anything else to do.

One young farmer named Ramey was especially obnoxious to McGurk because of his habit of jumping up on the engine when the engineer was busy elsewhere and giving the steam whistle a few toots. McGurk didn't say anything, but gave Ramey some angry looks. This tickled the young farmer, who was just beginning to feel his oats, and caused him to pull the cord with even more vigor.

Then we moved to young Ramey's father's farm, about a mile away, for a big job. Another threshing outfit was operating in the field adjoining our new location. The men, as was to be expected, were sore at us for what they considered an infringement on their territory. They expressed their feeling by making remarks about our broken-down outfit. Then, too, they heckled us with their steam whistle at every opportunity. McGurk didn't say much, but I could see by the way he glared at the rival outfit he didn't like it. Nor was he enthusiastic about having young Ramey around, especially since we were now threshing for his father, where Ramey felt more free than ever to loaf around the engine as much as he liked.

The steam engine from time to time had to be refilled with water. For this purpose a tank wagon was a part of our outfit, at the top of which was a hose long enough to draw water from a horse tank or creek and a hand pump that was used to force the water into the engine boiler.

Young Ramey became interested in the tank wagon after we had moved to his father's farm. After fooling around the engine as much as he dared under McGurk's glares, he climbed on top of the water wagon and began experimenting with the apparatus. McGurk watched Ramey fooling around with the tank's water pump. After watching him a while, he said, "That's a pretty slick thing you are looking at."

"Why, what is it?" asked Ramey.

"Well, sir, I don't tell everyone about it because it's an invention of my own, which I haven't gotten around to have patented yet. But if you promise to keep it a secret, I'll tell you."

"I won't tell a soul," promised Ramey, who was now so curious he couldn't stand still.

"Well, sir, that's a water compressor as well as a pump. It not only pumps water into the engine's boiler, but also squeezes up the water so twice as much can be stored in the same amount of space. The water in the tank at the present time isn't compressed because I forgot to turn on the compressor screw the last time I pumped it in."

McGurk then talked the young buck into trying out the water compressor by running both the intake and outtake ends of the hose into the tank. Then he proceeded to explain that if he worked the pump handle he would draw all the water past the compressor, which would squeeze the water so the tank would have twice as great a capacity as it had before. Well, sir, McGurk talked that fool Ramey into standing up on the water tank for over an hour pumping water out of the tank and back in again. No one paid any attention to what was going on because it all looked businesslike.

The rival crew across the way by now was tearing their hair trying to outdo us in the threshing. We, of course, were doing the same thing; consequently both outfits were really knocking out their jobs in jig time, with the whistles of the two big steamers blowing at full blast and the chaff from the straw flying in every direction.

McGurk, during the course of the day, kept becoming more and more angry at the rival outfit. He scowled in their direction every time they tooted their whistle, which was every few minutes. Then, late in the afternoon, he had an idea which, if it worked, would put the rival outfit out of business for a day. So, after watching young Ramey pumping water in and out of the water tank for a back-breaking length of time, he called him over to the engine, where he asked him if he had ever heard of a steam engine playing notes like a pipe organ.

Young Ramey was interested, so McGurk proceeded to tell him how it could be done with the rival outfit's engine, if he would carefully follow directions. McGurk then told him in detail how to sneak out to the other outfit and drop several large chunks of homemade soap into the tank of their water wagon. McGurk added that whistle soap was the best, but since they would have to send to town for it, the homemade variety would have to be used as a substitute.

Well, that kid followed McGurk's directions and loaded up the rival outfit's water tank with as much soap as he could lay his hands on. He could hardly wait the next morning for the steam engine to start up so he could hear the musical sounds.

Early the next morning the rival outfit quickly got its engine to steaming for the day's run, but as soon as they filled the boiler with the soapy water in the tank, all kinds of tricks began to take place. Enough soap foamed and bubbled out of the engine's cylinders to furnish washings for a hundred families!

The engineer of the rival engine of course discovered what was wrong and concluded that McGurk had had a hand in the business, although he couldn't prove anything. They spent all morning getting their engine in shape while the rest of the hands loafed around. We finished threshing that day, after which McGurk insisted that the outfit be moved to our next job on the same night. He was afraid the rival outfit would retaliate with similar tricks on him in revenge and did not wish to take any chances by remaining in their vicinity.

SKUNK OIL'S PUNKIN

Collected from Grant Essex of Lincoln. This tale, collected in many neighboring states, is clearly a folktale. The completeness and smoothness of the narration makes this version particularly attractive.

One of the first men I met after I had settled in Chase County [in the southwest corner of the state] in the '80's was an old fellow who had a claim on the Stinking Water River. He was a character who did a little bit of everything from trapping and hunting to farming, but what he excelled in the most was lying. He could think up more lies in less time than anyone I have ever known. And I have heard some pretty good deviations from the truth in my day. But this man was the champion.

I don't recall his real name, nor would it matter if I did because to everyone in the community he was known as "Skunk Oil." He had been given this name because of his constant claims that a skunk's oil had the power to cure all diseases. Besides, Skunk Oil carried a bad odor with him—caused, I think, by his lack of interest in bathing. Then, too, he was constantly sweating, even in the coldest weather. It wasn't a pretty sight—or smell! But it was, so to speak, Skunk Oil's trade mark, and as that you had to accept it.

One day when I was out looking over the land in preparation for spring plowing, I saw Skunk Oil ambling along an old buffalo trail which led past my place. I had only met him once before, and I knew I was in for another lie, since a newcomer to the county was always legitimate prey for Skunk Oil.

But Skunk Oil, after our preliminary greetings were over, fooled around a while talking about this and that before he got around to the whopper that I knew he was itching to tell. You

see, I had met up with him once before on the first day of my
arrival in the county, so I knew what he was leading up to. He
finally got started by asking what I thought of the country and
its possibilities. I answered by telling him I didn't think anyone
could raise much but grass and, with luck, maybe a little hell.

"Man, you're plumb wrong there," was his reply. "Ever hear
about them punkins I raised over by the river? Well, you ought
to have seen them."

I saw he was starting to warm up to his subject, so I looked
doubtful and said I didn't think they'd grow over there. He
didn't reply for a moment or so because he was busy biting off
a chew of navy plug that apparently was as tough as leather.
Then, after he had succeeded in chewing off a big piece, he
slowly replied, "I didn't think they would grow there myself, so
I didn't attempt planting any punkin seeds. But one day when
I was dropping some corn seed along the river, seven or eight
punkin seeds showed up in the poke of corn, so I naturally
planted those seeds with the corn and forgot about them. The
corn grew up and by the middle of the summer was better'n
shoulder high. But I didn't go over to the field for a long time. I
believed in letting good enough be, so let the corn take care of
itself. Besides, I was having a great deal of pig trouble at this
time."

"How was that?" I asked.

"Well, I had an old sow who had a litter of eleven little pigs
that I turned loose to forage for themselves. It saved me the
trouble of feeding them. For a while they stayed near the soddie,
but one day they didn't show up and it was the beginning of no
end of trouble. I spent several weeks looking for them, but
couldn't find so much as a trace of their whereabouts. Along in
September I went to my corn patch by the river, and what I
saw nearly made me doubt my sanity."

"Why, what had happened?"

"The eight punkin seeds that had been mixed in with the
seed corn I had planted had started growing in a big way, like
the bean in 'Jack and the Beanstalk,' only for me they followed
the ground. One punkin vine was especially big. It was at least
eight foot thick and took off across the river like a big green
snake, disappearing in a thicket on the opposite side of the river

bank. This vine was so enormous that its top was above my head. I followed it to the bank, where I crawled up on it and walked across the river. It made a natural bridge which was strong enough to hold a team of oxen.

"Well, believe it or not, I followed this vine for seven miles into the open prairie, where, at its end, I found a tremendous punkin which must have been at least thirty feet high. It was a beautiful reddish-yellow, ripening in the fall air. From a distance, with the sun shining on it, it looked very much like a harvest moon. I had never seen anything like it before and probably never will again.

"As I was walking around it, looking it over, I heard a grunting, squealing sound come from its insides. It was a peculiar, unearthly noise, which had me scared stiff for a few minutes until I happened to think of my missing pigs. It was them I heard. They were in the punkin, although I couldn't figure out how they had gotten there.

"So I hurried back to the soddie for a saw and axe, which I took back to the punkin. After two hours of sawing and cutting I managed to make a hole in the side. It was hard work, because the punkin's sides were hard as plate iron. After I had finished making a good-sized hole, I crawled inside where, sure's you're born, were those pigs. They had growed so it was difficult to recognize them. Must have weighed two hundred pounds apiece, while the sow probably tipped the scales at half a ton.

"Now that I had found my pigs, I was sure hankering to find out how they had gotten into the punkin. Nor did it take me long to get at the secret. The old sow had taken her litter to the corn patch, where, when rooting around, she'd dug a hole into the side of the vine and had gone inside, followed by her pigs. Here they stayed, feeding on the vine and growing along with it. In time it carried them across the river to the big punkin itself. This they made their headquarters. But there were many tracks in the vine itself, so they probably traveled back and forth a great deal.

"The punkin was too big to move, so I left the pigs there all winter and they used it for a snug, cozy hog house. I walked over once a week to see how they were getting along. When the weather was nice, I walked over on the top of the vine, but when it was cold, I lighted a miner's lamp, which I had purchased from an old peddler, and used the inside of the vine. It made a fine tunnel.

"When spring came, I hitched the team to my wagon and crossed the river on the vine—it was a perfect road—with the idea of loading one of the punkin seeds for another crop. I took Hank Billings, who lived up the river a ways, along to help me load the seed.

"Unfortunately we didn't have a rope and pulley so were forced to raise the punkin seed with our hands. The seed slipped during the process and caught Hank under it, breaking his leg. Naturally this accident made him good and mad since it meant he would be laid up for the greater part of the summer.

"So I was not surprised the next day when a committee of settlers called at my soddie and ordered me not to plant any more punkins. They said they were skeered of the punkin taking over the whole county if any more grew like the last one did, and there wasn't any sense in taking any unnecessary risks.

"I tried to answer their arguments by telling them what fine roads and bridges the vines would make and of the punkin houses and barns that could be made from the heads, but they wouldn't listen to me and burned all my seeds. So I calculate the only punkins we will have from now on will be the ordinary garden variety, which isn't good for anything except pies."

A COAL OIL CURE

Collected from Charley Woods of Lincoln, who was born in Otoe County in 1863. He told the following tale as typical of the German community there.

One of the big problems in the 1880's was head lice. It's funny, but everyone was afflicted, no matter how clean and careful they were. I remember having my hair filled with the insects, and every kid in school the same way. Our mothers were hard put to overcome the pests. Red percipity [precipitate] was rubbed into our scalps, but it didn't help much. Some people tried coal oil, but my folks were scared to use it because of the many stories or superstitions about its bad effect.

One story, which I never believed, was about a woman who used coal oil on her head in an attempt to get rid of head lice. She kept up her coal-oil treatment for a long time, many months, until she became sick with bad headaches. After a while, a liquid which looked and smelled like coal oil would leak out of her ears and eyes. As time went on, she kept on becoming sicker and sicker until she finally died. Doctors, when they cut her open, found on her brain a pint of coal oil which had seeped through her skull.

LINING THE HYMN

In pioneer Nebraska churches, hymn singing presented a formidable problem for the preacher. Hymn books were scarce, and even when they were available, few sod busters could read music. The problem was solved as it had been solved on the eastern frontiers: the minister "lined" the hymn—that is, he sang one or two lines and the congregation then repeated what the minister had sung, and so on, until the hymn was finished.

One preacher who had poor eyesight was unable to read without his glasses. One Sunday when he was conducting a service in a sod house he found that he was unable to line the hymn because he had forgotten his glasses. He tried to explain his predicament to the congregation: "My eyes are dim. I cannot see. I left my specs at home."

The congregation, thinking he was lining a hymn, burst into song and faithfully reproduced his words. The minister, now frantic, made another attempt to clarify the situation: "I did not mean that you should sing; I only meant my eyes were dim." But the audience, now warmed up to the singing, hastily repeated these lines. It is not known how he finally got them turned off.

GRASSHOPPER TALES

Collected from Thomas J. Hartnett of Hubbard, who was born in Dakota County in 1861. There had been "grasshopper years" in the '50's and '60's, but, as Everett Dick writes, the invasion of the year 1874 "surpassed anything before or since and caused such great damage that on the plains it is generally called the grasshopper year. The grasshoppers came suddenly. They traveled with a strong wind, coming with it and leaving with it. Rising high in the air with their wings spread, they were carried along with very little effort; they appeared from the North. Their ravages reached from the Dakotas to northern Texas and penetrated as far east as Sedalia, Missouri. . . . At times the insects were four to six inches deep on the ground and continued to alight for hours. Men were obliged to tie strings around their pants legs to keep the pests from crawling up their legs. In the cool of the evening the hoppers gathered so thick on the warm rails of the railroad that the Union Pacific trains were stopped. Section men were called out to shovel the grasshoppers off the track near the spot where Kearney, Nebraska, now stands, so that the trains could get through. The track was so oily and greasy that the wheels spun and would not pull a train" (7).

The grasshoppers came to Dakota County in such numbers in 1873 [sic] that they hid the sun. A cornfield would be completely stripped of all vegetation inside of two hours. They tell a story about a man who, when plowing in a field, hung his work jacket with a watch in it on a post. When he came back to his jacket after plowing the field, all that was left was his watch. The grasshoppers had eaten his jacket.

They tell, too, about a man who left his team in the field while he went to his well for a drink of water. When he came back, the grasshoppers had eaten up the team and harness and were playing horseshoes with the iron shoes the horses had left.

These stories are only exaggerated in their detail, because a swarm of grasshoppers, like a Kansas cyclone, could do anything.

TORNADO TALES

Tornadoes, commonly but incorrectly known as "cyclones" throughout the Middle West, can be as freakish as they are destructive. There are authenticated reports of straws driven through thick planks and of animals picked up in one field and set down unharmed in another. When a tornado struck the Fredericksburg church in Kearney County, July 18, 1886, the building was lifted off its foundation, carried about thirty feet, and turned upside down. Its walls were blown some distance beyond, the floor was completely demolished, and pieces of the church were found two hundred yards from where it stood.

The first of the following tales was collected from Keith Wallace of Gordon County; the second from Mrs. J. A. Milliken of Aurora; and the contributor of the third is unknown. All originally appeared in the Nebraska Farmer. *The concluding group of three were collected by George L. Jackson and appeared in his article "Cyclone Yarns" in* Prairie Schooner, *April, 1927.*

One of the funniest things that a recent cyclone did in this community was to blow our chicken house away. After the storm we all ran out to see about the chickens and found the only rooster we had in a half-gallon jug with his head sticking out, and not even a crack in the jug. We had to break the jug to get him out and found the handle on the inside.

One afternoon a whirlwind swept into our yard, struck the bee hives, and played swing your partners right and left with the bees. Then it spun the windlass of the well around like a crank and it followed the bucket and rope right down into the well. When the whirlwind reached the bottom, it shot the bucket sky high and blew the water out with a roar. The water fell a second later like a mighty cloudburst.

Pa found the old windlass blowed chuck full of bee stingers drove porcupine-fashion right into the wood. The well was bone dry and has never freshened since. The bucket was standing by the overturned bee hive and was full of clear strained honey.

In '98 we had a cyclone that did considerable damage. Among other capers it rolled up eighty-nine rods of barbed-wire fence, posts and all, and set it on top of a row of cottonwood trees. We had a cow that was so breechy she used to climb those trees, go through the barbed-wire fence and down the other side into the cornfield. I saw her do it time and again.

On April 30, 1888, a cyclone passed over Howard County. This cyclone was not of the mass of windstorms but was a whirlwind with personality. The idiosyncrasy of this twister was its avidity for water. Every well, stream, and watering trough that happened to be in its path was sucked dry of its moisture and left as parched as if on the Sahara. Some wells were dry for weeks; the water in the creeks flowed into the dirty sands never to be seen again; even the cows for several days gave never a drop of milk.

Near the end of a sultry afternoon on August 16, 1910, a tornado passed near Hartwell. An agent for a patented scrub brush was demonstrating a sample of his wares at the door of a farm home when the storm struck, whirling him in the air, and removing every stock and straw from the premises, with the exception of the house. The last gust of the storm dropped the agent once more at the house door. "As I was saying," he began, "this brush is a regular cyclone. It sweeps clean and does a thorough job. . . ."

On April 10, 1917, a very freaky cyclone devastated a section of the country near Mason City. At one place a farmer on the road with a wagonload of oats was picked up, wagon, team and all, and carried to Arcadia, twenty miles distant, where he was set down, team and wagon in good condition and not having lost an oat. At another place a woman had a hundred prize-winning Black Langshan chickens from which the cyclone plucked every feather and pinfeather from every bird in the flock. None of the birds was killed but that their experience had been horrifying in the extreme was attested by the fact that the feathers which grew back in were snow-white. At another place a farmer had just come in from a muddy field and was sitting with his feet in the oven of the kitchen range, drying his socks and reading the daily newspaper. The cyclone blew the socks off the man's feet and carried the stove out the door and five miles over the hills, but left everything else in the house untouched, not even tearing the newspaper that he held spread before him.

TALL TALES

The tales in this section were collected by FWP workers, but were not included in the Nebraska Folklore Pamphlets. The originals are preserved in the folders of Nebraska WPA material at the Library of Congress.

The Cloudburst

The three following tales were collected from E. O. Skeidler of Lincoln. Mr. Skeidler said that he had heard them from Mike Guninge, a German pioneer settler in Atkinson.

I came from Germany many years ago and settled in Atkinson and took up farming. In Nebraska in those days there wasn't very many good dogs, no dogs like we had in Germany, like the dachshunds. So I sent back to Germany to have one of my relatives ship me a genuine German dachshund. Several weeks later I received word from the depot that my dog had arrived.

I drove down to the depot and got my crate with dog in it. I thought that I wouldn't uncrate it until I got home, so I put the crate in the back of the wagon. As I started back to the farm, it began raining. I was driving two fast horses, so I whipped them and they started off with the speed of lightning. They ran so fast that the rain did not catch me or get me or the horses wet. The rain, as I saw when I looked back, was a cloudburst. I arrived at the farm, drove in the barn, and looked in the back of the wagon. Though the horses and me were not even wet, the poor dog was drowned.

The Buckskin Harness

I went down to the general store and bought a new buckskin harness. I put it on my horses and thought I would go out in the field and haul in a load of hay. Just as I was ready to return to my barn, it began to rain. It simply poured down. When I started up the team to get back, the new harness stretched and left me and the wagon there in the field while the horses went on clear to the barn.

As I was walking back to the barn, the rain stopped and the sun came out very hot. I found my horses standing by the barn, with the new harness still stretched from them out to the field. Then as the sun beat down, the harness warped—and here come the wagon with the load of hay, finally stopping just right where it belonged, behind the horses.

The Big Cyclone

I was out feeding my hogs one day when all of a sudden a cyclone came up and carried me and a hog a mile up in the air. There we was, way up in the clouds, the hog and me remaining stationary up there, held up by the cyclone. I had to think quick on how to get down safely to earth. We were on the edge of the cyclone, so I grabbed the hog by the tail and shoved him out of it. Down we went for about a hundred feet, and then I pushed the hog back into the cyclone. I kept on doing this, dropping about a hundred feet each time, until the hog and me were back on the ground again.

Prairie Chickens

This anecdote and the next one were collected from H. W. Sample of Hastings.

Six hungry hoboes were riding in an open coal car. Bang! Bang! sounded some hunters' guns in a cornfield to one side of the right-of-way, and the hungry hoboes envied the hunters their good luck in bagging several prairie chickens. Only six chickens remained of the flock, and this sextette came flying straight toward the train. Prairie chickens usually fly low, and when this flock was about to fly over the slow-moving coal car, the entire six broke their necks on the telegraph wire. But the momentum they had acquired in their frantic flight brought them tumbling into the coal car—a chicken for each hungry hobo.

Saved by a Horseshoe

Five Apache Indians were hot on Bill's trail and gaining on him. Bill had emptied his six-gun, all but one shell which he was saving to shoot himself with if the Indians overtook him. He well knew the Apaches' reputation for capturing whites alive and burning them at the stake. Just as his fleet steed crossed a narrow stream, the Indians caught up with Bill. At that moment one of his pony's hind feet struck a rock and the shoe flew off and hit the foremost Indian square on the head, killing him instantly. The shoe then bounded off him to hit the next

Indian with the same result, and kept caroming on till it killed them all.

Prairie Mirage

The following two items were collected from F. G. Elliott of Wilbur.

In the early days mirages on the prairie were frequent, and many an old settler was lost because of a mirage he had seen. But a mirage was what saved Nebraska from the prairie dogs.

On this occasion the mirage took the form of a large city. It was about noon of a hot day and I was standing out by the well on my claim, with about a million prairie dogs around me. Then suddenly there appeared this vision of a large city on the prairie in the distance. I knew it was a mirage, but the prairie dogs didn't. Now these billions of prairie dogs had been taking care of me, seeing that I didn't progress very far on my claim, and when they turned and saw that a city had been built—they thought—behind their backs, they just fell over and died of mortification. Most of them did, anyway.

Jud Smith's Granddad

At Swan City, Nebraska, in the early seventies there was a blacksmith named Jud Smith. Jud was pretty good at telling stories about how great his ancestors were. He didn't say anything about their brain power, but he did boast plenty about their strength. Jud said his grandfather was so strong that he used to spike his whiskey in good strong ale, and it was nothing for him to have a quart of whiskey as an appetizer for breakfast. When he went on a drunk, he always downed at least five gallons of whiskey. He said his grandfather was so strong he never used a hammer to drive nails in a horse's hoof; he always used his bare fists instead. Once when a cyclone hit the town, Jud's grandfather held onto his house with one hand so it wouldn't blow away. If there were any iron bars to bend, he didn't waste any time heating them but bent them over his knee. A person had to be careful around Jud's granddad because if he had to sneeze, anyone caught in the path of the sneeze was as like as not to be blown across the town.

One time they had a shot-putting contest, using cannon balls as the shot. When it came Jud's granddad's turn to cast the iron ball, he picked it up and let it loose with a grunt that scared horses all over town. The ball disappeared in the clouds and was never found—although people did wonder some when they read in the papers the next week about a strange cannon ball found buried on the Capitol grounds at Washington, D.C.

Professional Liars' Tales

Collected from the Hastings Daily Gazette-Journal, *August 6, 1887. The following extract appeared under the headline:* THE HASTINGS LIARS AND TALL TALE TELLERS HOLD ANOTHER IMPORTANT SECRET MEETING—SOME OF THE TRUE TALES THAT WERE TOLD.

The subject for discussion was the "windstorm" of the previous evening and the members of the association were invited to relate whatever personal reminiscences they might have with them. The discussion brought out the fact that Thursday night's storm was a comparatively tame affair.

Dave Evanso testified that during his recent visit to Oshkosh he saw a windstorm twist an eighteen-foot well so badly that the bucket had to be drawn up with a corkscrew.

Duke Thompson stated that while he was editing a Republican newspaper at Danville, Illinois, about a year previous to his removal to Hastings, he was caught in a gale which blew all the hair from his upper-crown shoot—a fact which accounted for his lack of hirsute ornamentation at the present time. He further stated that he returned to the spot the next day and gathered up what hair he could find, and has religiously preserved it in alcohol ever since as evidence of the fact that he was not born bald-headed.

Chaplain Ogden, who before he joined the Y.M.C.A. was considered the best lightweight amateur prevaricator in Geneva, New York, recalled the fact that while traveling in Texas some years ago he saw a windstorm blow three hundred bushels of corn through a knothole in the side of the crib—one ear at a time, of course. As each ear passed through the knothole, the kernels were scraped from the cob, and after the storm had subsided the farmer found his shelled corn in a pile outside the crib; the cobs had been thrown in a separate pile nearby. Mr. Ogden stated that the corn was somewhat injured by the rain but that the farmer obtained a good price for it at the nearest distillery.

The Chaplain's story somewhat staggered the members present, but they regained their equanimity after John Croth came to the rescue with a revamped story in regard to a Dakota zephyr which blew a two-hundred-barrel cistern inside out and spilled the contents over a quarter section of land.

Jack Reynolds recalled an incident which came under his observation while he was stumping the state of Kansas for St. John [one-time governor of Kansas and presidential nominee of the National Prohibition Party, 1884] during the last presidential campaign. He stated that while he was traveling over the Missouri Pacific railroad on his way from Wichita to Topeka, a sudden gust of wind carried a seventeen-mile section of track in a circular direction and set it down upon the ground without disturbing the ties, rails, or spikes. Owing to the blinding clouds of dust which accompanied the wind, said Mr. Reynolds, the engineer never noticed the mishap and kept the throttle wide open. When the train pulled into the next station, the astonished passengers discovered they were in Wichita—the town they had left some fifty-five minutes previously.

TALES OF FEBOLD FEBOLDSON

Collected by Paul R. Beath. In a 1948 article, "Nebraska Strong Men," Louise Pound has this to say about the origin of Febold Feboldson: "The stories of Febold published in the Writers' Project pamphlet [Number 5, July 1937] do not name the tellers or give place and date. They are not 'documented' in scholarly fashion. The fact is that Febold, the prairie hero, originated as a flight of fancy, patterned after Paul Bunyan, and he owes most of his fame, I think, to Mr. Paul R. Beath, who, though not his creator, has spun many stories about him and floated him into fame. . . . The character Febold, the strong man, and his name seem to have been created by Wayne Carroll, a local lumber dealer, who wrote a column under the name of Watt Tell in the now defunct Gothenburg, Nebraska, Independent. This series began about 1923. Later Carroll used Febold in advertising that he wrote for his lumber company. Febold could never have been made a lumber hero like Paul Bunyan, for there are no trees on the Great Plains. So he became a hero wrestling with the adversities of the prairie region, tornadoes, drouths, extreme heat and cold, Indians, politicians, and disease. Later matter concerning Febold from the pens of Carroll and Don Holmes and other contributors appeared in the Gothenburg Times, *1928–1933, and sporadically since.*

"Carroll may have had in mind for his creation of Bergstrom Stromberg, the fabulous person usually cited as relating the Febold tales, a real person, Olof Bergstrom, who founded Gothenburg, Nebraska. He is sometimes said to have founded Stromsburg also, probably through confusion with his brother who located there. Olof Bergstrom was a pioneer leader of immigrant Swedes into Nebraska, who had a somewhat hectic career and stories of whom, Mr. Beath says, were current when he was a boy.

"The Febold stories 'caught on' about 1928. After Wayne Carroll, not only did Don Holmes write them but contributions began to come in from readers of the Times. *From this mass Mr. Beath gleaned the stories which he wove into his version of Febold's exploits which appeared in the Nebraska folklore pamphlets and earlier in the Omaha* World-Herald *and the* Prairie Schooner . . ." *(20). Mr. Beath collected the stories in a volume titled* Febold Feboldson: Tall Tales from the Great Plains, *first published by the University of Nebraska Press in 1948. The three tales given here follow the text of the Writers' Project pamphlet, which differs in minor details from that of the anthology.*

Real American Weather

Somebody ought to do something about the weather. It's downright disgraceful that in most parts of the United States the climate is of foreign origin. Florida and California brazenly boast of Mediterranean sunshine. Winter resorts in the Adirondacks are only imitations of those in Switzerland. Even the famous blizzard of 1888 came from Siberia. In fact, there's only one place where you can get real, genuine American weather, and that's on the Great Plains between the Mississippi and the Rockies.

In the early days, I guess, it was even more American than it is now. At least that's what Bergstrom Stromberg says. He's 'way past ninety and has seen some big weather in his day. Besides, he's heard all about the climate of the early days directly from his uncle, the famous Febold Feboldson. Febold was the first white settler west of the Mississippi, not counting Spaniards and Frenchmen, who don't count anyway.

Take 1848, for instance. That was the year the Petrified Snow covered the plains all summer and held up the Forty-Eighters in their gold rush to California, with the result that they became Forty-Niners. At that time Febold was operating an ox train between San Francisco and Kansas City because the snow prevented him from doing anything else.

Since Febold was the only plainsman able to make the trip that year, the Forty-Eighters appealed to him for help. His secret was to load up with sand from Death Valley, California. The sands of the desert never grow cold, nor did Febold and his oxen. This sand he sold to the gold rushers at fifty dollars a bushel, and they were glad to get it.

Then the Forty-Niners began to swarm over the snow-covered plains in their prairie schooners. But before they reached the Rockies the jolting of the wagons scattered the sand and covered up every bit of the Petrified Snow. And that's the reason, according to Bergstrom Stromberg, that the prairies are so all-fired hot in the summer.

Febold cursed himself twenty times a day for twenty years for selling the Forty-Eighters that sand. Then he spent the next twenty years trying various schemes to moderate the climate. He finally gave up in disgust and moved to California. Thus he set an example which all good Middle Westerners have followed ever since.

Or take the popcorn ball. There's a genuine American product. Most people think that someone invented the popcorn ball, but it's actually a product of the American weather. It invented itself, so to speak, on Bergstrom Stromberg's ranch in the early days when Febold owned the place.

It was during that peculiar year known as the Year of the Striped Weather, which came between the years of the Big Rain and the Great Heat. This year the weather was both hot and rainy. There was a mile strip of scorching sunshine and then a mile strip of rain. It so happened that on Febold's farm there were both kinds of weather. The sun shone on his cornfield until the corn began to pop, while the rain washed the syrup out of his sugar cane.

Now the cane field was on a hill and the cornfield was in a valley. The syrup flowed down hill into the popped corn and rolled it into great balls. Bergstrom says some of them were hundreds of feet high and looked like big tennis balls from a distance. You never see any of them now because the grasshoppers ate them all up in one day, July 21, 1874.

But the Great Fog, I suppose, was the biggest piece of American weather that ever hit the Great Plains. It followed the year of the Great Heat which killed off the Dirtyleg Indians and Paul Bunyan's Blue Ox. Near the end of that remarkable year, according to Bergstrom Stromberg, it began to rain and it kept it up for the proverbial forty days and forty nights.

"But nary a drop of water hit the ground," said Bergstrom.

"Then what became of it?" I asked.

"Why, it turned into steam, of course. That there rain had no more chance of hittin' the ground than you have of spittin' into a blast furnace."

This steam, as Bergstrom tells it, cooled enough to turn into fog. The whole country was fogbound. It was so thick that people had to go around in pairs, one to hold the fog apart while the other walked through it. The pioneer ranchers didn't need to water their stock. The cattle would simply drink the fog. It looked funny to see pigs with their noses up in the air rooting for fish and frogs. But the dirt farmers were as mad as the stockmen were happy. The sun couldn't shine through the fog and the seeds didn't know which way was up. So they grew downward.

Things were getting pretty serious. All the farmers had just about decided to go to California when Febold came to their rescue. He hit upon the idea of importing some English fogcutters from London. But the English were so slow that Febold didn't get his fog-cutters until Thanksgiving, and then the fog had turned to slush. He finally got to work and cut up the fog and slush into long strips which he laid along the roads so as not to spoil the fields. In course of time the dust covered up the roads, and today you can hardly tell where Febold buried the Great Fog.

But many a rural mail carrier has cursed Febold and his English fog-cutters. For every spring, when it rains or thaws, that old Fog comes seeping up and makes rivers of mud out of all the country roads.

Post Holes

If there was one thing which Febold wouldn't have around the house it was a mail-order catalog. And it was all because Eldad Johnson's grandfather tried to beat Febold's record for digging post holes. For Febold did and still does hold the record. But let's begin at the beginning.

When Febold first came west in the early days, there was no need of posts or post holes because there was no cattle or cultivated land. But as the frontier pushed across the Mississippi and onto the plains the pioneers began to feel the need of fences. They were familiar with only the two kinds they had used back east, the rail fence and the stone fence. Since there were no stones or trees on the plains the early settlers were stumped. And they would be sucking their thumbs yet if it hadn't been for Febold and his post holes.

Just about this time barbed wire was invented, and Febold got busy and bought a few thousand miles of it. His problem now was to get posts to put the wire on. This he did by digging post holes in the fall and letting them freeze all winter. Just before the first spring thaw he would dig up the holes and varnish them. Then he would put them partially back in the ground and string the wire. In time the varnish would wear off and leave the bare holes standing there. Eldad Johnson says that many of Febold's post holes are still standing on the old home place on the Dismal River.

But Herebold Farvardson, another one of Febold's nephews, takes exception to Eldad's account. Herebold says he has never seen a frozen post hole above ground. It seems that there were some on the old home place in the early days, but that Febold had to use them all up driving wells during the Year of the Great Heat. That was before the invention of the well-digger. Febold would drive a post hole into the ground, and then another directly on top of the first one, and so on until he hit water. A hundred-foot post hole makes a very fine well. Herebold says that if anybody doubts his story just let him come up to the old home place some time and look at the well.

Luckily, it really doesn't matter what became of the frozen post holes because it wasn't long before the pioneers were shipping in real red cedar posts so fast that the problem now was how to dig enough real post holes. It couldn't be done by hand and there was no machinery. Finally Febold recollected that the dismal sauger had a cousin, the happy auger, which had a tail which just suited his purpose.

The happy auger* was a peculiar animal. It looked something like a kangaroo—that is, it stood on its hind legs and had a long heavy tail. This tail was the most peculiar part of this peculiar animal. It was shaped like a corkscrew, an instrument very common in those pre-cellophane days. Every time the happy auger sat down, it spun around on its tail and screwed it several feet into the ground. With this auger Febold used to dig enough post holes to keep hundreds of men busy setting the posts. After the auger was seated with its tail screwed into the ground, Febold would sneak up behind it and fire a six-shooter. The poor creature would jump twenty feet into the air and leave the prettiest post hole you ever saw.

Now Eldad Johnson's grandfather was one of those good-for-nothings who sit around all day long looking through last year's mail-order catalog. As long as he was looking at the underwear section in the pink paper he was happy and harmless. But when he got to the firearms section in the green paper he began to get crazy ideas. One of his ideas he actually carried out, and it made Febold pretty sore. What did that goofy grandfather of Eldad Johnson's do but order a machine gun from his favorite mail-order house. When it came, he loaded it up and hid it in the barn. Next morning he got up before Febold and sneaked the happy auger away and went out to beat Febold's record for digging post holes.

And that was the last of the happy auger. When the machine gun began to fire, the poor creature jumped at every shot. It jumped in circles, in triangles, squares, parallelograms, and

* Also known as the snollygoster. See *Febold Feboldson: Tall Tales from the Great Plains* (Bison Book ed.; Lincoln: University of Nebraska Press, 1959), p. 100.

swastikas. At every leap it left a perfect post hole. It finally jumped in a straight line directly for the Gulf of Mexico and hasn't been seen since. Old timers say that Febold caught Eldad Johnson's grandfather and made him fill up all the post holes.

But he didn't get quite all of them filled because in 1861 he ran away and joined the Confederate Army. So if anyone today finds a post hole with no post it's likely to be one of those which Eldad Johnson's grandfather made with the happy auger and his mail-order machine gun.

The Dirtyleg Indians

The Dirtyleg Indians were not only one of the meanest tribes of heathens west of the Mississippi, but also one of the cleverest. But Febold, in spite of his never taking a bath, was a white man and therefore more clever even than the Dirtylegs. At least he was if we want to believe Eldad Johnson's story about duck hunting in the early days.

When Febold first came west, the Dirtylegs were still getting their ducks as their grandfather did. They would get a herd of buffalo and drive them in a circle near a river until there was a large circular ditch made. Then when they saw a flock of ducks about to alight on the river the Indians would turn the water into the ditch. The ducks would follow the water round and round until they became dizzy and dropped to the ground. The Dirtylegs would then pick them up and wring their necks.

But during the Year of the Great Heat there was no water in any river, only a few sandhill ponds. Since the Dirtylegs could not make these ponds flow in any direction, Chief Tummihake appealed to Febold for help.

"Wal," said Febold, "you Injuns have allus been such gosh-awful braggarts, you oughta have big enough lungs to ketch a few ducks. So come along."

And Febold and Tummihake and the Dirtylegs went off to the sandhills where Febold stationed the Indians in the weeds about one of the ponds. When a flock of ducks were about to light on the pond, Febold yelled "Blow!" and the Indians blew all the water away. And there were the ducks stuck in the mud.

Febold then had the Indians dig tunnels under the pond and build fires there. Thus the ducks were roasted without being touched by human hands, and Febold was initiated into the tribe with the name of Old-Stick-in-the-Mud.

Among other things for which Febold and the Dirtylegs are responsible is the expression "being stung by the presidential bee." This is more than a figure of speech because there actually was such a bee in the early days when the expression originated. Febold raised them on his bee farm when he was crossbreeding bees and eagles.

Febold discovered the marvelous power of his bees quite accidentally. One of the no-account bucks of the Dirtyleg tribe, Standing Pat, tried to steal a bee one day and got stung. He swelled up to twice his natural size. The Dirtylegs were so amazed at his giant stature that they made him their chief. Febold saw great possibilities in his "Chief Bees," as they were then called, and began to peddle them to the Indians, one to a tribe, and that to the highest bidder. When, however, the United States government took over the Indian lands and put all the tribes on reservations, Febold's racket was ruined.

But Febold got a good price for his bees. He sold them to Tammany Hall and Wall Street; the new owners changed the name to "Presidential Bee" and went right on with the business. Herebold Farvardson says that Febold always did regret that deal because the New York politicians have always been so unethical about handling those bees. Instead of stinging one man and letting him be President, they sting a dozen and let them fight it out. And the bad part of it is, says Herebold, that the men who lose get stung the worst.

The Year of the Great Heat was a bad year for prairie fires, and Febold had to do some fast thinking to find out the cause of the fires and stop them. At that time Febold was living with the Dirtylegs as Indian agent. The grass was so dry that he forbade the Indians to have any campfires at all. But still there would be bad fires every week.

Since the fires never started in the Dirtyleg country, Febold began to scout around among the Pawnees and the Sioux. Immediately he found out the cause of all the trouble. The Sioux were great fighters, and when a Sioux warrior got real mad he had fire in his eye, and that was what was setting the prairies ablaze.

The problem was to keep the Sioux and other warlike tribes happy and peaceful. And that was too easy for Febold. He imported barrels and barrels of whiskey from the Kentucky mountains. He passed it around among the Indians who called it "fire water," not because it tasted like fire (as has hitherto been supposed), but because it stopped the prairie fires.

TALES OF ANTOINE BARADA

Antoine Barada "ranks second only to Febold as a legendary or mythical character of Nebraska" (1). In the article on "Nebraska Strong Men," referred to above, Louise Pound discusses the account of him (included here in full) given in the Writers' Project pamphlet and suggests that the Writers' Project authors may have drawn on an article by Robert Maher, "who wrote of [Barada's] remarkable deeds in the Sunday Journal and Star *of Lincoln, Nebraska, June 14, 1936, . . . or the two accounts may have been derived from the same source. . . . Mari Sandoz testifies that she knew stories of him when she was a child. He was a half-breed, she says, the son of Michael Barada, who 'was supposed to be of royal connections in Spain. . . . The town of Barada in Richardson County was named after Michael. . . . Around 1934, while I was working at the State Historical Society, a letter came in seeking information on the Barada family, to settle as I recall now, an estate. Whether this was another of the recurring Spanish inheritance hoaxes I don't know now. . . . There was also a Michael Barada in the Custer County region for a while, I'm told'" (20).*

Antoine Barada was the strongest man who ever roamed the shores of the Missouri River. His name was known and his feats of strength related in all the settlements along the river's bank. One who claimed him as a friend had a decided advantage in an argument where might made right. Even those who had never seen Barada had a greater respect for a person whose cause was championed by Antoine. As his reputation grew, the tales of his prodigious feats of strength became more and more exaggerated by frequent repetition, until, somewhat like Hall Caine's White Prophet, the superman became almost supernatural. In this way it came about that Antoine Barada, "The Bogeyman," was held in greater fear than the real Antoine Barada, and was credited with feats of strength beyond all reason.

Antoine Barada was the son of Count Michael Barada, a gay Parisian, and Laughing Water, a pretty Omaha Indian maiden, whose romance is said to be one of the most beautiful in history. Since she was of the Omaha tribe, the count and his wife resided in Thurston County, Nebraska. Antoine spent his later years on the reservation with them. He died in 1866 and was buried beside his wife in Richardson County, Nebraska, at the little village of Barada, which was named in his honor.

This Samson of the nineteenth century was no ordinary fellow. The legends of his feats have stubbornly persisted for almost a century, and his varied career as chief, captive, trader, scout, and pilot deserves more than passing notice.

He was born in 1807 near what is now Fort Calhoun in Washington County. When he was seven years old, he was captured by the Sioux and held for two years. Some traders finally bought his release for ten ponies, returning him to his parents. Colonel Rogers had permission from his parents to take Antoine to the Military Academy. In St. Louis he met his aunt, Madame Mousette, who took him to her home and dissuaded him from any military ambitions. He grew up in St. Louis, living with his aunt. He worked at many places in that city, eventually becoming superintendent of the quarries belonging to Withnell and Coats. He could lift a weight of 1,800 pounds clear of the ground.

When he was twenty-five years old, he left St. Louis and rejoined his tribe. In 1836 he returned to St. Louis, where he married Josephine Veien. After a trip to California in 1849, he returned via Panama and New York. He then began to farm in Richardson County, Nebraska, where he raised a family of three boys and girls. In 1875 he visited the Black Hills. He often paid visits to his tribe, and in his last years had a strong desire to return to them permanently. His application for an allotment of land for him and his family was rejected, however.

When he died, he had friends from the Missouri River to the Pacific Coast who remembered his good deeds, kind words, and generosity. He was buried in the Catholic cemetery east of Barada.

The real Antoine Barada was undoubtedly a man of unusual strength and, like others of his day who lived in this wild country, had many interesting adventures. But the legendary Antoine Barada, the strong man of the river, was in a class by himself. The tales of his superhuman feats of strength were like those of the *Arabian Nights*.

It was said that he discovered artesian wells in Nebraska, yet this remarkable discovery was entirely accidental and due largely to his great impatience. Like many men of great strength, he had the innocence of a child and the restlessness of a tiger. Once a boat was waiting to tie up while a forty-foot pole was being driven for a hitching post. After watching the pole-driver for some time, Antoine could stand it no longer. He picked up the derrick, hammer and all, and threw it over into Iowa. When he smote the big timber with his mighty fist, the pole disappeared, never to be recovered. Indeed, it went so deep in the earth that an artesian well resulted, spouting water fifty feet in the air. All in the vicinity would surely have drowned had not Antoine sat upon the hole until everyone had rushed to safety.

Many legends were merely Herculean. For example, when a boat became foundered upon a sand bar, the captain simply whistled for Barada. A rope was then thrown ashore, and Antoine pulled the boat out into deep water.

Because of his innocence and good nature, Antoine was a great favorite; no public gathering was complete without him. Picnics in the timbered groves were happy events in those early days. People sometimes drove all day and night to be present at such celebrations. Roast wild turkey, venison, barbecued bison, and other viands were prepared by the women; while the men pitched horseshoes, played kitten ball, or engaged in other contests.

It was at such a picnic that Barada established an all-time world record as a long-distance jumper. Late in the forenoon, while the women were laying the dinner upon split logs for tables, the men engaged in a broad-jumping contest. Antoine, always a modest man, waited until all the others had competed. The record so far stood at a distance of ten feet three-and-a-half inches; this, however, was made by a man who used weights which he threw behind him after he was well clear of the ground. Since this was a new mode of jumping, Antoine made up his mind to profit by this novel method of propulsion. Quickly picking up two boulders of about four hundred pounds each, he stepped to the line, swinging one on either side of him. With the third swing he leaped, hurling the stones over into Kansas. Spectators held their breath as they saw him disappear into the distance. He had leaped so high and so far that dinner had to be postponed for three hours while he walked back.

But it must not be thought that all of his contests of strength were with the local men in this sparsely settled territory. Antoine Barada met all comers from any point of the world who dared to meet him in any field where strength prevailed.

He was once matched to wrestle with Jean Palos, the Greek wrestling champion. The mighty Palos was notorious for his rough treatment of an opponent. Antoine won the match by pinching his opponent with his toes while he slapped him into unconsciousness with one blow on his ear.

Sandhills Version

Collected by Louise Pound in "Nebraska Strong Men." "Miss Sandoz says that she 'grew up on the Barada stories as told by half-breeds around Pine Ridge.' They were brought there, she suspects, by the Ruleaus and other families who used to live on what is called the Breed Strip in southeast Nebraska, and in the early 1900's still had relatives to visit there" (20). *This is the version she heard of one of Barada's exploits.*

Antoine Barada was a hurry-up man, always rushing, rushing, can't wait for anything. One time he got tired of watching a pile driver working along the Missouri with the hammer making the up-down, up-down, the driver yelling "Git up! Git up! Whoa! Back! Back! Whoa!" and then all of it over again and the piling going down maybe a half inch. So Antoine he picked up the damned thing in his bare hand, throws it high and far so it lights clear over the Missouri where it bounce and bounce leaving the ground tore up for miles and miles and making what the greenhorns call "Breaks of the Missouri." But at last it stop and if you dig down in them high ridges you find it is the damned pile driver with grass growing over him, a little poor soil, you understand, but it seems to satisfy them that ain't ever crossed the Missouri and don't know better. When Antoine had disposed of the Johnny Jumper hammer he sees that the piling that is left stands a mile higher than the rest, so he gives it a lick with his fist and it pop down into the ground so deep it strike a buried lake, the water flying out like from bung hole fifty feet high and like to drown out the whole country if Antoine he did not sit on the hole first.

Indian Tales

The twenty-one tales and legends collected here are representative of three tribes which figure prominently in Nebraska history—the Omahas, the Sioux, and the Pawnees. While some documentation for the Sioux legends is provided in the Nebraska Folklore Pamphlets, the introductory notes are vague about the sources of the Omaha and Pawnee materials. We are told only that the themes of the legends were "obtained from histories, folklore compilations, and unpublished manuscripts," and that "elderly Indians and early residents, scattered over the state, furnished from their memories the titles and fragments of the stories" (1). However, in some cases it has been possible to establish sources by textual comparison, and the general tenor of the materials seems to indicate that all the selections are truly examples of Indian lore.

OMAHA TALES

The Omahas, a Siouan tribe, were the most consistently friendly to the whites of all the Nebraska tribes. Originally located at the mouth of the Missouri, they migrated as far north as Minnesota but were driven off by the Yankton Sioux and headed westward into the region between the Missouri and the Black Hills. Finally, they turned down river and eventually established themselves in north-eastern Nebraska, where they stayed for more than two centuries. In 1856 they went onto a reservation in Thurston County.

Amos Two-Trees and Morning Star

Mission Point, the scene of this story, is a bluff about five hundred feet high on the west bank of the Missouri River a few miles north of Macy, on the Omaha reservation (see map, site 3). The Indians used it as a signal station, the French and Spanish as a camping place, and the pioneers as a boat landing and a land-mark. The "talisman" mentioned early in the tale is perhaps Amos's totem, described in a report on the Omaha tribe as "not an object of worship and only in a limited sense . . . a fetish. It was a token or kind of credential of the vision granted to the youth during his fast; he did not appeal to the thing itself, but to that which it represented, the form sent by [the Great Spirit], which could reach him personally, 'have compassion' on him, and therefore bring to him the help he required in his hour of need" (11).

Amos Two-Trees grew to manhood on the hills of the Missouri River near Mission Point. His talisman was a lone wolf. He chose an old playmate, a very beautiful girl, to be his wife. For her he constructed the finest tipi, caught the finest beaver, and made a couch of soft buckskin.

He returned from a long and successful horse-stealing expedition against the Sioux and went to the tipi of his sweetheart, Morning Star. He was expecting to marry her as soon as the feast, victory dance, and other festivals were over. He asked for Morning Star and her mother told him that she was at the trader's cabin. He went to see her, but she would not talk to him. He dared not show any emotion over a squaw, but all the happiness went out of his life.

Winter was over and spring came, and still he was alone in his tipi. One lonely night as Amos lay listening to the sleet and rain beating against the tipi, Morning Star came in and sat by the fire. She was moaning the Omaha death chant. As the fire burned down, she ceased the chant and came over to his couch and sat down. She felt of his face and caressed him with loving touches on the forehead. "Two-Trees, I am going away," she said.

"But why?" asked Two-Trees.

"When you went on your last hunt, you were in my heart night and day; but bad spirits were hovering over me. I was very lonely. I went to the trader's store, and he was kind to me. He gave me presents and persuaded me to go to his cabin and cook for him. He told me I was his woman, and I went to his couch and lived with him. When you returned, I was ashamed. I thought I could go away with the trader and you would forget me. But tonight, when I told him I was going to have a papoose, he beat me, called me a red squaw, and drove me out into the storm. I am exiled from my people, so I must go away."

"Go to your father's tent and wait for me," Two-Trees said. "I will go to the trader's cabin and place my hands around his throat. As the light fades from his eyes, I will tell him why his days are over. We will go away together, and I will call your papoose mine."

But Morning Star replied, "I am not worthy of so great a sacrifice. You are to be a great warrior and chief. If you killed the trader, the white men would kill you, and maybe our tribe would help them. Promise me you will not do this."

At length Two-Trees promised. But he said, "I will come to you in the morning."

Before she left, Morning Star crooned an Indian love song, talked of the Happy Hunting Ground, and gave Two-Trees a love pat on the forehead. Two-Trees could not sleep. As soon as it was light he went to her father's tipi, but her mother said she had not been there. Leaving the tipi, Two-Trees found her track. He followed it to the bluff above the river and saw where she had plunged into the water. He went back to the village and told her people. Later they found her body in the river.

No one ever knew of her visit to Two-Trees nor what she had

told him. But he wished revenge even though he had given his promise not to kill the trader. He went to the trading post; there was no sorrow in the eyes of the white man. Two-Trees concealed his hatred and used all his guile. One day he told the trader that he had seen a wolf on the Mission Point, and he invited him to go hunting. Suspecting nothing, the trader readily consented. When they reached Mission Point, Two-Trees seized him and tied him to a tree.

"Your time has come to die as Morning Star died," Two-Trees said. "When I have finished whipping you, you will be glad to jump into the river."

With his hunting knife Two-Trees cut the trader's clothes away and with an Indian whip he gave him forty strokes. Then he took him to the edge of the cliff and told him to jump or he would give him forty more strokes. Then, for the first time, the trader cried out. He pleaded, but the Indian would not listen. The Indian gave him forty more lashes, but the trader was a strong man and did not want to die.

The third time, Two-Trees slowed the strokes to increase the torture. The white man collapsed and hung lifeless in the thongs. The Indian threw some snow in the trader's face to revive him. Two-Trees again carried him to the edge of the cliff. He handed him his gun so that he could choose his death. With his gun in his hand the trader plunged into the river below.

Two-Trees told the people at the village that the trader had jumped from Mission Point into the river. The Council was suspicious and sent scouts to investigate and question Two-Trees, and they found that he told the truth.

Two-Trees began to hate all white men. But since his own people were friendly with the whites and knew nothing of his grievance, he went to the Sioux and for fifty years roamed the West fighting the white man. His life seemed to be charmed. He was with Sitting Bull at the Battle of the Little Big Horn and opposed Custer's last charge.

Later he fled to Canada. Once while on a buffalo hunt he was thrown from his horse and lay as dead. He thought that his spirit had gone to the Happy Hunting Ground, and that a great voice bade him to return to earth and obtain forgiveness from the white men for fighting those who had done him no wrong.

He returned to his tribe and buried the tomahawk, but his people seemed to have forgotten the teachings of their forefathers and they were like squaw men.

Once more he became a lone Indian—until a friendship sprang up between him and a white man to whom he told his story. He explained, "I have just returned from the Happy Hunting Ground. Last night while I slept, my spirit floated on until I came to a great wall. I could see the Happy Hunting Ground. All was light and beautiful. A silvery river flowed away into the distance. Everyone was happy, singing, dancing, hunting, fishing. No storms or cold. I could see my Morning Star, just as she used to be before I went on that fatal hunting trip. But I could not go in. A great voice bade me go back and be forgiven. As I floated back, I could see the faces of the white men I had wrongfully slain."

The white man clasped his hand with the friendship grip and said, "Two-Trees, I forgive you for the wrongs you have done. I give you my blessing and make you free to go to the Happy Hunting Grounds." The look of longing in Two-Trees' eyes changed to one of joy. He smiled and closed his eyes. The white man crossed Two-Trees' hands.

A group of Indians who had seen the signal fire made by the white man were waiting outside. The white man let them in. An old man came forward and with a piece of chalk made some markings on Two-Trees' forehead and chest. They made a bier of earth, carried him out, laid him on it—his head to the west— and made a small fire at his feet. After sprinkling some powder on the fire, the old Indian went to Two-Trees' head and spread over him a beautiful piece of buckskin with drawings on it. They sang a strange chant accompanied by motions to the east and west.

With great tenderness and care they placed the body on a stretcher made of willow poles and carried it away. The old man gave Two-Trees' pipe to his white friend and said, "This is the pipe of peace. Remember, he has buried the tomahawk."

That afternoon the white man, unable to put the memories of Two-Trees from his mind, went up to Mission Point and saw there the tree and the bluff as they were when Morning Star and the white trader had leaped to death.

The Cry on Blackbird Hill

Located eight miles north of Decatur (see map, site 4) on the Missouri River, Blackbird Hill served the Indians as an observation point. Here, according to legend, the Omaha chief Blackbird was buried sitting upright on his favorite horse. Four years after his death, on August 11, 1804, the hill was visited by the Lewis and Clark expedition. The belief persists that on the night of the October full moon, a woman's scream can be heard at the top of the hill.

One fall in the middle of the nineteenth century, the Indians discovered a wandering white man who was raving mad and nearly starved. They took him to the medicine man of the tribe. After the Indians had laid the man on a couch in the wigwam, the medicine man sent them away. Then he stroked the white man's forehead and murmured strange words. He selected some dried herbs from his medicine pouch and placed them on the live coals of his fire. Gently he fanned the smoke over the white man.

The man recovered and lived with the Indian for some time. Gradually he began to take an interest in life, and before he left for his home in the East he told the Indian this story.

He said that after he had finished his course in an eastern school, his father had sent him abroad on a business mission. On his way home he was shipwrecked and five years passed before he was able to reach his homeland. In the meantime his mother died; with her last words she asked for her boy. His sweetheart at first waited for him, but finally she yielded to a former suitor. They were married and moved west.

The young man who had been shipwrecked returned. His sister told him what had happened and he set out to find her, hoping that her husband, a boyhood friend of his, would release her. He went westward to California, where people were rushing in search of gold, but his efforts were fruitless. Discouraged, he again started for his home in the east. Sailing down the Missouri River he landed one evening at the foot of Blackbird Hill. A well-marked path led him to a cabin; here, to his great surprise, he found his sweetheart. They each told what had happened in the years since their parting, and the young woman promised to ask her husband to release her and said that she would go with him on the next day.

When the husband returned, the girl told him what had happened. He pleaded with her to stay. He became crazed and struck her with his hunting knife, almost severing her head from her body. Her former sweetheart was near the cabin and saw what was happening. Before he could recover from the shock, the husband had picked the girl up in his arms and had carried her to the edge of the cliff. With a scream he hurled himself and his dead wife into the river below.

The white man then became unconscious and first recovered on the couch in the Indian tipi. He returned to the East, never to be free from the memory of this harrowing experience. The story became known to all Indians. The blood dripping from the girl's body killed the grass on the trail from the cabin to the cliff, and the grass has never since grown on that path. And now, each year, when the October moon is full, that same piercing cry is said to be heard.

The Magic of Big Bear Hollow

Big Bear Hollow is a crater-like depression about five miles in diameter in the great sandstone bluffs along the west bank of the Missouri River in the northeastern part of Thurston County (see map, site 5). Except for an opening next to the river, the valley is surrounded by wooded cliffs, deep-cut ravines, and ledges. Black Bear's den was an almost inaccessible ledge far down the face of a steep cliff.

One spring some Indian boys were watching ice cakes float down the river which washed the edge of the hollow. Suddenly they saw a great black bear floating toward the shore on a cake of ice. The bear climbed up the high river bank and went up the bluff to the magic shelf about three hundred feet above the river bank. The shelf was about fifty steps long and ten steps wide. If an Indian or an animal lay down to sleep on this shelf he would be changed into some other animal. Once an Indian went to sleep on this shelf and when he awoke he was half wolf; he had jumped into the river and drowned himself.

The big black bear lay down on the shelf and went to sleep, and every day the Indian boys came to look at him. When he finally awoke on the fourth day, his head was like a man's and his paws were like arms. He crawled to the opening of the hollow and gave a great roar. All the bears came running to him and he put his magic on them. He made them climb trees and dig holes. Some brought him food—meat, honey, and fish.

One day, as two women were gathering fruit, the half man cast his spell on one of them and she followed him away. When the Indians called to her, she would not answer. Every year the bear came and took away a woman or girl. And when the Indians went by in their canoes, they saw that he threw the others into the river or gave them to the other bears to eat.

When the half man took White Feather's wife, White Feather said that he would bring her back. He went alone, and he never came back. The medicine man tried to make magic against the half man, but it was no use. They put out poisoned honey for him to eat; he ate it, but it did not hurt him.

The half man had lived in the hollow for about fifteen years when an Indian from the north, White Fox, came with his new wife, Songbird, to the village of White Eagle. White Fox and Songbird had fine furs, a tipi, and a canoe. He was a great hunter, trapper, runner, and wrestler. The village gave them a great welcome. They danced, feasted and had contests. The chief told White Fox about the half man and half bear, but he only laughed and said that the Omahas did not understand about bears.

One day when White Fox was out hunting, Songbird and another woman went to pick berries. Suddenly the big bear was standing in front of them. He cast his magic on Songbird and she went with him. Everyone had learned to love Songbird and they were greatly distressed. When White Fox returned, they told him what had happened.

But White Fox said only, "It is too bad for the half man." The chief and all the tribe warned White Fox of the magic, but as soon as daylight came he took his bow and arrow, tomahawk, and knife and went to get Songbird. Soon he came running back without his weapons. He was bloody with bites and scratches. Many were waiting for him at the opening of the hollow and they took him home, where the medicine man healed his wounds.

When he was well he said to the chief, "I know now I must have some magic to overcome Big Black Bear. I am going away, but I shall return and get Songbird."

The chief replied, "We will help you if we can. We have tried all the magic that my medicine men knew how to make. If your magic does not work, I shall move my village away from Big Bear Hollow."

White Fox left his tipi and Songbird's things with the Indians and he went away in his canoe. As soon as the ice broke in the spring, White Fox returned, bringing with him two grizzly bears. They were but half-grown and very tame. He kept them in his own tipi and made only this explanation to the Indians: "When I have them tamed and trained properly, I shall go and get my Songbird."

The Omahas did everything they could to help him. They could see that he was working very hard with the bears. He wrestled and raced and talked with them. They grew much larger than Big Black Bear. They learned to throw a buffalo and kill it. He had time for nothing but training the bears. The medicine men said that he was making very strange medicine.

At length he called a council of the Indians and said, "I am ready to go to Big Bear Hollow. I wish the women would set the tipi in order for Songbird. Tomorrow I shall lift the magic of Big Bear Hollow and Big Black Bear will be no more. I shall split the head of Big Black Bear and throw him into the river."

The Omahas listened and shook their heads, saying, "Strange Indian uses big words."

The next day White Fox set out for Big Bear Hollow dressed in his hunting clothes. He carried with him his knife and tomahawk. At his side walked the two bears. When the little bears of the hollow saw White Fox, they roared and ran at him, but the grizzlies knocked them down. They killed some of the little bears, and the rest became afraid and ran away. White Fox and the grizzlies then went on to the shelf where Big Black Bear lived with Songbird.

When they reached the shelf White Fox said, "Climb upon the shelf and hold the half man and half bear, and I will kill him with my tomahawk."

He held onto them as they climbed. When the big bear saw them coming, he roared, but no bears came to help him. He threw rocks from the cliff at the two bears, but the rocks bounced off. Nothing could stop them. When White Fox and his bears reached the top, the bears held Big Black Bear and the Indian made ready to split his head open.

White Fox said, "You have kept my Songbird and I am going to kill you." To Songbird he said, "Turn your head away." He split the half man's head with his tomahawk and then said, "Throw him into the river."

The bears helped White Fox and Songbird down from the shelf. When Songbird got back to the tipi she did not act right: she did not know White Fox and she could not talk. He called a medicine man, who gave her some strong medicine and she went to sleep. He said that she would be all right when she woke up.

She slept for three days, and White Fox sat by her side and waited for her to awaken. When she roused, she put her arms around White Fox's neck and said, "Why have you stayed away so long?" Songbird did not remember that she had been away, and White Fox told her a little at a time so that he would not shock her.

White Eagle's warriors went to the hollow and killed some of the little bears. Because they were able to do this, they knew that the magic was gone. They held a great feast and dance, and gave White Fox many farewell presents. He left the two grizzly bears in the hollow and took Songbird back north to his own people.

Weeping Water

Originally called L'Eau qui pleure, "The stream that weeps," by French traders and trappers, this beautiful little stream rises in Cass County and empties into the Missouri between Plattsmouth and Nebraska City. Two towns on its banks—Weeping Water and Nehawka (the Indian rendering)—take their name from it. In 1947 Louise Pound wrote that "the Nebraska Legend of Weeping Water has existed in printed and oral form for at least eight decades" (20). So far as she could determine the first printed mention of the tale occurred in 1871, in a poem "The Weeping Water" by Orsamus Charles Dake, the first professor of English Literature at the

University of Nebraska. In a brief prefatory note, the legend was summarized as follows: "The Omaha and Otoe Indians, being at war, chanced to meet on their common hunting ground south of the Platte River in Nebraska. A fierce battle ensued, in which all the male warriors of both tribes being slain, the women and children came upon the battle-field and sat down and wept. From the fountain of their tears arose and ever flows the little stream known as the Ne-hawka or the Weeping Water." Professor Dake, according to Miss Pound, added a love story, "not mentioned in his prefatory note, of the Otoe youth Sananona and Nacoumah, the daughter of the Omaha chief, Watonshie. When their union is forbidden by the Otoe chief Shosguscan, the spirited Sananona leaves his tribe to go among the Omaha. It is this situation that brings on the tribal conflict ending in the destruction of the warriors of both sides."

The legend next appeared in a History of Nebraska *by A. T. Andreas, published in 1882. The Andreas version, as Miss Pound noted, echoes the manner of the Dake poem and includes a basic love story, but the narratives are not identical: "One difference . . . is that the tribes and persons are not named in the Andreas version. And the young hero is the chief of his tribe, as though Dake's Sananona and Shosguscan are merged into one character. Another difference is that the youthful chief abducts the daughter of the chief of the rival tribe instead of leaving his own tribe." The Federal Writers' Project version, which follows, apparently was taken from Andreas'* History of Nebraska, *for the wording is virtually the same. The FWP editor identified "the powerful but peaceful tribe" as Otos, but assigns no name to the other tribe concerned—the Omahas in the original version.*

A powerful but peaceful tribe of Oto Indians once dwelt near the source of the river now known as the Weeping Water. Their laws were good, their chief mild-tempered and valorous. The braves of the tribe were as straight as their arrows and as fleet as the horses upon which they rode. And so lithe and lovely were their maidens that their beauty far exceeded that of the maidens of any surrounding tribe. Fairest of these fair maidens was the chief's daughter.

Though this tribe was indeed strong, it happened that an

even more powerful tribe lived to the west. The ruler of this neighboring tribe chanced one day to visit the Otos on some friendly business. He saw the chief's daughter and was captivated. He asked the girl's father for her, but the father refused. The chief, however, was determined to have this beautiful maiden for his wife; he decided to steal her. He prowled about the village night and day awaiting an opportunity to carry her off. On the third day he saw the chief's daughter and her companions going out to bathe in a still lake near the village. He quickly dashed up, lifted the chief's daughter to his horse, and rode away.

Her companions ran to the village and spread the alarm. Angered because this warrior had carried off their most coveted prize, the braves rushed out in pursuit, leaving the lodges in charge of the women and the infirm. They rode fast with great hatred in their hearts. In their anger they were reckless and the results were disastrous. The warriors of the other tribe came out to meet and aid their chief. Every one of the Oto pursuers was killed in the fight that followed.

For three long days and nights the Otos at the village waited for their warriors to return with the chief's daughter. On the fourth day they started out in search of their fathers, husbands, sons, and lovers. At length they found them—dead—upon the plains. Seeing their braves dead, the women began to weep. They wept so long that their many tears flowed together and made a stream that still exists—Nehawka, the weeping water.

SIOUX TALES

Like the Omahas, the Sioux (or Dakota) Indians are of Siouan stock; when first known to the white man, they were occupying the western half of the upper Mississippi Basin. By the seventeenth century the Sioux parent group was made up of seven major divisions, of which four tribes—the Wahpetons, Sissetons, Mdewakanton, and Wakpekute—were known collectively as the Santee. The other divisions were the Yanktons, the Yanktonnais, and the Teton. The Tetons were further divided into seven subtribes: the Oglala, Brule, Two Kettle, Sans Arc, Blackfoot, Hunkpapa, and Minneconjou.

With one exception, all the following tales concern the Santee Sioux. According to one authority, their name derives from the

Siouan word Isantee, *"knife lake"* (22), *while another source be-lieves that it stems from* Isanyati, *"they go for knives," because in their Minnesota home they went frequently to flint mines for knife-making materials* (14).

On August 16, 1862, six years of Plains Indian hostilities began with the uprising of the Santee Sioux on the reserve set aside for them along the Minnesota River. In 1863, after the uprising was put down, the Santees who had taken an active part in the fighting were kept under guard at Fort Thompson in Dakota Territory, near Crow Creek Agency. But the land was unsuited to agriculture, and in three months three hundred—nearly a fifth of their number—died of famine and disease. In June of 1866 the Santees were moved to the northeast corner of Nebraska, near where the Niobrara empties into the Missouri, but they stayed there only until the fall. They were then moved to the nearby Brazille Creek area, where they were allowed to remain.

The tales which follow, with the one exception noted, were col-lected from the files of the Word Carrier, *a missionary paper published by the Santee Mission School. The issues in which they appeared came out between 1883 and 1887, when the paper had a circulation of less than three hundred. According to the original introductory note: " As published in the Santee missionary paper, the translations were very rough and made no attempt at literary style. Consequently they have been subject to considerable editing to clarify their meaning, although every attempt has been made to re-tain the simple, almost childlike style of the original. . . . Certain references to large bodies of water not found in Nebraska, such as the sea mentioned in ' The Orphan Boy,' relate to the lakes of Minnesota, where the tribe originated"* (1). *Where the name of the translator is known, it is given in the headnote.*

The Spider and the Ducks

Translated by Peter Hunter. Although "the Spider" is here interpreted as the Santee name for "evil spirit," he is clearly the Trickster, of whom Stith Thompson says: " Undoubtedly the most characteristic feature of the tales of the North American Indians is the popularity of trickster stories. We cannot speak of a definite, all-inclusive trickster tale, or even with any strictness of a trickster cycle. Nevertheless, there does exist over the western two-thirds of the

*continent a considerable body of widely known anecdotes told in
various areas as the adventures of different tricksters"* (24).

The Spider was searching for food on the plains when he came
to the base of a high hill. Thinking to find food at its top, he
laboriously climbed one of its steep sides. When he reached his
destination, he saw before him a large lake which stretched
from the base of the hill into the distance as far as the eye could
see. Many ducks were floating on its shiny surface. The Spider,
becoming ravenously hungry at the sight of the waterfowl,
began to scheme how he could get some of them to eat. He
descended to the base of the hill, where he had started, and
gathered a bundle of hay which he carried to the hilltop.

This time he stood erect on the hilltop so that all the ducks
could see him. One of them said, "Hello, old Spider, what do
you carry on your back?" "Songs," replied the Spider. To this
remark they all answered, "You had better come down and
sing to us." The Spider immediately accepted their invitation
and descended to the lake shore near the ducks, where he proceeded to fashion a lodge from the hay he was carrying. When
he had finished the lodge, he invited the ducks to come in and
sit down. It took a long time for the ducks to get in because
there were so many of them.

When all of the ducks were seated, the Spider closed the door
and told them to shut their eyes. Then he began to sing:

> "Whoever opens his eyes
> Must have red eyes, red eyes,
> Whoever opens his eyes
> Must have red eyes, red eyes,
> Whoever opens his eyes
> Must have red eyes."

The ducks liked the song and began dancing to its tune. The
Spider kept on singing; at the same time he went from one duck
to another and twisted off its neck, until the necks of half the
ducks in the lodge had been twisted off. Then he came to a swan,
who had been visiting the ducks on the lake and had followed
his companions into the lodge to hear the Spider sing, and attempted to twist his head off. But the swan's neck was too long

and strong for the Spider to break it off. So the swan, who was badly frightened, said, "Quack! quack!" One of the young ducks, upon hearing this warning, opened his eyes and at once saw many dead ducks in the lodge. He cried out in alarm: "Open your eyes, all of you, the Spider has killed almost the entire flock!" All of the remaining ducks opened their eyes when they heard what had happened to their companions. Their eyes immediately became red, as the Spider had said they would. This is the reason why ducks, to this day, always have red eyes.

The Fox

Translated by Julia LaFramboise, a teacher and missionary in the Santee Normal Training School. Again the central figure is the Trickster, who uses his powers to destroy the ideal existence of a fellow creature. Concerning the role of Trickster stories in Indian culture, Paul Radin observes that "laughter, humor and irony permeate everything Trickster does. The reaction of the audience in aboriginal societies to both him and his exploits is prevailingly one of laughter tempered by awe. There is no reason for believing this is secondary or a late development. Yet it is difficult to say whether the audience is laughing at him, at the tricks he plays on others, or at the implications his behavior and activities have for them" (21).

Part I

A fox, who had spent many days searching for something to eat, was on the point of starvation when he came to a large tent of buffalo skins. Although at first afraid to venture into the tent, in which he could hear two men were talking, his hunger finally compelled him to do so. The first thing he saw, after he had entered, was a pot of venison cooking over a fire. On either side of the fire sat two old blind men; they were discussing old times while waiting for their meat to be cooked. The fox, perceiving that they were blind, grew bolder and, seeing a rib sticking out of the pot, slyly took it out and picked off the meat. Then he took another and still another, until nothing was left but a pile of bare rib bones. These he replaced in the pot.

At last one of the blind men said, "Well, I think this meat must be done." He removed the pot from the fire but found it contained nothing but bones. He then said to the other old man, "You artful, good-for-nothing fellow! You thought to cheat me out of my dinner." The other man, in great surprise at the accusation of his companion, became enraged. Each accused the other of being the guilty one, in loud and angry tones. The fox meanwhile took up a stick and, going very stealthily up to one of them, struck him with it. The blind man at once turned and accused the other man of striking him. The fox then struck the other man. Both blind men thereupon flew at each other in great wrath, which so excited the fox that he giggled. The blind men ceased fighting and inquired who had come. The fox, smoothing his face, answered, "A traveler."

The old men, very much ashamed of their quarrel with each other, resumed their respective places and welcomed the stranger. They told him to partake of the dried buffalo meat which was packed away in skins in great piles around the tent. The fox accepted their invitation and ate until he could eat no more. Then said the old man, "If you are without provisions for the way, take one of the sacks of buffalo meat." So the fox selected the largest and went on his way rejoicing. The meat was so good, however, that he stopped every little while to eat. Very soon he had nothing left but the skin in which the meat was packed; this he rationed out so it would last for two days. When the last mouthful of this was gone he was as famished as ever.

One day, when he thought he would die of hunger, he saw a fat buffalo feeding on the green grass. The fox immediately hid in the tall grass, and was trying to devise some way of killing the buffalo when the animal looked up and saw him. He said, "What do you want, my young brother?" The fox came forward and answered, "Ah! my brother, you see how starved I am. Oh, that I were a buffalo so I could feed on green grass and grow fat like you!" The buffalo, hearing his wish, replied, "Would you indeed be a buffalo if you could? Since you would be, you shall. Do you see yonder knoll? Go and sit upright on it and I will come up the hill and jump over you." The fox obeyed the buffalo and took his position. The buffalo, with staring eyes and foaming mouth, came galloping up the hill, frightening the fox so much that he jumped to one side. The buffalo said, "You have now spoiled it all. You can never be a buffalo if you don't sit still and let me jump over you." The fox was very penitent and promised to sit still the next time if the buffalo would try once more. Again the fox sat on the knoll, but when he saw the buffalo coming at him so fiercely he jumped aside a second time. The buffalo, now angry, said, "Since you are such a coward it is best that you remain a half-starved fox." But the fox entreated him to try once more. This time the fox sat still. The buffalo, as he jumped over him, knocked him over with his hoof, causing the fox to tumble down the hill. When the fox got up from his fall, he was a buffalo. He immediately began to eat the green grass, which grew profusely in the vicinity.

Part II

The Spider was hunting in the prairie with a quiver full of weeds and a tall weed for a bow. During his hunt he met the buffalo, to whom he said, "Why, the last time I saw you, you were a poor hungry fox." The fox then told him how a kind buffalo had turned him into a buffalo so that he might not be hungry so long as there was grass to eat. Unktomi [the Spider] answered, "This, indeed, has been a hard year. Famine is in all the land. Turn me into a buffalo that I may not be hungry." "Well," said the good-natured fox, "get up on yonder knoll and I will jump over you." Unktomi did as he was told, but when he saw the fox-buffalo running toward him, he jumped aside. The fox-buffalo then said, "You will never be a buffalo if you are such a coward." Unktomi sat down on the knoll again, and as the fox-buffalo jumped over him, he hit Unktomi; but instead of turning the Spider into a buffalo, he was himself turned back into a fox. After Unktomi had seen what had happened, he sat down and laughed immoderately while the poor fox sneaked out of sight.

The Beaver

Once Unktomi [the Spider] was going along the bank of a river when he saw a little beaver fast asleep on the shore. Unktomi, chuckling to himself, said, "Now I'll have some fun." He took the bark from a nearby tree and with it carefully tied up the little beaver. Then he carried it a long way off to a high hill, where, after untying it, he woke it up by asking, "Why, brother, how did you get here?"

The little beaver, half asleep and thinking he was still by the riverbank, turned over and attempted to dive into what he thought was water. After making several attempts to dive into the ground, he opened his eyes and saw that he was a long way from home. Meanwhile, Unktomi laughed and laughed until he nearly fell over.

It took the little beaver a long time to get to the river. The grass had been burnt off and the soles of his feet were cut by the stubble. Unktomi followed at a distance, making the most of his practical joke. After this occurrence, Unktomi traveled for many days. One day when the weather was very warm he lay down to rest and fell asleep. The little beaver found him asleep and said, "Now I'll have my revenge."

He dug a tunnel from the nearby river which ran water to Unktomi. The beaver kept on digging until there was a vast lake around his enemy, with nothing but a small island in the center, on which Unktomi slept. When the beaver finished, he said to Unktomi, "Why, my brother, how did you happen here?" This question caused Unktomi, who was partly aroused, to turn over. In doing so he splashed into the lake that the beaver had built. The beaver left the vicinity before Unktomi came to the surface. His surprise was so great that he was nearly drowned before he recovered his presence of mind. When he rose to the surface, he tried in vain to climb up on the little island. But with every effort a piece of the earth would cave in, until the island was completely demolished. Then, nearly exhausted, he struck out for the shore, reaching it shortly before his strength gave out. He stretched himself out on the bank to rest. When he had recovered from his experience, he looked around to see if the little beaver was laughing at him; and sure enough, there was his face grinning above the surface of the water.

The Unvisited Island

The introductory element of "The Unvisited Island" is one of the oldest recorded folktale plots, the two-brothers motif. According to Stith Thompson, the twin-brothers tale was "discovered in 1852 in a papyrus dating from about 1250 B.C. and once belonging to King Seti II. The story is given in great detail and is much like a modern folktale. There are two brothers. The elder, Anup, is married; the younger, Batu, lives in his house. The wife tries in vain to seduce Batu and then accuses him before her husband. Anup believes her" (24). At this point the similarities end, but how remarkable it is that two societies so far apart in space and time—the Santee Sioux and the Egyptian—have an identical story.

A young warrior once lived with his elder brother, who was married. The wife of the elder brother was a bad woman who often tried to entice the younger brother. But he always answered, "How can I do a thing that will shame my brother?" By and by this unfaithful woman brought false charges against the younger brother to her husband, who believed her, and ordered his brother to be exiled on the Unvisited Island. The Spider [the Trickster] was commanded to carry out the order, and for his reward was to marry the false wife's sister.

The Spider enticed the younger brother to the Unvisited Island with the pretext of an egg hunt. Then, when the younger brother was gathering eggs on the shore, he turned the head of the canoe and paddled away. The younger brother called after him with cries and entreaties, begging him to bring the canoe back. But it did not avail. Then he cursed the Spider as a mean deceiver. The Spider replied by telling him that he would meet with a Gray Bear, the Arm-Awls, and the Two-Women, then left him. Thus the younger brother was left on the Unvisited Island.

When he met the Gray Bear he made himself into a dead fish, which the bear swallowed whole. Then, after he was inside of the bear's body he stabbed the bear in the heart, cut his way out, and took off the paws for trophies.

The Arm-Awls were two old hags who sat all day outside their tent. The younger brother, before visiting them, folded up his blanket; then, without paying any attention to them, went into the tent. They looked daggers at him, but did not say anything because they meant to pierce him with their arms when he came out. He knew this, so threw out his blanket, which they pierced through and into each other. In this way they killed each other.

He had now met and vanquished the majority of his enemies, but the worst was still ahead in the form of the Two-Women. He took, before he went to their tent, a tooth and a bundle, which represented the gopher and the badger. With these he hoped to circumvent the wiles of the Two-Women.

So, armed and warned, he came to their tent. They were cannibals, who boiled and set before him man-flesh. But he, doing as he had been instructed, looked to the earth and prayed, "Grandmother, where are you?" His prayer was answered by a white pail, which came out of the ground, into which he emptied the contents of the pot that had been set before him. Then came the second trial. When he lay down they covered him with blankets to smother him. But he bored a hole through the blanket with his teeth so he could breathe freely. Then he made the hole larger, after which he talked to the Two-Women until they were persuaded to give up their cannibalism. After this had been done he married them.

It turned out that the Two-Women, who were the daughters of Ooktahee, the Great Spirit of the Waters, had been changed into cannibals by the Evil Spirit. They were very happy with the younger brother and bore children for him. But, by and by, he began to pine for his own country. The Two-Women, upon seeing something was the matter, inquired the cause. So he told them. "Oh, is that all!" they said. "We will take you back." So they called their mother and told her to bake pumice stone. When the pumice stone was baked and ground to powder, they said, "Call father." So they stood by the water and said, "Old man, come; the girls want to go to the mainland." Then immediately something floated up on the water and came to the shore. This was Ooktahee, the Water Spirit. They filled his eyes with the burnt stone, then put the younger brother in the sack and hung it on one of the numerous horns of the Great Spirit of the Waters. Then they and their boys got on and paddled for the mainland. But Ooktahee was very uneasy. He felt that shadows were coming over. He bade them look out for the Wakinyan [the Thunder Spirit] who was his immemorial enemy. "No, father, the sky is blue," they said. But indeed there were thick clouds and a great storm coming. No sooner had they landed and gotten to shore than it burst upon them. Then they said, "Father, hurry away, the Thunder is near." "Alas, my daughters, I thought so," was the reply. Just then the Thunder hurled his bolts at him and all the water was turned into blood. The younger brother said, "Alas for my poor father-in-law!" But the Two-Women said, "He will not die of that. He never dies."

They were now in his own country, but he saw no one until after the tent had been put up, when he saw a woman walking to a nearby spring for water. She looked like his sister, but she was so disfigured it was difficult to recognize her. It was only after she had approached closer that he knew for certain who it was. He said, "My sister." She answered, "My brother," and they embraced each other. Then he asked of her welfare, and why her face was scarred. She told him that her husband treated her very badly—that when she came for water and returned he charged her with having been courted by someone and put hot ashes on her face. Moreover, he had destroyed all the people of the village. After giving her brother this information she picked up her water pitcher and went home. The Spider, who was her husband, was very angry when he saw her and said, "Now, someone has been courting you again." To which she replied, "See, you have destroyed all the people; who is there to say anything to me?" and she dashed the water on him. He only laughed and said, "Woman, has my brother-in-law come home?" "If you had been left on the Unvisited Island would you ever have returned?" she asked. Then she left him and went to her brother's tent. Here she took a bath, was given beautiful clothes to put on, then told to retire to the back part of the tent.

Then the younger brother said to his two boys, "Go, call Spider." They went and said, "Spider, we call you." He said, "Oh, how beautiful my nephews are," and following them went into the tent. He was hoping to see his wife, now dressed so nicely and seated in the back part of the tent; but the younger brother said, "Spider, sit there in the door," to which he made answer, "Yes, brother-in-law, I will do what you tell me." It was now the younger brother's time to take vengeance. So he said, "Spider, weave tamarack roots; weave a basket over the fire." Spider squirmed, but did as he was told. He was killed by the smoke, after which the younger brother cut out the Spider's heart, dried it, then pounded it up fine and made a medicine from it which he gave to his two boys, saying, "Go and scatter it on the ruins of the village."

When the next morning came, he said to them, "Go and see what has happened to the medicine you have scattered." They returned and said, "Father, all over there are crawling worms." He sent them again the second day. They returned and said, "Father, the things are now very large." The third day they brought word: "Father, they are now little men, and we heard them say to each other, 'Stand up, you are crooked.'"

On the fourth day the people were perfected; and at the early dawn, with loud voices, beating drums and proclamations they came and pitched their tents around the tent of the younger brother, who was made their chief. In this way all the people of the tribe, whom the Spider thought he had destroyed, were brought back to life.

The Two Hunters
Translated by Julia LaFramboise.

Two hunters started out from camp on a day when the snow was deep and game was scarce. One of them was successful in his chase, but the other hunter did not succeed in finding any game. When the fortunate man sat down on a log to rest, the other man came over to sit beside him. They smoked their pipes and talked about the events of the day. The unfortunate hunter expected, according to Indian hunters' courtesy, the successful hunter to share his game with him. But the successful hunter, after having smoked his pipe, took up his deer and walked off without further ceremony. This insult was deeply resented by the other man, who decided to have revenge. He at once resolved to kill the other hunter's daughter, as his *Wakan* [sacred medicine] would enable him to do so without detection, since he was a medicine man.

When he came to his tent, he opened his medicine bag and prayed to his gods to send a disease that would immediately kill the successful hunter's daughter. The prayer of hatred was answered and the hunter's daughter died. The successful hunter, who knew his daughter had died an unnatural death, desired to find out who had caused her death. When she was laid on a scaffold in the top of a tree [which was the way the Santees buried their dead], he lay down beside her, knowing that the man responsible for her death would come in the night to cut off the tongue of his victim. He did not have to wait long. As soon as the sun had gone down he heard a rushing sound like that of a whirlwind. A winged man flew over him and lit beside his daughter's corpse. The father scanned the countenance of the man who was preparing to cut out his victim's tongue, and recognized the features of the slighted hunter.

As the medicine man proceeded with his terrible work he asked the corpse: "Do you still eat of your father's venison?" Whereat the enraged father seized him, saying, "Yes, she still eats of it!" The struggle between the two powerful men was long and terrible, but when the beams of the pale moon shot out from behind a cloud, the stricken father was avenged.

The father of the dead girl cut up the corpse of the medicine man and took it home, where he told his wife he had brought fresh meat for her to put in the pot. After it was put on to boil he called all the members of the medicine fraternity to a feast. The host did not speak until after the last man was through eating and the pipe was passed around the group. Then he said: "You all know that my daughter has been killed by medicine; 'tis useless to deny it." They all answered, "Yes." Then the host went on: "My daughter's death was the work of one of your fraternity, of one of your greatest medicine men, whom I called to attend this feast and who did not come. But I caught him, and it was of him you have made such a hearty meal. I am avenged."

The medicine men all looked grave as their chief speaker stood up and said: "It was just. Since he was so bungling as to be caught he deserves his fate."

The Rabbit

An old man lived with his squaw and two daughters, for whom he used to fetch wood. One day, when he was chopping wood, he heard someone whistling. Upon looking around he saw, sitting by a distant tree, a rabbit motioning for him to come over. The rabbit, upon his approach, gave him an acorn and told him to crack it open in his stable when he went home. The old man, when he came to his stable, did as he was told. To his surprise a wagon came out of the acorn.

The next day, when again he went after wood, he met the same rabbit, who gave him another acorn. This time it contained a harnessed team of horses.

The rabbit on the third day gave him an acorn that was to be cracked open in the tipi. It contained a pack full of clothes for his two daughters.

The old man told his daughters on the morning after they had received their clothes that there was a young man who had been very good to him and wanted to know which one of his daughters would marry him. They both thought they would like to. The old man went to the tree and found the rabbit and asked him to come home with him. The rabbit, now very bashful, did not want to go. So the old man picked him up, put him in the wagon, and took him home by force. When they got there, he took the rabbit out, carried him into the house, and said to his daughters, "Here he is." The daughters looked at the rabbit and said they did not want him. This made the rabbit feel ashamed, so he crept under the bed. Before long he crawled out as a young man, dressed in gray clothes. Then they both wanted to marry him. But the younger one said to the older, "You must not marry him, because you hate him so." So the younger daughter and the young man were married.

After they were married the young man cracked an acorn which caused a large tent to rise up a short distance from where the old people lived. The young couple moved into this tent, which was completely furnished. The only request the young man made of his bride was that he should not be called "Rabbit," but "Caske." She complied with his request and called him Caske, but one day she forgot and called him Rabbit. This made him so angry that he left her. She felt very badly and cried for many days.

At last one day she put on her finest dress, prepared some lunch, and went away. The first person she met on her journey was an old woman who lived in a grass tent. The old woman said, "Grandchild, whoever you are, come in." When she went in, the old woman took a handful of wild beans from under some hay, and a few pieces of dried-out tallow, which she gave to her for her meal. After she was through eating the old woman asked her where she was going. The girl answered, "Nowhere in particular; I am just walking around." Then the old woman said, "No, Grandchild, I know where you are going and what you are going for, but I prefer my sister to tell you." The old woman told her where to find her sister, who lived down the road in another grass tent.

But the second old woman did as the first one had done— gave her beans and tallow to eat, asked her the same questions, and told her to go to her sister who lived still farther down the road. She visited five old women, all sisters, who lived in grass tents and gave her wild beans and tallow to eat, and asked her the same questions. The only exception was the fifth sister, who said, "You are going after your husband, who is not far from here. Go down the road until you come to a place where some young women are washing and laughing as they wash. Among their clothes you will find those that belong to your husband. Take them with you. These young women will tell you where your husband is."

She followed the old woman's directions and found the place where the young women were washing. Here she saw Caske's clothing and asked the young women if they could tell her where Caske was. They replied that he had gone to a dance where he was going to be married. They directed her to the dance, where she found Caske dancing with a very pretty girl. She watched them for a long time, until Caske turned around and saw his wife looking at him. He came over to her and took her away from the people. When they were alone, he took an acorn out of his pocket and cracked it. It contained clothes for his wife, as hers were all ragged from her travels. Caske cracked another acorn and got horses and a wagon. They then rode home, where they lived happily together for a long time.

The Orphan Boy

Translated by Julia LaFramboise. This tale poses a problem to the reader: What are Pegasus, palaces, and keys doing in a Santee

Sioux story? In some cases, such elements can be explained as translation problems: that is, a translator familiar with the European fairy tale might translate a word meaning "a long lodge with many rooms" as "a splendid palace with many hundreds of rooms." But here the rooms, keys, and flying horses are integral motifs in the tale and therefore, assuming that the translator did not fabricate these elements, they must have been part of the original tale. They might well have been borrowed from folktales told the Indians by early French trappers or British soldiers.

At one time, long ago, a friendless orphan boy lived in a large village on the seashore. One day, becoming tired of his surroundings, he got into a large canoe and paddled out to sea. A terrible storm came up and cast him upon a lonely island, where he lived in solitude until one day a large canoe containing several men landed. They told the boy, who met them at the beach, that they were going to a distant shore where there was a well which, when salt was thrown into it, would create gold. The men had their canoe filled with salt for that purpose. The boy was glad to take passage with them.

They were on the ocean many days before they came to the well. When they arrived, they threw in their salt and got a great deal of gold, yet they wanted more. So they sent the orphan boy down in a sack, in spite of his cries and screams, threatening to keep him in the bottom of the well until he had filled the sack with gold. They used all their ropes in an attempt to get him to the bottom of the well; then they fastened poles together. At length, after many poles had been fastened together, the boy reached the bottom of the well where he found many gold coins at the mouth of a huge cave. He filled two sacks with gold coins and attached them to a rope with himself on the top of the sack. After this had been done he signaled to the men at the top by jerking the rope that he was ready to ascend. They commenced to pull him up. He was almost within reach of the mouth of the well when the rope and poles gave way, letting the boy drop to the bottom of the well again.

When the boy recovered consciousness, he heard a great noise above him which sounded like a whirlwind. To his terror he found that it was coming nearer down the well. He crept into the large sack, but was soon conscious of being carried upward, past the mouth of the well and high into the air. He now knew for certain that he was the captive of a large bird. After what seemed to be ages he was put down. When he crept out of the bag he saw that he was in an eagle's nest.

The old eagle was about to tear him to pieces but, seeing the boy's wretchedness, took compassion on him and brooded him with her young. The nest was in the top of a very tall cottonwood tree which stood alone on a plain. One day when the old eagle was gone he commenced climbing down the tree. It took him a long time to slide down, and when he reached the ground he was scarcely able to move. The branches had torn his clothes and skin so badly that his flesh was exposed and raw. Yet he knew it would be certain death to remain where he was, so he crept away, rested for a while, and moved on a little farther, until he reached a river, where he quenched his thirst. Shortly after he came to the river two beautiful young women appeared along the river bank and took compassion on him. They bound up his wounds and fed him; and when he was able to walk they took him home with them.

They lived in a splendid palace with many hundreds of rooms in it, each filled with curious and beautiful things from all parts of the world. Here they took care of him until he was well again. After he was well, they adopted him for their brother, and for the first time the poor boy was very happy.

One day his sisters told him they were going away from home for the day. Before they left, they told him he could amuse himself in any portion of the house with the exception of one room, which he was never to enter. Then, after giving him the keys to the palace, they departed. He went from room to room, admiring the many beautiful things he saw. When night came his sisters had not returned and he had not yet seen all the rooms in the palace.

The next day he went over the other rooms. At length he came to the forbidden room, where he paused a long time on the threshold. He put the key into the keyhole, then pulled it out with a shudder at thought of the possible consequences, and passed on. Yet when he had seen all the other rooms he returned to the forbidden one. This time he opened it and saw a fiery steed, milk white with golden markings, wondrously beautiful. Its eyes flashed as he led it from the palace and mounted it.

He had scarcely gotten firmly seated before the horse flew into the air with the boy on its back. The speed of its flight took his breath away and he fainted. When he recovered consciousness he was lying wounded and bleeding on the seashore. Raising his head, he looked around and recognized the place from whence he had embarked months before. An old woman came along and took him to her home, where he told of his experiences. She immediately retold his tale to the great chief of the town, who had him brought to his palace for an interview. After he had told his story a second time the chief said, "Those young women that you call sisters are my long lost daughters. They were carried away by a man one day, years ago, when they were swimming. The horse that flew away with you is my long-lost horse. When he came near home he left you by the seashore, where you were found. Through you I have gotten back my beautiful horse, and he has told me where my daughters can be found."

The chief sent men in canoes after his daughters. There was great rejoicing in the town on the day when they were returned. The lonely orphan boy became the chief's son, and was made chief over all the warriors in the country.

Canktewin—The Ill-Fated Woman

An interpretation of this tale appears in brackets at its conclusion.

Part I

Once there was a large village in which lived an honorable man who was called to all the great feasts. He took an active part in the dances to the Sun and the Heyoka [anti-natural deity]. He had ten sons, all of whom were handsome braves, and two fair daughters.

Now, as spring drew near, and according to their usual custom, they started out on their spring hunt. The young braves took their two sisters with them. The five eldest brothers were to hunt game for the elder sister and the other five for the younger sister. After traveling a long distance they selected their camping ground. Day by day the brothers vied with one another in bringing to their sisters the choicest game.

As time wore on the younger sister, who was the more amiable of the two, became the favorite. To her white deerskin tent came the choicest game of forest and lake. So, in consequence, jealousy grew in the breast of the elder sister. One morning after the departure of her brothers she decked herself in fine clothes and trinkets, after which she picked up an axe and told her sister that she was going to get firewood. She followed the well-worn path of her brothers through the forest until she came to a tall tree, where she perched herself among its thick branches. There she waited until evening, when her eldest brother came in sight, heavily laden with a deer. As he passed beneath her she struck his head a blow with her axe that broke his skull. Then she descended from the tree and dragged him into the bushes, after which she resumed her hiding place before the second brother appeared. She disposed of him in the same manner, and the same with the next and the next, until all of the ten brothers were killed. Then she went home to her sister and affected great distress and uneasiness for their non-appearance. The really distressed younger sister looked in vain for their coming that night.

Next morning the younger girl, upon awakening, saw that her sister was busy outdoors by the fire. To her horror she saw that her sister had the ten heads of her murdered brothers; she was scalping them and sewing together the scalps for a mantle. Then she heard her exclaim, "What shall I do? I lack just one scalp of finishing my beautiful mantle. Oh! I'll complete it with my sister's scalp!" The younger sister, upon hearing these words, fled in terror from the tent to the deepest recess of the forest, where she wailed out her anguish, calling on the Wanaghis [ghosts] to avenge her lost brothers.

When night came and darkness spread over the earth her attention was attracted by a low whistle, then another whistle, longer and louder; then one to the north of her; then another to the east; then to the south and to the east; then to the south and west. Afterward came a stillness that even the insects dared not disturb, while close by her a voice said, "Sister, it is your murdered brothers that whistled. Go home and go to bed! In the night you will hear whistling, as you did just now, but fear not. When you hear this whistling your elder sister will say, 'My sister, get up and light the fire,' but do not heed her though she implores you to get up."

So she went home, where her sister still worked on the scalp mantle. After a while they both retired. They were awakened at midnight by the whistling. At the first sound the elder sister called to the younger, whose name was Canktewin, and entreated her to light the fire. But Canktewin slept until morning. When she awakened she found that her sister was already up and about. When Canktewin came out of the tent her sister cried angrily at her, "Go back, or I will kill you with this!" wielding a human leg. It was one of her own legs that the ghost of one of her brothers had pulled off. The elder sister's face had become so distorted during the night that Canktewin found it difficult to recognize her. The elder sister, after threatening Canktewin's life, sat down again, muttering to herself in the manner of witches. At length she arose and hopped off on one leg, carrying the other one under her arm.

The elder sister had hardly gotten out of sight before Canktewin left the tent and fled for her life. She ran until out of breath, but when she paused to rest she heard a voice in the distance which she recognized as her sister's, who was pursuing her. Upon looking back Canktewin saw the unsightly creature hopping toward her at the rate of one or two yards at a hop, with her scalp mantle streaming behind her. She had nearly overtaken the helpless Canktewin when they encountered a small swamp. The one-legged creature, in trying to extricate herself from the mire, pulled the other leg off. Unable to proceed further, she died there.

In the meantime Canktewin came to the shore of a beautiful lake. Off in the distance, on the surface of the lake, gleamed something which, when it came closer to the bank, proved to be a metal canoe with a single boatman. She hid in the bushes, but was too late to escape the sight of the boatman, for he landed just below her, walked up to her hiding place and commanded her to get into his canoe. But when she began to step into the canoe she saw a hundred snakes in its prow, each of which hissed at her. She drew back in terror, only to be driven forward by her captor. Again the snakes jumped toward her. When their master commanded them to be silent they obeyed him, and Canktewin got into the canoe and seated herself among them. The man then got in and paddled until the sun was on the west side, when they came in sight of a very high precipice. As the canoe drew nearer a door flew open and the man ordered her to get out. She stepped into a great stone hall, where a little old woman was sitting by a huge fire and an immense pot containing a stew.

Next morning, as the man was starting out in his metal canoe, he said to the old woman, "Grandmother, have another stew ready on my return." After his departure the old woman wept and said, "Oh, my grandchild, why did you come here to the man-eater's house? This man has eaten a great many young men and women, and you are the fairest of them all. I cannot kill you. Take this tomahawk and cleave open this old head of mine. My life has been long, but what use is it to me now? Take my body, put it into the pot and make a savory stew for the man-eater. Then take my severed arms and the axe to yonder island, tie them to a tree, and fly for your life. Go toward the east; run night and day until you come to a bright metal house."

Poor Canktewin wrung her hands in agony and said, "I cannot! Oh! I cannot! It is better that you do your work and kill me."

"Ah! My grandchild," said the old woman, "it would be but one of your kindest acts to take me away from this den to the happy land of the spirits, where all my kind have preceded me. I am nothing but a lightning-blasted tree whose center has been rotted out with age. Take, oh take, my grandchild, this weapon and kill me." But her pleadings were in vain. Canktewin would not kill her. The old woman then threw herself into the boiling pot.

Canktewin, upon seeing what the old woman had done, became horrified and wept until the declining sun reminded her that she must escape before the man-eater returned. But before leaving she severed the arms of the old woman, which, together with the axe, she carried to the island where she tied them to a tree. Then she fled.

Soon after her flight the man-eater returned to find his grandmother gone. In answer to his call he heard her voice from the

far-off island. Again he called her. This time he heard her
answer that she would come as soon as the wood was chopped.
He sat down to wait, listening to the strokes of her axe. After a
while he became angry at her delay and started after her. When
he arrived at the island, he found only her arms, which were
chopping wood. He knew then that Canktewin had escaped. His
anger was so great that he foamed at the mouth as he started in
pursuit.

In the meantime Canktewin ran night and day until suddenly
a bright light dazzled her eyes. After she had become used to
the strange light she discerned a metal house. Her limbs by now
were so tired that she could scarcely stand up. But she was
quickly aroused from her pause by a yell of rage. Turning
around she saw the man-eater running toward her with a flash-
ing tomahawk in his hand. He was only a few steps behind her
when she reached the metal house, by the steps of which sat a
man carving a large pipe. Carven images were fastened to his
ears; they winked and blinked at her when he turned his head.
She cried, "Save me and I'll be your cousin!" Still he was silent.
She screamed in desperation, "Save me and I'll be your sister!"
The man-eater almost had her in his grasp when the silent man
sprang to his feet and pushed her into his metal house. "Why
did you not say you were my sister before?" he asked.

In the meantime the man-eater, shouting angrily at the top
of his voice, kept running around the house. This annoyed the
silent man, so he said, "My pets, go and eat him up; he troubles
me." He opened a side door that let out a lion and a tiger, who
immediately sprang upon the man-eater, tore him to pieces,
and commenced to devour him. But each piece that touched
the ground became a man-eater, and it was only when they ate
up the ground on which his blood dropped that they were
victorious.

Part II

Canktewin was very happy to become the silent man's sister.
The many rooms of her brother's house were decorated with
braided belts, moccasins, quilled blankets, and leggings. Some
of the articles were unfinished. "These," said her brother as she
was surveying them, "are the handiwork of my former adopted

sister, who was deceived and killed during my absence. Now I am going to leave you, but do not on any account open the door to anyone while I am gone." So saying he set out on a journey to a far country.

One day, when Canktewin was working on one of the unfinished belts, she heard a pleading voice at the door saying, "Aunt, do let me in ere I perish with cold. I am the silent man's child and he sent me to you." This wailing voice repeated its demand for admittance at regular intervals until her sympathizing heart could withstand it no longer. She admitted a small boy with a large mouth. His strange deformity made her shrink back, but when she remembered that it was her protector's child she led him to the fire and warmed him, where he fell asleep. She sat and watched him. As he slept his mouth opened wider and wider until she saw a man's feet coming out of his throat. She immediately awoke the ugly creature, saying, "Get up, my nephew, and fetch some wood; our fire is going out." As he stepped out she closed and barred the door. The boy, who was but a demon in disguise, saw that he had been fooled. He raged and raved at the door for a long time, but it was to no purpose. Canktewin would not let him in a second time. When her brother returned he praised her wisdom in escaping the wiles of such an enemy.

She lived with her brother many happy years, but after a time she began thinking of her lonely parents, bereft of their children, and became seized with the desire to return and comfort them. When she made known the cause of her unhappiness to her brother he told her to go at once. But before she left he gave her instructions on how to avoid the many dangers she would find on her journey.

One day, when she was traveling through a large village, she was chased by the men, women, children and dogs who inhabited the place. But she looked straight before her and did not heed their uproar. When she came to the outskirts of the town there was a furious earthquake which nearly swallowed her up. She ran in order to get away from the new danger, but on looking around saw a large spotted dog which was fiercely pursuing her. She was nearly out of breath when the dog also became tired out and abandoned the pursuit.

Shortly afterwards she heard a childlike voice calling her name. She looked around and spied a dwarf in the branches of a tree. He tried in every way to make her speak. She had nearly passed out of sight when his extreme insolence made her command him to be still. Whereupon he came down and told her that she could not pass until she had shot arrows with him. She shot arrows with him and lost them. He led the way in the hunt for them until they came to an enclosure, where he told her she was his slave. Looking around, she found every avenue of escape closed and barred. All she could see was a large field, where hundreds of scalpless young women were toiling. The dwarf left her to give an offering to the Tahkushkanshkan [the motion god] for permitting him to find another slave. When he was preparing for his ceremony he retired to his round hut and called for Canktewin to bring his heated stone. When she was handing it to him he pulled off her scalp. After the dwarf finished his offering he bound Canktewin and seated her in the center of his round house.

After she had been seated there a while she saw a large black stone slowly descending toward her from the top of the roof. To save herself she threw up her hand, in which was a small sharp stick. The stick pierced through the soft center of the stone, which contained the dwarf's heart, immediately killing him. She then ran out to the field and proclaimed freedom to the poor scalped creatures. They all went to a nearby lake where they bathed their heads in the water. Their scalps were immediately restored to their heads. Then she continued on her way homeward, while the other slaves, after thanking her for freeing them, returned to theirs.

One day, while still on her journey, she walked along the shore of a lake, where she met two young women who asked her to bathe in the lake with them. Before doing so they informed her that the fates had decreed that whoever dove up from beneath the surface of the water in the center of the lake, which was marked by a tuft of wild rice, would be taken as his wife by Wahmnuhahtahghosha [the Pearl Spitter]. Canktewin was the only one who succeeded in coming up at the tuft of wild rice. Then they proceeded on their journey together until they saw a beautiful canoe come to the shore, out of which a young man stepped, saying, "I am the Pearl Spitter." Then, as Canktewin was getting ready to step into the canoe, the two young women pushed her aside and stepped in themselves.

Canktewin was now alone again. She followed the lake's shore until another canoe came in sight. This was far more beautiful than the first, and the boatman far more handsome than the other. He sprang ashore and began to spit beautiful pearls of all sizes. This proved him to be the real Pearl Spitter, the first one being an impostor. She eagerly gathered the pearls. Then they entered the canoe and paddled to the opposite side, where there was a large village, the Pearl Spitter's home. Here they lived in great happiness, until one evening when there was a grand feast to which they were both invited. While they were at the feast her two rivals in the diving contest saw her with the real Pearl Spitter, whereupon they were filled with envy and jealousy. They followed Pearl Spitter and his wife home, where they drove Canktewin out of the house and occupied it themselves. The counterfeit Pearl Spitter came in great wrath and called the real Pearl Spitter a coward, whereupon they had a fight. They destroyed the village during this struggle, also all the trees by the lake, and shook up the waters of the lake so that it was never clear from that time on. But at length, by cowardly wiles, the counterfeit Pearl Spitter overcame his noble antagonist. Poor Canktewin stayed long enough to wail over the grave, then went home and comforted her father and mother all the days of their lives.

[*In this "peculiar character study the name 'Ill-Fated Woman' was chosen to express the original Santee meaning.* Canktewin *gives only a part of the native idea.* Cankte (*the* win *is the feminine termination in proper names*) *in Dakota means a tree that has been blasted by lightning. It is also used as an attribute of the great Thunder God, who kills the trees by his flash. By figure of speech it seems to be used of this young woman who, though amiable and full of good intent, always brings disaster on those with whom she is connected as well as on herself. But as for herself she miraculously escapes every time, only to fall into new dangers and stir up more trouble. Thus by her amiability she captivates her brothers and arouses the jealousy of her sister, causing the death of them all. She falls into the hands of the man-eater, only to cause the death of the good grandmother who befriends her and shows her how to escape. She is nearly recaptured because she fails to say the right word in time. She almost brings ruin to her new benefactor, the silent man, and death to herself by opening his house to the demon. On her road home, by failing to keep still one moment longer, she falls into the hands of the wicked dwarf and loses her scalp. And later, as seen in the second part of the story, she brings disaster on her lover and the village and country in which he lives by the jealousy she arouses in her rivals. Consistently fortunate herself, she brings misfortune to the people who are connected with her. True, she liberates the scalpless maidens toiling in the fields of the wicked dwarf, and at last goes home to cherish her parents in their last days. But these are only incidents, not main points of her life. Doubtless other ideas, mythological and philosophical, may be traced in this story. Its most evident meaning, however, is as a study in character"* (1).]

The Hunter

Tales like this one are folk histories, invented to explain a geographical feature, a name, or (as in this case) a custom. They may or may not be based in fact and they are classified as legend, for they have a single theme and are generally told as fact.

In the olden days, long before the first paleface set foot in this country, a small band of Indians were camped near the Cypress Hill, where they were well supplied with wood and water. There they had good pasture for their ponies, who were very scarce and highly prized by the Indians. One of the Indians who lived in this village, named Arrow-Point, was a hunter who provided meat for his wife and the little Arrow-Points. To do this he had to spend many days away from his home, traveling great distances to secure sufficient game for his family's needs. There, in strange hunting grounds, he was in constant danger of being killed by the war parties of other tribes. In those days the only weapon was the bow and arrow; he had to use a great deal of cunning in order to get near enough to the game to kill it.

One day, when he was stalking a herd of antelope, he was surprised by a band of Blackfeet Indians, who were out on a horse-stealing expedition. Arrow-Point had to run for his life. No matter how fast he ran the Blackfeet kept gaining on him, so it became evident that unless some help came he would soon be slain. As he ran he called on his feet, "Oh, my feet, run, or I will be killed by our enemy." But his feet answered back, "Call on your head. When you eat you give all to your head and never think of us." Again Arrow-Point called out, "Oh, my feet, run, and I shall always remember you when I eat." But still his feet remained stubborn. So, seeing that all was lost, he threw himself on the ground and said, "All right, when I am killed my head will be placed on a pole and all the Blackfeet nation will dance around and admire it, but you, you will be cut off and thrown to the dogs." With that threat his feet began to jump and hop, in a great fright to get away. He sprang to his feet and flew over the ground, quickly outdistancing his pursuers.

He soon reached his home in safety, and in fulfillment of the promise to his feet he had them bathed in buffalo fat for two days and nights. He was now the swiftest runner in his tribe, often beating his companions' fastest horses. The Indians changed his name to Eagle-Foot. Remembering his narrow escape from death, he always wiped his hands on his feet when through eating. This is a custom that has been observed by the Indians to this day.

The Flint Chief

Perhaps, in your search for prairie flowers, you have chanced upon bits of flint and wondered how they came to be. The tradition of our tribe tells us that they came from the Flint Chief, who once lived in our midst. This was many years ago, before the coming of the palefaces.

The Flint Chief, as tradition tells us, was a very large and unusual man whose head and shoulders were made of iron, his belly and thighs of flint, while his legs were of two granite boulders. His huge size forbade his joining the chase or following the warpath. But none in the tribe was more skilled in the mysteries of the hunt or knew more about the arts of war. He was also wise in the council, where he decided the arguments which arose from time to time among his people. It was he who furnished his tribe with the sinews for war and the implements of the chase, because, during the days when the braves were absent, he carved arrowheads. This is why he was called the Flint Chief.

One day when this kindly old chief sighted his arrows for balance and straightness of line, bending his head this way and that during the process, he dropped his knife against his left thigh. Immediately a happy thought came to him, causing his eyes to twinkle merrily as he laughed in a low chuckle that sounded like the gurgle of a mountain brook. Then he laughed again, this time so loud and long that the rocks and weeds vibrated with echoing joy. You see, his knife, falling against his thigh, had set off sparks, ending his lifelong search for fire.

The discovery of fire had been the Flint Chief's greatest ambition. It could only be obtained by lighting sticks of wood to trees or bushes that had been ignited by lightning. The fire, when once secured in this manner, sometimes went out and the tribe had to wait for weeks before another tree or bush was set on fire by the great Thunder Bird. So some means of making fire at will was of great importance to the tribe. Now the Flint Chief had found that he carried this great gift within his body, ready for instant use. What could be more precious to his people than this? All they had to do now in order to obtain fire was to carry a piece of flint that had been chipped from his body.

As soon as his warriors had returned he called them together, showed the piece of flint he had broken off of his body, and explained its use. Their joy became great when each in turn became the possessor of a piece of flint.

And so it came about that ever after they supplied themselves, as occasion required, from this never failing source. One precaution, however, was necessary. The Flint Chief had explained to them that while they might smite him on either thigh with impunity, a blow in the belly would prove fatal. But the unerring eye and unfaltering arm of the warriors feared naught.

Happy chief, fortunate people! Alas that perfection does not dwell on this earth! Into this fine harmony came a discordant note in the form of Matoschecha [Bad Bear], who brought upon them the calamity that still survives in the tradition of our tribe after so many generations have passed.

After one of their grand hunting expeditions the warriors came home laden with great packs of buffalo meat, robes, and skins. While the women made moccasins, gaily bedecked with ribbons and beads, the pot was kept boiling for the young braves. Chaskay, one of the tribe's best warriors, was eating lazily from his wooden bowl on top of his bearskin when he good-naturedly asked his pretty girl-wife to tie his moccasins. As she complied with his request he felt as if he had attained the total sum of human happiness. But he little knew of the dreadful tragedy in which he was to play a part. It was caused by Matoschecha, the warrior who tattooed his tally of scalps on his right arm and, with equal faithfulness, tattooed the number of bears he had slain on his left arm. He was an evil-eyed, ill-conditioned man whose violent temper brought disturbance and unhappiness to everyone with whom he came into contact.

That evening he was bitter and morose. He felt that his twenty-one bearskins availed him nothing so long as Chaskay possessed the beautiful bearskin on which he was eating his meal. Its large size and unusually fine fur made Matoschecha insane with jealousy. So he walked over to the good-natured Chaskay and claimed it for his own, accusing Chaskay of stealing it. Chaskay, with an expression of bewildered surprise, told Matoschecha that he was mistaken, but was willing to let the Flint Chief settle the argument.

The Flint Chief, as soon as he was told of the quarrel, decided in the ease-loving Chaskay's favor. Matoschecha, with vengeful look and heedless hand, immediately threw a large stone at his enemy. But Matoschecha, in his blind fury, missed his aim, and the stone intended for Chaskay struck, with great force, the Flint Chief's stomach.

The Flint Chief immediately let out such a piercing scream that he caused low rumblings to come from under the ground and the hill to shake as he fell to the earth among a heavy shower of flying flints which came from his body. He looked with reproachful eyes on Matoschecha; then a flame of fire began consuming his body as his great head and granite shoulders rolled away, covering the form of Matoschecha from the face of day. All that was left was a pile of flints, which to this day has been used by our tribe for making fire.

Neeshu

Translated by Charles Hoffman. This tale, with its animal helpers and courtship tests, is very much like European fairy tales.

Part I. Neeshu as a Young Child

A long time ago there lived in a big village an old man who was always alone. If a visitor went into his tent, he was never seen afterwards, and no one knew what had become of him, it being supposed that he had been killed.

The chief heard so many complaints from his people about these strange disappearances that one day he sent five warriors to bring the old man to him. When they came back with him, the chief told the warriors to tie his hands and feet and put him into prison.

The next day the chief and some of the people who lived with him went away from their home, leaving no one behind but Neeshu, the chief's little son, who was about ten years old. Neeshu played with an iron ring outside his father's tent. He would roll it around to see how far it would go without falling over. After a while he rolled it a long way and it went into the prisoner's tent, where the old man had been put the day before. Neeshu peeped in, and asked to have his plaything back. The old man answered that he would do a great many things for him if he would only come in and untie his hands and feet. Neeshu said he did not think his father would like it if he did that. But the old man told him that he would take him to live with him if his father said or did anything to him. Neeshu was so anxious to get his ring back that he untied the tent door and went in to let the old man out. The old man, before escaping, told Neeshu how to find his home. He said he lived on an island in the river, but that Neeshu need not be afraid of the water when he came to see him because he could walk on it without the risk of drowning. When he came, he would be met by the old man.

Neeshu, after helping the old man to escape, played around the tents all day until late in the evening, when the chief and his people returned to the camp. The first thing the chief did was to look into the tent where he kept the prisoner. He became very angry when he found it empty, and immediately sent for everyone in the camp to stand in a line in front of him. Then he took a magic glass out of his pocket which, by looking through it, gave him the power to distinguish the innocent from the guilty.

The chief put it up to his eyes and looked a long time at each member of his tribe, but all were innocent, since they appeared the same when he held the glass up to his eyes as they did before; and he knew that when he held it up before the guilty man he should see him as he appeared when he was untying the old man's feet. But he kept them all standing there, wondering what to do next, when someone said, "Your son, Neeshu, ought to be examined as well as us." So the chief had someone awaken him and bring him out to where the others were. Neeshu stood before his father and the chief raised the glass instrument to his eyes to have a good look at his son. He peeked through his magic glass for a long time. When he put it down, he was too surprised to speak, but finally said that he had seen his son untying the old man's hands and letting him out of the prison.

This raised a shout, as he had said that he would certainly kill the one who had done it. But he could not kill his own son, so he said that he would give him a severe whipping and keep him shut up for a long time.

Neeshu did not like to be shut up and did not feel very good after the whipping he received, so made up his mind to run away to find the old man he had helped to escape. So, after the stillness of night had come upon the camp, Neeshu took a blanket and ran as fast as he could to the river. When he came to the bank he waited a few minutes, wondering if he could really walk on the water, as the old man had told him. At last he took a step or two and found that he got along all right. He kept on walking on the water until he came to the island, where the old man met him and took him to his large tent.

They lived together on the island for a long time. Neeshu, during the years, grew very rapidly. The old man, whom Neeshu now called grandfather, was what the Indians call *wakau*; that is, he possessed the power to make things grow as much in a day as they would have done in a year under ordinary conditions.

One day, when they were hunting, they went to a part of the island where Neeshu had never been before. Here he saw four pools of water of different colors; the smallest was yellow, the others were red, black, and white. The grandfather told Neeshu to put his head into the yellow water and see what it would do. He did so, and found that it made his hair very long and yellow. He was delighted, and coiled it up on top of his head and covered it with a deerskin cap. Then he told him to step into the large pool of black water and to cover himself all over with it. When he came out, he was dressed in black and was on a splendid black horse that had fine black skins thrown over its back. Then he went into the red and white pools of water, from which he came out with clothes and horses the same color as the water he had gone into.

He was very careful of all the new things he had; he put the clothes away and found good places for his three horses, of which he was very proud.

Part II. Neeshu as a Young Man

One evening when Neeshu and his friend were sitting by the tent talking, his grandfather told him of a beautiful young woman who lived six suns away and who was much admired by all the men, young and old. A number of men had endeavored to win her for a wife, but none of them were ever seen after their first visit to her because her father and mother were *wakau* and always did something with all the young men who came to see her. Nevertheless, Neeshu made up his mind that he would go to see Sunapahat anyway. The old man was a little afraid to have him go, but admired the boy's courage so much that he did not say much against it.

Soon after this discussion Neeshu set out to find the home of Sunapahat. He had walked about three miles when he saw a lion, a bear, a hawk, and an ant sitting around a buffalo which they had killed. They were now trying to decide how to divide the spoils.

The ant, as soon as she saw Neeshu, asked him if he had a knife. He answered that he had, so she asked him to cut up the buffalo for them. He agreed to do it and after skinning it divided the bones between the lion and the bear, gave the flesh to the hawk and the head to the ant.

After finishing his work he was about to leave them when the ant again spoke to him, saying, "We know where you are going and know that you have a difficult task before you. So, to show how grateful we are for the help you have given us, we will do everything we can to make your journey easier." So saying, she took one of her little legs, wrapped it in a deerskin, and handed it to Neeshu, telling him that if he was ever in trouble and wanted to escape to take out this little foot and say, "I will be an ant," and immediately he would be one, and could slip away unnoticed. The lion and the bear gave him one of their claws, telling him the same that the ant had: that whenever he required their service to take out these claws, call to them, and they would be there to do anything that he wished. The hawk gave him one of her wing feathers, saying, "When you want to go very fast, produce this feather and say, 'I will be a hawk,' and you will find yourself flying away as fast as I can. Should you get hungry," she continued, "you can kill something and eat it; that is the way I always do."

After leaving these strange friends he walked a short distance, then became tired because the day had been long. At this moment he happened to think of what the hawk had told him. So, taking the feather from the deerskin, he said, "I will be a hawk," and in a moment was delighted to find himself flying away in the air, up above the tallest trees.

He flew so fast that it did not take him very long to come to the village where Sunapahat lived. He circled above the tops of the tents, trying to determine where she was. After hunting for some time he found her sitting in a little arbor of boughs, sewing. Her beauty took his breath away. She was even lovelier than he had expected. As soon as he found where she was, he began wondering where he should go to transform himself from a hawk to a man again. Finally he found a quiet place where he made himself ready to see Sunapahat.

When he arrived at the door of her tent, he was greeted by Sunapahat's mother, who said, "Did you come to see my daughter?" "Yes, I came to see her," he answered. She said, "I am glad to see you; walk in." After he had entered the tent she gave him something to eat, and although he was much too excited to be hungry, he ate all she set before him. When he had finished eating, she told him she would have something for him to do the next day. He answered that he would go into the village, but would be back to spend the night with them.

In the village he met some men who asked him what his business was. He told them that he had heard much of Sunapahat and had come to see her. They were much surprised and told him that it would do him no good; that all who ever went to the house for the purpose of seeing Sunapahat were always killed. Neeshu said he meant to try anyway, and perhaps he would succeed.

He talked with the villagers for a while, then went back to where Sunapahat lived. The first one whom he saw was her mother again, who was a dreadful-looking old woman. She told him his bed was ready, showed him where it was, and then went away. He sat quietly for a long time, wondering what would befall him on the morrow. While in the midst of his thoughts Sunapahat herself came into the room. She was pleased with his appearance, and decided to help Neeshu perform the tasks that her mother and father would require of him. She knew that the next day her mother would ask him to do something that seemed impossible for him to do; still, if he did not do it he would be killed, just as many others had been. After telling him what she knew she left him.

In the morning the mother called to him, saying his breakfast was ready. He followed her to a room where two large kettles full of the flesh of the former suitors of Sunapahat were boiling. As the old woman prepared to leave she warned him that unless he ate the entire contents of both kettles he could not have her daughter.

Neeshu looked with disgust at the dreadful stuff the old woman had placed before him, then slowly unrolled the bear and lion claws from the deerskin, and said, "I want both of you to come and eat this up for me." They immediately came and did as he requested, leaving only a few bones in the kettle and the two claws, which he carefully wrapped up in the deerskin.

When the old woman came back, she was thinking, "I suppose he is dead by this time and we shall not hear any more of him." Consequently she was much surprised to see him sitting there, smiling. She did not show her surprise, but said, "I am glad that you could eat all that I had cooked for you." Then she went away to find her husband to tell him what had occurred. He listened patiently, then said he was afraid that the man was *wakau*.

That evening Neeshu's beloved, Sunapahat, came to him to tell him what he would have to do the next day. She said, "My father will give you an axe and tell you to level a high hill that is nearby. When you are ready to go, be sure to call me, since I think that I can help you."

The next morning her father told him that he had always had the desire to see a long distance without climbing to the top of the great hill in front of the tent, so he wished Neeshu would take the old axe and level it off.

Neeshu took the axe and climbed the hill, wondering all the way how he could ever dispose of so much earth. He sat down to think it over, but could not hit upon a good plan. Then he remembered that Sunapahat had told him to call her as soon as he got to the hill. He felt ashamed that he had forgotten her request for so long. As soon as he had called she appeared to him in a cloud, so that none but he could see her. She asked for the axe, which he handed her, then waved it back and forth over the hill until it gradually became level and flat. Sunapahat then went away as she had come, concealed in a cloud.

Neeshu went to the old man and told him that his work was done. The old man went to his tent door, where he became sad when he saw that the hill had actually disappeared. He and his wife talked about it a long time and were sorry that Neeshu had been able to comply with their foolish request, since the hill belonged to them and had been covered with good timber. Now that it was leveled they would not have so much wood. Still, they did not want Neeshu to know that they were not pleased with his work. The father was afraid that Sunapahat had helped him, but her mother would not believe his suspicion. The father then went to Neeshu and told him that he had one more thing for him to do, and that he would tell him in the morning what it was.

So in the morning the mother took Neeshu to the door of her tent and pointed to the lake, saying, "Whenever I want to go anywhere, that lake seems to be in my way. I wish that you would drain all the water out; here is a thimble to do it with."

Then she went back into the tent while he slowly walked to the lake, trying to think of some way out of his difficulty. He sat down upon the bank and thought of many different ways until he remembered what Sunapahat had said to him the evening before. He had forgotten her again. He was ashamed to call her, so dipped a few thimblefuls out, but soon saw that he could do nothing that way. Then he called her and she came as she had come to the hill on the previous morning, hidden from everyone but him. She asked for the thimble, held it a certain way in her hand, then waved it back and forth over the water. With every motion the water gradually lowered until there was only a little water left at one side. This she told Neeshu he must dip out with his thimble. Soon after she had gone her mother came to see how Neeshu was getting along and was surprised to see him dipping out the last few thimblefuls and supposed that all the water had been disposed of in the same way. She merely said that she was glad he had done as she had asked him to do and went to find her husband to talk it over. They agreed that they had done a very foolish thing. Yesterday the hill with most of their wood had gone and now the lake where they got water and fish had also disappeared. They were convinced that Neeshu was *wakau* and did not like to give Sunapahat up without one more test of his powers. The mother said that she would have a plan ready by morning.

That evening, as before, Sunapahat came to Neeshu, saying that she did not know what her mother and father would ask of him next but that he could rely on any assistance from her that she could possibly give.

The mother came to him in the morning and said, "We will do something together this time; we will see who can fly the higher and who will remain in the air the longest." Then they went a short distance off, where they were to take off, and found the entire village assembled to witness the trial. The mother took a richly embroidered deerskin, wrapped it about her, and sailed into the air. Neeshu then took out the hawk feather and said softly, "I will be a hawk." He was immediately flying above the heads of the people. He went up and up until he seemed but a small speck among the clouds. The old woman, meanwhile, did not know that Neeshu had flown above her and, getting tired of gliding, started down. After she had once started down she descended very rapidly. The village people were so disgusted with her flight that as soon as she had landed they put her and her husband to death.

When Neeshu came down, he was greeted with cheers and shouts of delight from the villagers. He had been successful, so he took Sunapahat, who was now his bride, and returned to his island home, where the old man lived who had done so much for him.

The grandfather was very glad to see Neeshu and asked him if the young woman with him was really Sunapahat. Being told that she was, he told Neeshu that he was a brave, good boy; and then, after telling Sunapahat that he was glad to have her there, began to arrange things for her comfort.

The three lived together for a long time until one day the grandfather asked Neeshu if he would like to go back to see his father and mother. He answered, "Yes, I would like to go." So Neeshu packed the clothes that he had gotten in the pools and took the three nice horses, with which he and Sunapahat left the island to go back to his old home. The grandfather went with them a little way.

After a short journey he came to the camp of his people, where the first one he saw was his mother. He said, "Mother, don't you know me?" She looked at him a moment, then embraced him. She was also glad to have the beautiful girl, Sunapahat, with them and made her welcome.

The Great Fish Who Is Called a Sand Bar

Since the Santees did not live along the Missouri until the 1860's, this tale may originally have been told about the Minnesota or some other river familiar to them. At any rate, the very general nature of the tale permits it to be applied to virtually any river, or section along a river, which was constantly choked with sand bars and mud flats.

A party of warriors were winding their way homeward along the bank of a muddy river after a successful invasion of the country of their enemies. Their war paint and dancing eagle plumes gleamed in the last rays of the setting sun. Toward the right of the party walked a couple of stalwart braves. There was a tenderness in their manner to each other that at once revealed a close comradeship, since the love of two men who have faced danger together often surpasses their love for women.

They had been on the warpath for many days and nights, and now over forty-eight hours had passed since their last morsel of food had been consumed. So it was with much pleasure that Chaske, one of the two friends, caught a large pike in the river.

Chaske quickly prepared the fish for his friend, Hepan, who was weaker than he. But after it had been prepared in perfect Indian style Hepan refused to eat it. In vain Chaske urged, hoping to overcome his friend's reluctance to share his meal. At length, being unable to resist the pleadings of Chaske, Hepan said, "My friend, I do as you urge because you love me; but if I eat the pike don't become weary of bringing me water from the river during the night." So, with this understanding, the two joyfully partook of the fish. But the meal was scarcely over before Hepan said, "Chaske, bring me some water." Chaske joyfully brought his friend water, since he was happy to do any service for him. But soon the large pailful was empty and his friend was still panting for water.

Chaske, in an attempt to allay his friend's painful thirst, made frequent trips to the river. But the thirst, instead of becoming quenched, became more and more intense; and as the night wore on the flagging energy of Chaske suggested an easier and surer method of quenching his friend's unaccountable thirst. It was to move him to the bank of the stream where he could drink his fill. Upon proposing it his friend agreed to the idea, but at the same time exclaimed, "My friend, you have undone me." So Chaske carefully helped Hepan to the river's edge, and then left him to snatch an hour's rest before the dawn came.

Chaske had scarcely dozed off before the voice of his friend awoke him with the words, "Behold me." When Chaske reached him, the upper half of his body had turned into a pike. In distress and anguish, Chaske upbraided himself for bringing about his friend's misfortune by taking him to the river's edge, but it was too late to help now; the fish part was already submerged in the river, and the remainder of his body was following fast until the last vestige of a man had disappeared, having been replaced by a great pike that stretched across the mouth of the river. As time sped on, the sand washed upon it until to casual observers it looked like an ordinary sand bar.

Many canoes, during the years that followed, were wrecked on the big fish. These accidents kept on occurring until one day an Indian maiden, who had been Hepan's beloved, came slowly down the stream in a birchbark canoe that was loaded with beaded moccasins and all kinds of maiden handiwork, which she dropped into the water for her lost lover. The large fish, as a token of acceptance, did the one thing it could do: submerged itself under the water.

The paleface, who now use the Missouri, call the great fish a sand bar because their river boats are sometimes left stranded on top of it. Only we, the Indians, know it is a great fish who was once a man.

The Legend of Porcupine Butte

There was a young warrior, many years ago, who was often seen wandering about with a very downcast expression upon his face. He had a sufficient reason for his forlorn countenance, because for many days and nights he and his companions had been carrying on an unsuccessful search for buffalo, whose meat was needed for their starving tribe.

The young man slowly climbed up to the top of a very high hill, where he looked over the landscape for a buffalo herd. But it was of no avail. He could see nothing but the wide country, its hills and valleys, and the pine trees dotting the hillsides here and there. His face grew more downcast and his vision more troubled than ever. Suddenly he was startled by a voice which broke the stillness. "Why are you so sad at heart?" it asked.

The young man gazed about him in astonishment. He had seen no living being. "Who spoke to me?" was the thought. He looked around, but didn't see anyone. "I must have been dreaming," he said to himself, and again his countenance fell. But again the same voice spoke. "Why are you so sad? Why is your face so sorrowful?"

Again the young man looked about him carefully. No human being was visible. The only living thing he saw was a porcupine, lying with its head in a northerly direction. "But the porcupine could never talk," the young man said softly to himself. However, the porcupine spoke once more, and urged the young man to tell him why his countenance was so sad. Then the young man answered that it was because they could find no buffalo. "And my people are starving," he finished. The porcupine then said to him, "Take notice the way in which I am lying, and where my head points. Follow on, in that direction, and you will surely find buffalo." The young man believed what the porcupine had told him, and gathered the warriors together. Once more they started on their quest for buffalo. This time they were successful. The porcupine had spoken truly. Never were buffalo more abundant. So the tribe, which had been starving, had more buffalo meat than it could eat.

The hill, in gratitude to the porcupine, was named *Pahinsintela Paha*, or Porcupine Butte, and so its name remains to this day.

How Gold Came to the Black Hills

Translated by Walking Elk. An interpretation of this tale appears in brackets at its conclusion.

A man had four children, all of whom were young men. But they were poor, and it seemed as if they would die because of their poverty. So one day the husband said to his wife, "Behold, old woman, I feel the greatest pity for my youngest child, who may die because of hunger. Let us, therefore, seek the Great Spirit and beg him to take care of our youngest son for us."

The old woman replied, "Yes, old man, you say well; we will do so." The couple then went on a journey westward in search of the Great Spirit. One day, after they had climbed a very high hill, they met a man who was sitting on its top. This man asked, "What do you seek?" The old man answered, "Alas, my friend, I want to give my child, whom I pity, to the Great Spirit, so I am seeking him." The man then answered, "My friends, I am the Great Spirit. Give him to me. I will take him to my home and care for him."

So, after the old couple had given their son up, the Great Spirit took him to his home in the clouds. Here, after they had arrived, he said, "Examine this house as much as you like. Make yourself at home. My only request is that you take good care of this horse and keep away from the small hut that adjoins my mansion. Never, under any condition, go inside of it." After this warning he gave the young man the keys to the rooms, adding, "Watch and protect this place carefully, because I am going on a long journey." The Great Spirit then went away.

When evening came, the Great Spirit returned. He had many men with him, who filled the house. When they had been there a long time, one of the men said, "The boy is good; that is enough." After saying this he went out. All the other men, in a like manner, left for their homes. Then, again, the Great Spirit said, "I am going on a long journey. You stay and keep watch."

One day, when the young man was watching over the palace in the way his benefactor had requested, the horse spoke to him. He said, "Friend, go into the small hut into which you are commanded not to look. You will find something yellow in the middle of the floor. When you come to it, dip your head into this yellow liquid—only make haste, before the Great Spirit comes back. Because when he returns, he will bring many men with him who will eat both of us, but I, like you, am unwilling to die in such a horrible manner."

So the young man went into the little hut, where, in the middle of the floor, stood a pool of yellow liquid into which he dipped his head. His head immediately became golden and the house was filled with a shining light. Then he went out and jumped on the waiting horse, and together they fled.

After they had traveled a long way, a distance of many suns, the man who called himself the Great Spirit caught up with them. He called out, "You bad rascals, stop! You shall not live. Whither will you go in such a small country as this?" Saying this, he came toward them faster than ever and they became very frightened. Again he called out, "You are bad rascals! Stop! You shall not live." And indeed it seemed as if they would not live.

Then the horse said, "Wave your right hand rearward." The young man did as he had been told, whereupon the whole

breadth of the country became a sea, so that he who had followed them came to a standstill and said, "Alas! my horse,
have mercy on me and take me to the other side; if you do I will
value you very much." But the horse replied, "Ah! I am not
willing to do that." But he who called himself the Great Spirit
continued to plead with his horse, to no avail. Whereupon the
man who called himself the Great Spirit became drowned, while
the horse, still carrying the young man, kept on swimming until
they sighted land.

So it came about that one day, after they had traveled a great
distance, they came to the dwellings of a tribe who lived in high
hills. Here both the horse and the young man settled down.
They lived here for many years in peace; but one day they were
attacked by many warriors from an enemy tribe. The boy,
during the course of the battle, turned his head around so his
enemies could see the portion that was covered with gold. The
gold blinded the enemies, making it easy for the young man to
kill them, one by one, until only a few were left alive. But those
who remained made a second attack; this time he destroyed
them all. The young man was much thought of by the hill
people after his victory.

[*"A complete understanding of the fable may be difficult because
of the many double meanings it contains. The word* head *for instance means* head-hair *or* scalp *when more literally translated;
and the same word also means* hill. *This double meaning is apparent in the fable. The desire for gold is the great temptation.
Gold, to the Indian, was forbidden by the Great Spirit. For this
reason the Black Hills were sacred ground. But even the Indian
comes to desire it, and mysteriously clothes himself with its power.
So he is obliged to flee and is pursued by the white man, who in the
fable is called the Great Spirit. The head, or hill, of gold is the cause.
The Indian, though he flees, obtains the victory once more, notably
in the Custer massacre, and, in consequence, is much thought of by
the people in whose land he finds a home. This is Sitting Bull's
tribe. Neither party is to be blamed—certainly not the Indian. He
wants only to live. First he hopes to accomplish this desire by
nestling himself in the bosom of the Great Spirit. Disobeying, he is
obliged to flee. But in all the destruction he wreaks on his enemies*

his only object is self-preservation. He cannot be blamed for wanting to live. And, on the other hand, the white people wanted the Hill of Gold, for which they too were not greatly to be blamed" (1).]

A Dog's Revenge

At one time there lived an old woman who had stored away a large supply of dried buffalo meat. A hungry dog, who knew where the meat was stored, tried to creep into her tent one night when he supposed the old woman was asleep, with the purpose of stealing some of it. But the old woman was aware of his coming and kept watch. When the dog thrust his head under the tent, she struck him across the face and made a great gash, which swelled greatly.

The next morning a companion dog came and attempted to talk with him. But the injured dog was sullen and silent. The visitor asked, "Tell me, what makes you so heartsick?" The injured dog replied, "Be still; an old woman has treated me badly." "What did she do to you?" was the visitor's next question. "She had a pack of dried meat, which I tried to take away in the middle of the night, when I supposed her to be asleep. But when I poked my head under her tent, she cried out, 'Shoo! What are you doing here?' and struck me on the head and wounded me, as you see."

The visiting dog, upon hearing the story, said, "Alas! Alas! She has treated you badly; verily we will eat up her pack of meat. Call an assembly. Call Rain Mist, call Bite Off Silently, call Strong Neck, call Sharp Knife." The injured dog invited them all for a council.

When all the dogs were assembled, the companion dog, who presided over the council, said, "An old woman has treated our friend badly, so bestir yourselves before the night is past. We, in a group, will attack her tent and eat up the dried meat which she prizes so highly."

The dogs, after working out their strategy, began their attack on the old woman in this manner: Rain Mist caused it to rain throughout the day. This drenched the tent and softened the tent pins. Then Bite Off Silently bit off all the lower fastenings so quietly that the old woman didn't know what was taking place. Strong Neck then came and seized the pack with his mouth and carried it far away. After this had been done Sharp Knife ripped the pack through the middle. The remainder of the night was devoted to the feast, during which they ate up all the old woman's dried buffalo meat.

The moral of this myth is that a common sneak thief becomes more dangerous after he has associated himself with daring companions.

Lovers' Leap

Collected from Mrs. A. H. Rulkoetter by Louise Pound. A similar account appears in Grant Lee Shumway's 1921 History of Western Nebraska and Its People. *The Lovers' Leap of this tale is just south of Long Springs Branch, near Harrisburg, Banner County, in the Nebraska Panhandle (see map, site 6). Other Nebraska lovers' leaps are located near Fullerton in Nance County (site 7), on the White River in Dawes County (site 8), and about four miles west of Niobrara in Knox County (site 9). They are discussed by Louise Pound in "Nebraska Legends of Lovers' Leaps" (20). The tribe of the ill-fated lovers in this tale is not identified; the maiden's suitor is an Oglala, one of the subtribes of the Teton Sioux.*

Situated on a little tableland just south of a little creek, then unnamed, stood a Sioux Indian village. Thither had come an Oglala brave with his finest ponies to exchange for the chief's beautiful daughter. Tomorrow he would claim his bride.

The daughter loved a brave of her own tribe and was determined not to marry the Oglala. Secretly leaving her father's lodge, she found her sweetheart and persuaded him to run away with her when night came. They mounted two of the ponies tied before her father's lodge and rode away. They were seen leaving the village and were soon overtaken. The angry chief had his daughter whipped and the lover put to death.

The next morning the Indian maiden donned her wedding finery and went humming through the village, wending her way to the south. The people seeing her wondered at her taking her lover's death so lightly. The Sioux braves watched her with admiration and envied the Oglala his good fortune. He, too, looked on in admiration and anticipation and rated his prize the more highly since he had nearly lost her.

As she went up Table Mountain her song took a sadder strain. She paused at the eastern extremity where ages of weathering had made a perpendicular wall to the cliff. All the people were watching her now. She raised her arms to the sun and commenced to sing again. Her song, weird and sweet, was instantly recognized as her death song.

A dozen braves rushed after her, but before they could reach her she threw aside her blanket and stood for a moment as a statue of bronze in the morning sun. Then, with a cry to her dead lover, she leaped over the cliff and was crushed to death on the rocks below. Thus the cliff received its name.

PAWNEE TALES

Members of the Caddoan Language group, the Pawnee people are called among themselves Chahiksichahiks: *men of men. They originally migrated from the south and were living in Nebraska, particularly on the Loup, Platte, and Republican rivers, as early as 1673. The Grand Pawnee Nation was made up of a confederation of four bands: the Chaui, or Grand; the Kitkehaki, or Republican; the Pitahauerat, or Tappage (sometimes called Noisy); and the Skidi, or Wolf Pawnee. The Grands were generally recognized as the leading band.*

The Pawnees never joined other Indians in war against the United States, but their contact with the white race brought new diseases which reduced their population from about ten thousand in the early nineteenth century to as few as 646 in 1905 (since that time there has been an increase). By the terms of the 1857 Treaty of Table Rock, the Pawnees ceded the last of their lands to the United States in exchange for a reservation on the Loup fork (see map, site 10) and a cash annuity. The government also promised to protect the Pawnees from their hereditary enemies, the Sioux, but the protection was soon withdrawn. In 1873 a Pawnee hunting party was attacked and massacred by Oglala and Brule Sioux in a canyon near Trenton, in Hitchcock County, and by 1875 most of the tribe had removed to Indian Territory (Oklahoma). The Pawnee reservation was formally exchanged for lands there in 1876.

In the late 1880's the noted naturalist and author George Bird Grinnell visited the Pawnee Agency and took down the history of the Pawnees and their tribal tales. The collection, Pawnee Hero Stories and Folk-Tales, *was first published in 1889; it was reprinted in a paperback edition in 1961 by the University of Nebraska Press. A number of these tales, with some alterations in wording, were collected in the Nebraska Folklore Pamphlets. The two selections which follow are presented in unedited form, as they originally appeared in Grinnell's text.*

The Dun Horse

Although their permanent villages were in the eastern half of the state, on their hunting expeditions the tribe roamed to the south and the west. The scene of this tale is near Courthouse Rock, on the south side of the Platte in Morrill County, about five miles southwest of Bridgeport (see map, site 11).

Many years ago, there lived in the Pawnee tribe an old woman and her grandson, a boy about sixteen years old. These people had no relations and were very poor. They were so poor that they were despised by the rest of the tribe. They had nothing of their own; and always, after the village started to move the camp from one place to another, these two would stay behind the rest, to look over the old camp, and pick up anything that the other Indians had thrown away, as worn out or useless. In this way they would sometimes get pieces of robes, worn out moccasins with holes in them, and bits of meat.

Now, it happened one day, after the tribe had moved away from the camp, that this old woman and her boy were following along the trail behind the rest, when they came to a miserable old worn out dun horse, which they supposed had been abandoned by some Indians. He was thin and exhausted, was blind of one eye, had a bad sore back, and one of his forelegs was very much swollen. In fact, he was so worthless that none of the Pawnees had been willing to take the trouble to try to drive him along with them. But when the old woman and her boy came along, the boy said, "Come now, we will take this old horse, for we can make him carry our pack." So the old woman put her pack on the horse, and drove him along, but he limped and could only go very slowly.

II

The tribe moved up on the North Platte, until they came to Court House Rock. The two poor Indians followed them, and camped with the others. One day while they were here, the young men who had been sent out to look for buffalo, came hurrying into camp and told the chiefs that a large herd of buffalo were near, and that among them was a spotted calf.

The Head Chief of the Pawnees had a very beautiful daughter, and when he heard about the spotted calf, he ordered his old crier to go about through the village, and call out that the man who killed the spotted calf should have his daughter for his wife. For a spotted robe is *ti-war'-uks-ti*—big medicine.

The buffalo were feeding about four miles from the village, and the chiefs decided that the charge should be made from there. In this way, the man who had the fastest horse would be the most likely to kill the calf. Then all the warriors and the young men picked out their best and fastest horses, and made ready to start. Among those who prepared for the charge was the poor boy on the old dun horse. But when they saw him, all the rich young braves on their fast horses pointed at him, and said, "Oh, see; there is the horse that is going to catch the spotted calf;" and they laughed at him, so that the poor boy was ashamed, and rode off to one side of the crowd, where he could not hear their jokes and laughter.

When he had ridden off some little way, the horse stopped, and turned his head round, and spoke to the boy. He said, "Take me down to the creek, and plaster me all over with mud. Cover my head and neck and body and legs." When the boy heard the horse speak, he was afraid; but he did as he was told. Then the horse said, "Now mount, but do not ride back to the warriors, who laugh at you because you have such a poor horse. Stay right here, until the word is given to charge." So the boy stayed there.

And presently all the fine horses were drawn up in line and pranced about, and were so eager to go that their riders could hardly hold them in; and at last the old crier gave the word, "*Loo-ah*"—Go! Then the Pawnees all leaned forward on their horses and yelled, and away they went. Suddenly, away off to the right, was seen the old dun horse. He did not seem to run.

He seemed to sail along like a bird. He passed all the fastest horses, and in a moment he was among the buffalo. First he picked out the spotted calf, and charging up alongside of it, *U-ra-rish!* straight flew the arrow. The calf fell. The boy drew another arrow, and killed a fat cow that was running by. Then he dismounted and began to skin the calf, before any of the other warriors had come up. But when the rider got off the old dun horse, how changed he was! He pranced about and would hardly stand still near the dead buffalo. His back was all right again; his legs were well and fine; and both his eyes were clear and bright.

The boy skinned the calf and the cow that he had killed, and then he packed all the meat on the horse, and put the spotted robe on top of the load, and started back to the camp on foot, leading the dun horse. But even with this heavy load the horse pranced all the time, and was scared at everything he saw. On the way to camp, one of the rich young chiefs of the tribe rode up by the boy, and offered him twelve good horses for the spotted robe, so that he could marry the Head Chief's beautiful daughter; but the boy laughed at him and would not sell the robe.

Now, while the boy walked to the camp leading the dun horse, most of the warriors rode back, and one of those that came first to the village, went to the old woman, and said to her, "Your grandson has killed the spotted calf." And the old woman said, "Why do you come to tell me this? You ought to be ashamed to make fun of my boy, because he is poor." The warrior said, "What I have told you is true," and then he rode away. After a little while another brave rode up to the old woman, and said to her, "Your grandson has killed the spotted calf." Then the old woman began to cry, she felt so badly because every one made fun of her boy, because he was poor.

Pretty soon the boy came along, leading the horse up to the lodge where he and his grandmother lived. It was a little lodge, just big enough for two, and was made of old pieces of skin that the old woman had picked up, and was tied together with strings of rawhide and sinew. It was the meanest and worst lodge in the village. When the old woman saw her boy leading the dun horse with the load of meat and the robes on it, she was very much surprised. The boy said to her, "Here, I have brought you plenty of meat to eat, and here is a robe, that you may have for yourself. Take the meat off the horse." Then the old woman laughed, for her heart was glad. But when she went to take the meat from the horse's back, he snorted and jumped about, and acted like a wild horse. The old woman looked at him in wonder, and could hardly believe that it was the same horse. So the boy had to take off the meat, for the horse would not let the old woman come near him.

III

That night the horse spoke again to the boy and said, "*Wa-ti-hes Chah'-ra-rat wa-ta*. To-morrow the Sioux are coming—a large war party. They will attack the village, and you will have a great battle. Now, when the Sioux are drawn up in line of battle, and are all ready to fight, you jump on to me, and ride as hard as you can, right into the middle of the Sioux, and up to their Head Chief, their greatest warrior, and count *coup* on him, and kill him, and then ride back. Do this four times, and count *coup* on four of the bravest Sioux, and kill them, but don't go again. If you go the fifth time, may be you will be killed, or else you will lose me. *La-ku'-ta-chix*—remember." So the boy promised.

The next day it happened as the horse had said, and the Sioux came down and formed a line of battle. Then the boy took his bow and arrows, and jumped on the dun horse, and charged into the midst of them. And when the Sioux saw that he was going to strike their Head Chief, they all shot their arrows at him, and the arrows flew so thickly across each other that the sky became dark, but none of them hit the boy. And he counted *coup* on the Chief, and killed him, and then rode back. After that he charged again among the Sioux, where they were gathered thickest, and counted *coup* on their bravest warrior, and killed him. And then twice more, until he had gone four times as the horse had told him.

But the Sioux and the Pawnees kept on fighting, and the boy stood around and watched the battle. And at last he said to himself, "I have been four times and have killed four Sioux, and I am all right, I am not hurt anywhere; why may I not go again?"

So he jumped on the dun horse, and charged again. But when he got among the Sioux, one Sioux warrior drew an arrow and shot. The arrow struck the dun horse behind the forelegs and pierced him through. And the horse fell down dead. But the boy jumped off, and fought his way through the Sioux, and ran away as fast as he could to the Pawnees. Now, as soon as the horse was killed, the Sioux said to each other, "This horse was like a man. He was brave. He was not like a horse." And they took their knives and hatchets, and hacked the dun horse and gashed his flesh, and cut him into small pieces.

The Pawnees and Sioux fought all day long, but toward night the Sioux broke and fled.

IV

The boy felt very badly that he had lost his horse; and, after the fight was over, he went out from the village to where it had taken place, to mourn for his horse. He went to the spot where the horse lay, and gathered up all the pieces of flesh, which the Sioux had cut off, and the legs and the hoofs, and put them all together in a pile. Then he went off to the top of a hill near by, and sat down and drew his robe over his head, and began to mourn for his horse.

As he sat there, he heard a great wind storm coming up, and it passed over him with a loud rushing sound, and after the wind came a rain. The boy looked down from where he sat to the pile of flesh and bones, which was all that was left of his horse, and he could just see it through the rain. And the rain passed by, and his heart was very heavy, and he kept on mourning.

And pretty soon, came another rushing wind, and after it a rain; and as he looked through the driving rain toward the spot where the pieces lay, he thought that they seemed to come together and take shape, and that the pile looked like a horse lying down, but he could not see well for the thick rain.

After this, came a third storm like the others; and now when he looked toward the horse he thought he saw its tail move from side to side two or three times, and that it lifted its head from the ground. The boy was afraid, and wanted to run away, but he stayed.

And as he waited, there came another storm. And while the

rain fell, looking through the rain, the boy saw the horse raise himself up on his forelegs and look about. Then the dun horse stood up.

V

The boy left the place where he had been sitting on the hilltop, and went down to him. When the boy had come near to him, the horse spoke and said, "You have seen how it has been this day; and from this you may know how it will be after this. But *Ti-ra'-wa* has been good, and has let me come back to you. After this, do what I tell you; not any more, not any less." Then the horse said, "Now lead me off, far away from the camp, behind that big hill, and leave me there to-night, and in the morning come for me;" and the boy did as he was told.

And when he went for the horse in the morning, he found with him a beautiful white gelding, much more handsome than any horse in the tribe. That night the dun horse told the boy to take him again to the place behind the big hill, and to come for him the next morning; and when the boy went for him again, he found with him a beautiful black gelding. And so for ten nights, he left the horse among the hills, and each morning he found a different colored horse, a bay, a roan, a gray, a blue, a spotted horse, and all of them finer than any horses that the Pawnees had ever had in their tribe before.

Now the boy was rich, and he married the beautiful daughter of the Head Chief, and when he became older, he was made Head Chief himself. He had many children by his beautiful wife, and one day when his oldest boy died, he wrapped him in the spotted calf robe and buried him in it. He always took good care of his old grandmother, and kept her in his own lodge until she died. The dun horse was never ridden except at feasts, and when they were going to have a doctors' dance, but he was always led about with the Chief, wherever he went. The horse lived in the village for many years, until he became very old. And at last he died.

The Ghost Bride

In a place where we used to have a village, a young woman died just before the tribe started on the hunt. When she died they dressed her up in her finest clothes, and buried her, and soon after this the tribe started on the hunt.

A party of young men had gone off to visit another tribe, and they did not get back until after this girl had died and the tribe had left the village. Most of this party did not go back to the village, but met the tribe and went with them on the hunt. Among the young men who had been away was one who had loved this girl who had died. He went back alone to the village. It was empty and silent, but before he reached it, he could see, far off, some one sitting on top of a lodge. When he came near, he saw that it was the girl he loved. He did not know that she had died, and he wondered to see her there alone, for the time was coming when he would be her husband and she his wife. When she saw him coming, she came down from the top of the lodge and went inside. When he came close to her, he spoke and said, "Why are you here alone in the village?" She answered him, "They have gone off on the hunt. I was sulky with my relations, and they went off and left me behind." The man wanted her now to be his wife, but the girl said to him, "No, not yet, but later we will be married." She said to him, "You must not be afraid. To-night there will be dances here; the ghosts will dance." This is an old custom of the Pawnees. When they danced they used to go from one lodge to another, singing, dancing and hallooing. So now, when the tribe had gone and the village was deserted, the ghosts did this. He could hear them coming along the empty streets, and going from one lodge to another. They came into the lodge where he was, and danced about, and whooped and sang, and sometimes they almost touched him, and he came pretty near being scared.

The next day, the young man persuaded the girl to go on with him, and follow the tribe, to join it on the hunt. They started to travel together, and she promised him that she would surely be his wife, but not until the time came. They overtook the tribe; but before they got to the camp, the girl stopped. She said, "Now we have arrived, but you must go first to the village, and prepare a place for me. Where I sleep, let it be behind a curtain. For four days and four nights I must remain behind this curtain. Do not speak of me. Do not mention my name to any one."

The young man left her there and went into the camp. When he got to his lodge, he told a woman, one of his relations, to go out to a certain place and bring in a woman, who was waiting there for him. His relative asked him, "Who is the woman?" And to avoid speaking her name, he told who were her father and mother. His relation, in surprise, said, "It cannot be that girl, for she died some days before we started on the hunt."

When the woman went to look for the girl she could not find her. The girl had disappeared. The young man had disobeyed her, and had told who she was. She had told him that she must stay behind a curtain for four days, and that no one must know who she was. Instead of doing what she had said, he told who she was, and the girl disappeared because she was a ghost. If he had obeyed the girl, she would have lived a second time upon earth. That same night this young man died in sleep.

Then the people were convinced that there must be a life after this one.

III. CUSTOMS

Some Old Nebraska Folk Customs

Louise Pound

[*The following article, somewhat abridged, is reprinted from* Nebraska History, *28 (January–March, 1947), 3–31.*]

The customs to be recorded here are from the nineteenth century, though most persist into the twentieth and are, indeed, familiar to the majority of us today. Some have been noted from as far back as the 1850's, when Nebraska was still a territory. It became a state in 1867. Most were gathered from comparatively late in the century. All are really much older than their appearance in Nebraska; in the main they are legacies from the British Isles or from the European continent. That they still exist among us is, however, no reason for excluding them. The Fourth of July celebrations and the political rallies seem those customs most indigenous to the United States; but of course political or civic festivities of much the same type have existed elsewhere, associated with other occasions.

As regards sources, a large part of what I have recorded derives from my own recollection or is of my own assemblage from oral sources. In the days when I was interested in folksong, its origin and transmission, I liked, for some reason, to gather other folklore matter as well, perhaps as background. But I owe very much to many individuals, notably to Dr. Ruth Odell, Mrs. A. H. Rulkoetter, Mari Sandoz, Grace Tear, and to student contributors, such as Ruth Milford, Florence Kellogg, Josephine Hyatt, Jeanne Allen, and others too many to name. Testimonies concerning frontier days I owe to various newspapers and documents, territorial and later, preserved in the Library of the State Historical Society. I have not attempted to make my assemblage exhaustive; but as a preliminary survey it may be complete enough to serve its purpose. Sometime in the future there may well be appropriate supplementation of my chroniclings, extending the records for Old Nebraska as contributing somewhat to its history as well as its folklore.

The customs regarding which I have gathered materials may be grouped for convenience under these headings: Civic Customs; Customs for Special Days or Occasions; Social Activities; Sports; Literary, Debating and School Activities; Singing; Play-Parties and Dances; Theatricals and Related Entertainment; Food; Addenda.

Civic Customs
Fourth of July

Among older civic customs, those of the Fourth of July may well take priority and should have treatment in considerable detail because of their historical place. Beyond question, the celebration of the Fourth was the great occasion of the year in frontier days. Stock features were the program, the big dance or dances, and the dinner. The whole region around about was invited to attend and take part. Settlers thronged in, coming in wagons horse-drawn or ox-drawn, on horseback, or even on foot. At times the vehicles were decorated with green boughs or with flowers. Often there was a dance on the night of July third, sometimes one outdoors "on the green" on the afternoon of the Fourth, and nearly always a large dance that night. The Fourth might be ushered in by the firing of salutes, or the ringing of bells. Children set off firecrackers or torpedoes, after these were to be had at stores. At about ten o'clock there was a march or procession, sometimes with the escort of a military company, to a nearby wooded place or grove where the formal program was held.

Preparations were often very elaborate. The Brownville *Advertiser* of July 5, 1856, commented in its editorial column: "The Fourth Attendance from our own and adjoining counties of this Territory and Missouri was large . . . . Vocal music under the supervision of Captain Thurber and Lady was fine as we ever listened to. The Declaration of Independence was read by Mr. Lake in a clear, audible and impressive manner." Of the dinner it was remarked that "All the delicacies and substantials of the season weighed down the tables: Buffalo Meat, Venison, Barbecued Ox, Roast Sheep, Hogs and Pigs enough to have fed the whole Territory." "Sentiments" and "responses" were delivered. In the evening there was a "Ball in McPherson's Hall, a new and commodious building rushed through to completion for the occasion" . . . . "The 'fiddle and the bow', the 'merry dance' continued until toward the 'wee hours' when all repaired to the large room below, where C. W. Wheeler had prepared a supper" . . . . "The dance went on 'until broad daylight' . . . ."

Of the Fourth of July celebration at Nemaha City, the Brownville *Advertiser* of July 2, 1857, in its Weekly Review column gave as the program: "1st. Vocal Music, American Ode—by the Choir. 2nd. Prayer—by the Chaplain. 3rd. National Glee—by the Choir. 4th. Reading of the Declaration of Independence—by A. D. Kirk. 5th. Freedom's Choice—by the Choir. 6th. Oration—by C. E. L. Holmes. 7th. Star Spangled Banner—by the Choir. 8th. Remarks—by Invited Guests. 9th. Dinner. 10th. Toasts. 11th. Dance on the Green." On July 11, the same newspaper commented: "The celebration of the Fourth at our sister town Nemaha City was a grand affair—we say without hesitation it was the most magnificent affair of the kind we ever attended. The table was four hundred feet long, and perfectly groaned beneath the weight of eatables placed thereon. There were over two thousand persons present, and after all were abundantly fed, there was yet 'enough and to spare'. There was a grand attendance of the fair sex . . . ." The celebration was held in the "new Hotel building." After the exercises, with numbers by the choir and an oration, there was a "dance on the green." In the evening "all hands adjourned to Brownville, where the merry dance was kept up . . . ."

The Nebraska City *News* of June 25, 1859, announced that the "Nebraska Harmony Singing Association have made arrangements to give a Grand Ball and Supper including singing, reading the Declaration of Independence, etc., on July 4. The Sidney Brass Band has been engaged for the occasion."

The Omaha *Nebraskian* of July 21, 1860, has among its Territorial Items: "The Cass County *Sentinel* estimates the numbers in attendance upon the Fourth of July celebration at Plattsmouth as from 1200 to 2000. Only two drunken men were in attendance." The same newspaper, July 7, 1860, tells of the Fourth at Omaha. The exercises "commenced at about nine o'clock by the presentation to the Hook and Ladder Company . . . of a magnificent ladder carriage." There was a presentation speech, a procession, an amateur band made music. At the grove there was the prayer, the reading of the Declaration of Independence, national songs were sung, an oration was delivered, and cannon were fired at the close. There was a "small display of pyrotechnics in the evening."

At these celebrations the dinners and toasts came at noon. At Bellevue in 1854 the toasts offered were as follows: "The Fourth of July," "George Washington," "President and Acting Vice-President," "Spartan Mothers of the American Revolution," "The Union," "Nebraska," "Our Friends Crossing the Plains," "The Press," "Bellevue," "The Ladies." Next came nine volunteer toasts to various persons, including the Indian Agent and the ladies who made ready the food.

In Lincoln from early times onward the Fourth was celebrated in much the same manner. There was the usual prayer by a minister, an oration, the reading of the Declaration of Independence, and songs were sung. Indeed, there might be speeches all day long. In many places in later decades of the century there might be an initial parade, with a pretty girl as Goddess of Liberty leading the floats. Or there might be a militia parade, a band concert, or a flag pole dance.

Staple sports, when these made their appearance, were ball games, horse races, foot races, wheelbarrow races, sack races, obstacle races, three-legged races, potato races, fat men's races, donkey races, greased pole climbings, and greased pig races. On the Fourth, sometimes on other days, men might spin silver dollars at a mark, occasionally half dollars or quarters. Children sometimes imitated them with dimes, nickels, and pennies.

Picnics were often planned for the Fourth. For these there was often a Marshal of the Day riding a horse, with perhaps a large red scarf draped from shoulder to hip. Almost always at Peru, Nemaha County, a young girl, selected for her beauty, posed as the Statue of Liberty. Old soldiers' picnics were held on this day, sometimes on other days; at these reminiscences were called for. Or there was a big dinner or barbecue with buffalo meat, occasionally catfish, the main eatables. At night fireworks, mainly Roman candles, pinwheels, and rockets, became a fixed custom. In the 1880's balloon ascensions were a frequent attraction.

In the later half of the nineteenth century, "water fights" were part of the day's entertainment on the Fourth, or perhaps on Memorial Day or at the county fair. In towns too small to maintain full-time fire departments, fire protection was furnished by so-called volunteer fire departments. These developed not only into fire-fighting organizations but also into social, fraternal, and insurance benefit societies. Water fights were staged between teams of two to four men against teams of like number. Each had a hose into which water was turned at top pressure. The object was to drive the opposing team over a certain line by water. Not only did the contestants get thoroughly soaked but very often the spectators. Lincoln had local competing teams in the 1880's.

The celebration of the Fourth of July was resumed in Lincoln in 1946, after having lapsed with the outbreak of the Second World War. Out of town picnickers were present but there was no reading of the Declaration of Independence, no oration, no official prayer. There were qualifying trials for the Mid-West Championship automobile races, then the competitive races for $2,500. One man was killed in these. A night show was given in front of the state fair grandstand, revues and stage acts were presented by producers from Chicago, and carnival shows and rides on the midway preceded the fireworks.

Political Rallies and Elections

Political rallies were marked by torchlight parades. The marchers carrying torches wore rubber capes to protect them from sparks. If there was an evening program, it might be started off by Roman candles.

A testimony early in the present century from Hebron, Nebraska, told that when the polls are closed on election day, the clerk goes out on the main street and calls, "Hear ye, hear ye, the polls are now closed." This is the official closing. This custom was observed at Omaha and other places also.

Oysters were shipped into the middle states in November, and sometimes there were oyster suppers at churches for those who came down town to learn the November election news.

Oratory

My mother, who came from New York to Nebraska in 1869, crossing the Missouri River on the ice, was fascinated by the pioneer eloquence she heard in early Lincoln on the Fourth of July and sometimes at political and other gatherings. Here are two examples she often quoted "verbatim" to her children. She had the "fabulous memory" that my brother Roscoe inherited. The first was from a Masonic orator, I think:

> In the course of human events since man's earliest history each presents an embodiment of compartments subordinate to the result of an ultimate one grand temple.

The second was from a newcomer to Lincoln, a German, who seems to have known his Latin and accenting carefully his long penultimate syllables.

> The diffi'culties and excellen'ces of a man's charac'ter are never known till he is laid in his sepul'cher.

Curfews

A curfew was tolled in Central City by the city fire bell at nine o'clock in the summer and at eight in the winter. This practice is not now followed. The children were told that they must be indoors when the curfew rang, or the town police would "lock them in jail." At McCook a nine o'clock whistle was sounded as a warning that "small girls should be at home in bed." This was true in Lincoln for a time. An eight o'clock curfew was reported from Fullerton and a nine o'clock from Fairbury.

Special Days and Occasions

Customs for Hallowe'en, Thanksgiving, Christmas, New Year's Day, Easter, May Day, Decoration Day may be omitted as pretty staple, widely recurrent, and varying little and in minor matters. The once flourishing custom of New Year's calls at the homes of friends where cards were left and often drinks served died out with the coming of the twentieth century.

Arbor Day

Arbor Day, a day set apart for the planting of trees or shrubs, was instituted by J. Sterling Morton of Nebraska City who was later the United States Secretary of Agriculture. On his motion, it was founded by the Nebraska State Board of Agriculture January 4, 1872. Prizes were offered by the Board for the best essay on agriculture and for the largest number of forest and fruit trees planted on Arbor Day. It was devoutly believed in those days that "rain follows the plow" and that the way to ensure more rainfall on the western plains was to plant more trees and to break more land. The day originally fixed upon was the second Wednesday in April, April 10, 1872. In 1885 the Nebraska legislature changed it to April 22 and made it a legal holiday. The first Arbor Day proclamation was made by Governor Robert W. Furnas in 1874. Alabama, Maine, and other states took up the Nebraska idea and by 1890 it had spread over the United States and, indeed, to other parts of the world. Its observance now comes late in April or early in May. It is still a legal holiday, though less widely observed. Schools recognize it by programs or ceremonies.

Birthday Customs

In southern Nebraska near Red Cloud and the Kansas line a neighborhood observed a birthday in a rather peculiar way. "It was unusual for a birthday to pass without a surprise party. Young and old gathered at the home of the family of the person whose birthday it was. As the high point of the party the unfortunate whose birthday was celebrated was thrown into the watering tank, usually none too clean. Cattle and horses might be frightened from their drinking as the shrieking person was tossed into the tank. Possibly this custom was of Kansas rather than of Nebraska origin."

It was the custom in some Nebraska towns to butter or grease the nose of a member of the family or a friend on his or her birthday. This was a Buffalo County testimony.

Occasionally it is the thing to pinch a person on the day after his birthday. Or, oftener, to pat or slap him on the back, or to paddle him, as many times as the years of his age "with one to grow on."

Gifts from the family were customarily placed under a person's plate at the breakfast table.

When a birthday cake is brought in, it is placed before the person whose birthday it is. On it are as many candles as the number of years of her life is supposed to be. If she blows out all the candles at her first trial she will be married within the year. If not, the number of candles left burning indicates how many years it will be before she is married.

Widely customary is the singing of "Happy Birthday to You," by those about the table, at the entrance of a person whose birthday is announced.

It was a pioneer custom for the mother to hold a child on each of its birthdays and rock it like a baby. A contributor testified that her mother always sang to her on such an occasion the lullaby she sang to her children when infants, Dr. Watts' cradle hymn, "Hush my dear, lie still and slumber."

Weddings
[See also " Love and Marriage," pages 268 ff.]

A familiar old custom is the shower of rice which usually takes place at the depot as the bride and groom depart by train. If they leave in a car, the shower comes as they leave the house.

The tying of an old shoe to the baggage, or of a white slipper, is supposed to bring good luck.

The bride throws her bouquet as she comes down the stairs to go away. The girl who catches it is supposed to be the next to be married.

A penny, a thimble, and a ring are baked in the wedding cake. The person getting the penny is to be wealthy, she getting the thimble will be a spinster, and the getter of the ring will be a bride.

The carriage, car, taxi, or automobile in which the newly married are leaving is placarded to let the public know of the wedding and bring embarrassment to the couple.

The saying that a bride should wear—

> Something old, something new,
> Something borrowed, something blue.

is not merely lore but is a custom religiously carried out by present-day brides.

In earlier days the "genteel" always had home weddings. In some rural sections there were no ordained ministers. The local justice of the peace often officiated. "The bride always had to have two dresses. Her second day dress, so-called, was to wear at the 'infare', which was always held at the home of the groom while the wedding was in the bride's home. The traditional gift of a farmer to a daughter was a cow."

"At some Bohemian weddings of Northern Nebraska, it is the custom to decorate the bridal car with streamers of the bride's chosen colors. The bridal party usually drives to the county seat for the marriage. The car with its gay decorations attracts immediate attention. Free dancing for the community is part of the wedding festivity. The town hall is frequently rented for a big free dance."

"A curious custom was followed till recent times in the German-Russian settlement at Lincoln. At the wedding dance the bride was the center of attention. She danced, not with her husband, but with other men. Each man who danced with her was expected to pin on her dress a bill. The money she collected in this strange way was used to pay the bridegroom, who customarily advanced the money for the bride's wedding finery. Feasting was another feature of the dance."

The Shivaree

In frontier days a wedding was always followed by a shivaree (charivari), and the custom is far from extinct. The shivaree took place at dusk or later, on the day of the wedding, or sometimes in the evening of the next day, at the new home of the couple. Friends or young people of the neighborhood gathered to serenade the bride and groom with the beating of tin pans, oyster cans, the ringing of cowbells or sleigh bells, with whistles, the blare of horns, firecrackers or shooting, or the utilizing of any other noise-making devices that might be available. This was kept up till the young couple appeared before the serenaders to treat the crowd. The crowd might be asked into the new home to be served pumpkin pie and watermelon or other eatables; or the groom might hand the men cigars. One contributor testified that sometimes he might actually "buy off" the boisterous crowd. Others doubted this. Another contributor wrote as follows:

> I distinctly remember my first shivaree. I was six years old and had come to live in Gothenburg in the fall of 1912. The local druggist had just been married. After dark a crowd of boys gathered down town for a march on the newly-weds' home. As we progressed the crowd grew. Arrived at the house, we began to yell and beat upon cans and otherwise make a noise until in a while the bride and groom appeared on the front porch. Then the groom told us what we had been waiting for, that he had instructed the local candy kitchen to treat us to ice cream. As I grew up, in the next ten years, I participated in many more shivarees. At least once but occasionally more than once, a popular newly-wed couple was shivareed by the local youngsters. I recall only boys participated; it was a little bit rowdy and too late at night for little girls.

Belling and warmer are other words for the customs that were used in Nebraska in the 1870's. Mari Sandoz says that the latter is still current in the sandhill region. Calithumpian, a name often used elsewhere, has not been common in Nebraska. See "Charivaria," by Mamie J. Meredith, in *American Speech*, VIII (April), 1933, 22–24. For instances of belling and warmer she cites the Lincoln *Daily State Journal*, January 1, 1878, and November 22, 1874.

The Nebraska shivaree is far from extinct. In 1936 the Louisville *Courier* of March 5 described a local shivaree on the preceding Sunday evening, and the Plattsmouth *Journal* of May 25, 1936, described another of local occurrence.

A news item from Hastings printed in the *Morning Journal* of Lincoln of June 16, 1946, read as follows:

There'll be no more of the old-fashioned charivari parties on Second Street here. They're getting out of hand, in the opinion of Police Chief C. W. Cawiezel.

Here's what has been happening, Cawiezel said:

1. The bride sometimes is placed on one fender of an auto and the groom on the other, forcing them to hold hands across the hood to keep from being thrown off.

2. The bridal couple is hauled in a small trailer, which is zigzagged and whipped, forcing the couple to hold on tightly to keep from being thrown out.

3. The newly-married pair is forced to ride on the running board of an auto.

The chief assured citizens the police will not interfere with "reasonable" community celebrations of marriages.

The shivaree has often been played up in western literature, for instance, in the play "Green Grow the Lilacs" by Lynn Riggs, given by the New York Theater Guild in 1931. This play was the predecessor or inspirer of the popular "Oklahoma."

The Infare

Another necessary accompaniment of frontier life was the *infare* (usually but less properly spelled *infair*) which took place on the day following the wedding. "It consisted of a visit of the bride and groom, the bride's folk and perhaps others of the wedding party to the home of the parents of the bridegroom." Sometimes the infare was a sort of housewarming or party of welcoming to their new home by the bride and groom and the bride's parents. Not infrequently the young girls attending rode horseback, riding behind their escorts, or on separate horses. Or the coming of the guests was by wagons.

In the frontier period an extended honeymoon was out of the question but sometimes "the couple loaded up a grist and drove gaily across the prairie to the mill, camping along the way while awaiting their turn. Or perhaps they took a two or three days trip to the County seat to buy a few articles for their scanty housekeeping."

Deaths and Funerals

A widespread custom at a death, as at Fullerton or Fairbury, was to toll a bell the number of years of the life of a dead person.

In early frontier days the corpse might be wrapped in a blanket or sheet. It was not unusual for caskets to be made from floors or cupboards if no lumber was to be had. In some instances coffins or rough boards were blacked with shoe polish, or lamp black or soot were applied to the coffin. When saw mills came coffins might be made to measurements. Such coffins were "somewhat triangular in shape, wide at the shoulders and narrowed to a peak at the feet." "In towns the casket for an older person was nicely covered with black alpaca, those for children with white cloth." If the death came too late in the day for burial, friends "sat up" with the body, keeping the face of the corpse wet with vinegar in order to delay mortification as long as possible. No actual "wake" was held. Neighbors came in and sat with the dead. "In our neighborhood," said an informant, "among the Protestants sitting up with the dead there was no drinking. Polish neighbors sat drinking at the home or drunk." If there was opportunity for formality or effort, all blackness possible was availed of for the burial. Usually little funeral equipment was to be had. There were services by the preacher at the grave as well as when the funeral was conducted at the home of the dead person.

While the family was at the burial many brought food to the home. In Nance and Thurston counties, for example, "a sort of elaborate dinner was given, with roast meat, fowls etc. provided. Everybody stepped in and partook and there was something of a reception afterward."

Throughout the century mourning was worn for months. Those not able to afford new mourning garments borrowed black garments in order to show respect for the dead. Horses in a funeral procession were always driven at a walk, no matter how great the distance to the cemetery. Letters from those in mourning must always be edged in black.

Whisker Vogue

Whisker vogue still characterizes the celebration of certain days. As a reminder of frontier times, men sometimes dispensed with barbers and let growths of whiskers, beards, "sideburns," handlebar mustaches, or goatees cover their faces. As late as August 18, 1935, for the Fiftieth Anniversary Picnic at Diller, Jefferson County, this practice was observed. For the same or similar occasions the daughters of pioneers went about the streets in garments of old style, poke bonnets, hoop skirts, lace mitts, such as their grandmothers wore. The Golden Spike Celebration at Omaha, April 26–29, 1939, honoring the anniversary of the completion of the Union Pacific Railroad, was made an elaborate occasion. It was marked by both masculine and feminine reminders of frontier days, whisker growth for the men and old fashioned apparel for the women. The shops too were made up to suggest pioneer times.

SOCIAL ACTIVITIES

Church Occasions

When a new preacher moved to town there was a pound party. Everyone took a pound of something to a welcome party in his home. Hunters shot wild animals to provide meat for the winter for the preacher, as a deer or a buffalo. Such parties were held in Dawes, Thurston, and Nance counties and elsewhere. There were donation parties also, later, when the preacher seemed hard up. Those who called brought an offering of food or other gifts.

Church activities included Junior or Christian Endeavor groups, choir practice (the night when young persons dated), prayer meetings, missionary societies, Ladies Aid societies. Some churches had "socials," some "sociables," as did rival churches at Fullerton. In season these might be ice cream or strawberry socials (sociables) held on lawns, with Chinese lanterns lighting them. The Omaha *Times* of June 17, 1858, tells of a strawberry festival given by the Methodist Episcopal Church.

In all, there were five types of church dinners: ice cream festivals, strawberry festivals, oyster stews, mixed suppers, and box suppers. "Soliciters," always young girls and their "beaus," drove from house to house listing what each housewife would bring to the church.

Church "bazaars" and "raffles" were popular, though the latter were ultimately stopped, as were lotteries in general.

The Omaha *Times* of June 24, 1858, tells of a ladies' fair, at which fancy work, cakes, and edibles were sold.

On Sunday a child whose birthday had occurred during the week advanced to the front of the church and dropped in a box there as many pennies as the number of years of his or her life.

Other Customs and Social Occasions

A popular event was the box social or mystery lunch or supper box party. Boxes or packages were brought by the girls and bid for by the boys. Usually there was some secret means of identification, by the ribbons or other decorations, communicated to the escorts so that the right box would be chosen. At Columbus sometimes as high as fifteen dollars were bid. The money went to the church.

Taffy pulls were of frequent occurrence at homes, sometimes at school houses. The participants took turns at pulling boiled-down sorghum till it was thin enough to stretch out.

Pasture parties were held now and then in scattered places. These were a type of picnic given in what seemed at the time a preferable location.

Surprise parties had vogue in some regions. Merrymakers went by wagon or horseback to some cabin or isolated home in pioneer days. Hayrack riding was a popular institution and so was the bobsled party.

Quilting parties at which quilts were pieced were also popular. They were held at homes. "Log cabin quilts" reportedly 80 years old are said to be still in existence in Nebraska. Watermelon feeds also deserve mention.

Mari Sandoz tells of feather stripping. "A dinner plate was placed upside down in the lap of each person. My mother gave each one a little knife and paper sack to be held in the lap, or a 'poke' made out of an old newspaper. The child then reached in under the plate and took out one feather, (a handful of feathers had been placed under the plate), stripped it, and carefully dropped the quill on the floor and the strippings in a paper bag. Riddles and jokes were told during the feather stripping. When phonographs were had there was dancing to the music."

Miss Sandoz tells also of bean picking. A bushel sack was emptied at a table. The guests separated the good from the bad and refilled the sack. Merrymaking followed.

According to the Dannebrog *News* of October 8, 1936, the big social event of the early days was the housewarming when a new home was built. There were drinks, almost invariably punch, just after midnight, at which time numerous toasts were offered and songs sung and speeches made. This was for the men. The women were served coffee, chocolate, and cake. All the rest of the night until daylight, sometimes till sunrise, was devoted to dancing the rapid, whirling, muscle-exercising Danish round dances, with one or two quadrilles thrown in for American flavor. These sociables or dances were immensely popular.

In rural communities and small towns, the general store served as a meeting place or social center, and it still may.

Along the Missouri River, as at Nebraska City or Brownville, it was an exciting social occasion when steamboats, especially the first steamboat of the season, arrived. At Brownville the young people were known to desert even church services to rush down to the banks when boats came in.

Courtship customs were pretty standardized in early days in Nebraska. Young persons "kept company." Sunday was "beau day." "In the evening a boy called upon a girl quite formally. He was shown into the parlor and there he and the girl spent the time, while the rest of the family kept away. He never stayed late. If he took a girl to evening church or to a party they were not to sit out in the buggy or sleigh after reaching her home, not if her parents were obeyed. He must bring her to the door but not enter. Neither must he come during the week unless for a brief call at the door. Mothers did not want their girls 'talked about.'"

"Long engagements were common, sometimes lasting for years. The engagement was never announced even to the parents until near the wedding day. The engagement ring was usually a carved gold band. It was not worn until a short time before the wedding and then served as wedding ring also. To be an 'old maid' was regrettable. To be a divorced woman was to be shamed, no matter what the provocation had been."

SPORTS AND GAMES

[*See also "Children's Games," pages 281 ff.*]

Outdoor Sports

In the sandhill country the wolf hunt or coyote hunt has been described by Mari Sandoz. It was planned in advance. Sometimes a few friends took part. Sometimes it was a community affair.

Riding and hunting were popular over the prairies from the first. Horse races were arranged and aroused much interest. The natural prairie grass made an excellent track. Bets were made freely. Backers might place fifty or a hundred dollars on each side. Outsiders bet considerable sums as well as local men. When the horses were from different towns, citizens exhibited their "loyalty" by backing the home town. The races might be running or trotting races. Occasionally there were "ladies contests," these on side saddles, with side saddles likely to be the prizes.

Ball was played in simple form from the first. By the early '70's baseball had appeared and prairie towns had their competing teams. Milford played Seward a game lasting from 2:00 till 6:00, August 18, 1871. Baseball was a well organized competitive sport by the 1880's.

Pitching horseshoes (quoits) was common from early days.

Croquet came rather late.

The bicycle arrived in the 1880's, and the vogue of roller skating reached Nebraska in due course.

Traditional outdoor games played by young persons were: hide and seek; pom pom pullaway; run sheep run; dare base; steal sticks; old witch; London bridge; farmer in the dell; drop the handkerchief; ring round Rosie; pussy wants a corner; crack the whip; cross tag; shinny; one-two-three o'cat; tin tin. Over fallen snow, fox and geese or dog and deer were played.

There were contests in broad, high, standing and running jumping and in wrestling and racing. Men's races on special occasions might include a three-legged race, sack race, fat men's race, potato race, peanut race, and wheelbarrow race.

Indoor Games

Popular indoor games were: postoffice; hide the thimble; charades; guessing games; spin the platter. Card games were euchre, poker, hearts, high five, five hundred, flinch, and there was some duplicate whist played at the turn of the century. Auction and contract bridge belong to the present century. Authors were played and checkers, more rarely chess. Parchesi and tiddledewinks, etc., were transient amusements.

Statuary (one person strikes a pose. Others guess who or what he is supposed to be) was played either indoors or outdoors. So was paying forfeits. ("Heavy, heavy hangs over your head. What shall the owner do to redeem it?" The judge, seated in the circle, asks, "Fine or superfine?" The person holding the forfeited object answers "Fine" if it belongs to a man, "Superfine" if it belongs to a woman. The penalty or sentence is then pronounced by the judge.)

LITERATURE AND DEBATING SOCIETIES AND SCHOOL ACTIVITIES

These had various names, Literary Society, Lyceum, Debating School, or Debating Society, and Athenaeum. Leading citizens, ministers, lawyers, and others participated in the debates, which offered good experience for youths. The Brownville *Advertiser* records that on February 8, 1857, the territorial legislature incorporated the Brownville Lyceum, Library, and Literary Association, intended to promote interest along these lines. The capital stock was $50,000, to be sold at $5.00 a share. The membership fee was $1.00 a season. The *Advertiser* had a notice of a meeting of the Library Association in its issue of September 9, 1859, and of a meeting of the Lyceum, December 12, 1859. In 1864 the Society raised $400 to improve the building in which the meetings were held. The Nebraska City *News* records a Library Association there December 4, 1858. The *News* of December 3, 1859, mentions the Webster Debating Society "composed of young gentlemen connected with Mr. Raymond's school." The Falls City *Broadaxe* tells of the Richardson County Lyceum in the issue of January 1, 1861. The Omaha Lyceum was organized in 1860. The Omaha *Nebraskian* announced, December 12, 1860, as a subject for debate

December 22 at the Congregational Church, "Resolved that the Legislature of Nebraska has the right and it is its duty to prohibit slavery in the Territory." In 1876 in Harmon's Grove on the Nemaha River was debated, "Resolved that Water Baptism Is No Part of the Plan of Salvation." In general, questions concerning governmental and economic topics were debated, such as "Popular Election of Presidents," "Missouri Compromise," "British Colonial Policy." Other questions debated were "Resolved that the Nebraska Legislature should pass a law releasing persons from debts outside the Territory after a residence of 60 days in the country," "Resolved that the Legislature should pass a herd law restraining all kinds of stock from running at large," "Resolved that men and women should be equal before the law in respect to legal rights and liabilities."

Often lecturers were invited to meetings to present some special subject.

Some topics discussed at Brownville in the days when Brownville College had been planned were: "Manifest Destiny," "Philosophy Greek and Roman," "The Historian, Statesman, and the Divine." These and other topics were mentioned in the *Advertiser* of February 25, 1857. The place of meeting was the Methodist Church.

As a rule, meetings of literary societies were held in schoolhouses. The programs were made up of debates, declamations, dialogues and music, and there was usually a paper telling "jokes" about those present.

Spelling Bees

These were popular among grown-ups in the '60's and '70's and they are still popular for children as an educational exercise. Words were given out by school teachers or other available persons. Marks for spellers were registered as points for each side. At the end of the evening tallies were counted for each side, where two or more groups competed. The person who lasted longest before missing "spelled down" the others. Friday afternoon was the usual time for spelling contests for schools. McGuffey's spelling book was relied upon and memorized by the zealous.

Bret Harte described a spelling contest in his "The Spelling Bee at Angels, Reported by Truthful James." It was organized by grown-ups who sat around the bar-room stove. "The Spelling Bee" was reported as a new game in Frisco. The schoolmaster said he knew the game and would give instructions. The words he called for were: separate, parallel, rhythm, incinerate, phthisis, gneiss. Bret Harte's bee ended in a shooting affray.

A district spelling contest (these are no longer called "bees") was held at Wilber, Nebraska, April 9, 1946. There were written and oral contests, each won by a girl.

Figure downs were held at times on Fridays after school hours. Arithmetical problems were placed on the board and pupils strove to finish first.

General school exercises might be held Friday afternoon also, with recitations, dialogues, essays, songs, etc., featured.

A school exhibition ended the school year. This was more elaborate than the "last day of school" program. It was often given at night and in a church or hall to accommodate the large crowd. A basket dinner served in the schoolhouse, a "surprise for the teacher," was a frequent event on the last day of a country school.

Singing

[See also "Songs of Trail and Prairie," pages 3 ff.]

There was much more singing in Nebraska in the early days and through the nineteenth century than there is now, though instruments were few. The liking for music had to be met by singing. As time went on there might be a violin, accordion, banjo, guitar, or organ for accompaniment, or alongside the singing. Pianos were almost unknown for some decades. The songs were of two groups, sacred music, religious songs, and "opry songs," as they were sometimes called. The religious songs often sung were "Amazing Grace," "On Jordan's Stormy Banks I Stand," "Beulah Land," "Bringing in the Sheaves," "Throw Out the Life Line," "Pull for the Shore," "Work for the Night Is Coming," and other gospel hymns from the books used for church or Sunday school. There was more group than individual singing. Groups gathered Sunday afternoons, especially at homes where there was an organ. There were also singings at country schoolhouses, and sometimes "teams" from whole counties or from various communities sang in rivalry.

Testifying regarding the early songs reaching the old sandhill region in the northwest section of Nebraska, an old buffalo and cattle country, Mari Sandoz states that Indian songs came first, of course, then those of the French fur traders, mostly French-Canadian dance songs. The Texas cattle trail group came next. Few of theirs could be called "cowboy songs" (songs of the open range) today. The real trail songs were softly melancholy spirituals and ballads, sung with no accompaniment beside animal bawlings and howlings. Then settlers from the East came with their songs. They brought copy books full of pieces, many similar to those of the Texas trailers. A Scotch-Irish family from Kentucky sang "The Cowboy's Lament," at a literary, a dance, or a shivaree. Later came "The Old Chisholm Trail," "Old Paint," "When the Work's All Done This Fall," "Little Joe the Wrangler," "The Little Old Sod Shanty," "The Lone Prairie," "Nebraska Land," and, alongside these, current popular songs such as "Puttin' on the Agony, Puttin' on the Style," "The Unfortunate Miss Bailey," and sentimental pieces.

The Frontier County Scrapbook, II, p. 96, in the State Historical Society Library, tells that at the Kester Schoolhouse, Arch Heater was accustomed to sing "The Steam Arm," "Shelling Green Peas," "Putting on the Agony," and other pieces. At Morrill Schoolhouse Andrew Johnson sang "When I Ride My Little Hump-Back Mule." He said "oomp" and "mool."

THE DANCE

[See also "Square Dances," pages 80 ff.]

Dance parties of various types in pioneer and later days were given various names, "barn dances," "hops," "stepping bees," and, for play-parties in certain regions such as the Sandhills, "bounce arounds." "Hoedowns," "shindigs," or "shindies" were rather rough and boisterous yet were occasions having some standing. "Hog wrassles," on the other hand, were characteristically cheap and rowdy. In Nebraska newspaper usage, nineteenth century dances might be alluded to as "terpsichorean performances" or "pigeon-wingings" or gatherings for "tripping the light fantastic" into the "wee small hours."

In many small towns and rural communities the "best families" never danced. One contributor told of being a guest at an infare party. She did not dance, but her Methodist minister told her that she was unfit to enter his church, and from that day she never did. In pioneer times gambling, dancing, saloons, and vice were always closely associated and hence were banned by the church.

The play-party games popular into the present century over the western plains thrived in regions where dancing was thought improper and was tabooed by the church. Neither the participants nor others ever called them dances. They were a lively and zestful species of social diversion for young persons in country regions or isolated towns and villages. They were at their height so long as there was little other amusement. In patterns they showed little change from those of the traditional English and Scottish games from which they descended. As communities became less isolated, and dancing floors, management, and musicians were to be had, such games waned in popularity, disparaged by city dwellers as childish or rustic. From their accepted position as a popular feature of social custom, the recreation of grown-ups, they passed into the tradition of the schoolhouse and playground and now linger in the dramatic games of Nebraska children played in open spaces outdoors.

Primarily the dancing was to song only. Largely the Nebraska play-party games were circle or ring dances or long line reels, with someone who knew the songs and tunes serving as leader. Later, various musical instruments, the fiddle, guitar, banjo, harmonica, even the organ or piano were availed of. The tunes were those handed down. When the older traditional songs, ballads or narrative songs among them, were utilized, they tended to shorten, disintegrate, or merge. As time went on, the texts and tunes became more and more westernized and more and more use was made of indigenous American tunes. The conduct of play-party games was noisy, but lively and spirited rather than boisterous. Additions to the songs were introduced and local matter or allusions improvised.

Play-parties might be held in front rooms, or yards, in school-houses or schoolyards, or in barns. They were characteristically open to all in the region round about. They were especially enjoyed on moonlight nights outdoors. Participants might come from a dozen or more miles away. Cider or lemonade or coffee with doughnuts was served. Intoxicants were not favored. The main refreshments were cake, cookies, roasted apples, pies, etc. Men wore shirts of various colors, sometimes stiff collars and cuffs of celluloid. Women were in long dresses of calico or gingham with shawls. As quadrilles or square dances replaced the play-party for group dancing, and when dances were held in hotels or halls, there was more formality in dress and re-freshment.

Among the inherited songs that were popular were "Needle's Eye," "Oats, Peas, Beans, and Barley," "Farmer in the Dell," "The Miller Boy," "Green Gravel." American of origin were "Buffalo Gals," "Old Dan Tucker," "We'll All Go Down to Rowser's," etc. Nebraska's most popular play-party game seems to have been "Skip to My Lou," ("Maloo," "Malue," etc.).

Changed conditions and a more tolerant attitude on the part of the church gradually weakened the taboo on dancing which had given vitality to the play-party. The lessening of com-munity isolation and the growing competition of other forms of amusement helped to break it down. Such dances as the waltz, polka, schottisch and two-step, and square dances (quadrilles, lancers) gained favor. The later play-party games were in-fluenced by and finally replaced by them. Early in the present century the play-party was still fairly common in outlying places, but it is hard now to find it surviving. The present re-vival of folksong and folkdance in general, especially of the square dance, has brought with it the revival of many dances of the old circle and line type, and it may bring the renewal to some extent of the play-party. But if so, it will be conducted in more sophisticated surroundings than in pioneer days with the accompaniment of music.

THEATRICALS AND OTHER ENTERTAINMENTS

With the coming of "opera houses," visiting troupes reached the larger towns. They played such dramas as "Uncle Tom's

Cabin," "East Lynne," "Ten Nights in a Barroom" and "The Count of Monte Cristo." Amateur theatrical societies were often formed which sometimes attempted to play Shakespeare. At Nebraska City a dramatic society was organized as early as October, 1859. An item in the Nebraska City *News* of December 31, 1859, read, "The Dramatic Society gave its second representation. Mr. J. G. Abbott as Othello, and Mr. Story as Cassio sustained the characters excellently." The Dramatic Society of Brownville gave its first performance April 23, 1876. At Fullerton amateurs presented "Othello," "Macbeth," and "The Merchant of Venice."

Frank A. Harrison wrote an account of "Nebraska History Plays" in *Nebraska History and Records of Pioneer Days* (1918), in the State Historical Library. Mr. Harrison tells of his first experiment in Garfield County, a spectacle play in which Indian battles were acted out. Some weeks later he gave one at Bellevue, and a year later he gave a history play at North Platte.

The Omaha *Nebraskian*, June 2, 1860, mentions the Philharmonic Society as in its sixth year.

At times a director was imported to a town and a cantata or pageant of some type was locally presented by local children.

The coming of the professional circus with its morning parade and its afternoon and evening performances was always a great event. Also, somewhat later, the street fair and the carnival.

Children got up imitative dramatic performances which they wrote, directed, and acted themselves. They gave circuses also. Admission to these affairs was usually by some fixed number of pins.

FOOD

[See also " Pioneer Cooking," pages 307 ff.]

Buffalo meat and venison were early forms of meat provided by hunters, and sometimes catfish were caught. Wild duck and turkey and geese were plentiful and so were prairie chickens and quail. Codfish and mackerel were brought in later. Jerked (dried) beef and salt pork became staple. Canned oysters were a real delicacy. Other staple food consisted of potatoes, hominy, cornbread or johnny cake, flapjacks, pancakes, buckwheat cakes. Sorghum gravy was made by browning flour and lard together, adding water, and boiling. Dried apples and navy beans were relied on, as were barley coffee and sorghum molasses. Occasionally a bee tree gave up a store of honey. Fruits were choke cherries, ground cherries, wild plums, wild grapes, mulberries, gooseberries and crab apples. Ice cream and the sundae were late delicacies. The sundae and its name made their appearance at about the end of the century.

Mrs. Kittie McGrew, writing of "Women of Territorial Nebraska" in the nineteenth volume of *The Nebraska State Historical Society Publications*, left a description of a pioneer log cabin built in 1855 which was superior in many ways to the majority in the locality. She said of the kitchen (pp. 97–98):

> The kitchen was a very attractive place, with a good stove and other conveniences not usually found in pioneer cabins. Its walls were hung with strings of red peppers, mangoes, popcorn and some choice seed corn tied with the husks and slipped on slender sticks. A great variety of gourds hung from wooden pegs driven into the walls. Some of the gourds were used for dipping water and some, with openings near the slender handles, held rice, dried corn, berries, or other household necessities and made fine receptacles. A sputtering two-lipped grease lamp, with cotton flannel wick, or perhaps candle wicking gave a fitful and feeble light . . . . In the yard was a well with a long wooden beam from which hung a chain and the old oaken bucket, a gourd dipper conveniently near, and a huge excavated log for a watering trough. Nearby was the great ash leach or hopper where the lye could be run off into the log trough to be made into a choice brand of soft soap. Near the kitchen door stood a split log bench where the family might have the tin basin for an early morning wash. There were great iron or copper kettles, suspended on poles or forked sticks, which were used in making soap and hominy and for heating water for the family washing and for butchering. All these were considered necessary adjuncts to a well regulated pioneer household.

ADDENDA

It is customary when a boy or girl shows up with a new pair of shoes for other boys or girls to spit on them.

Deserving of mention are the pioneer photograph album and the autograph album. In the latter, sentiments or verses were written as well as signatures. The vogue of collecting autographs lasted through the century.

Water-witching, attempts to find water by a divining rod, have been reported at various times, for instance from Platte County and Jefferson County. Rather peculiar old men searched for water with a forked stick of willow or other wood. The stick was much like a "sling shot" or "nigger shooter." It was held by the two forks and the point was supposed to point downward at the sought for spot.

Sayings, Proverbs, and Beliefs

Of all the forms of pioneer folklore presented in this collection, none has shown itself to be so persistent as the sayings and proverbs and some, at least, of the beliefs presented here. Most of these examples of folk wit and wisdom are as common today as they were three generations ago; indeed, it is astonishing how frequently they occur in everyday conversation. When someone wants to make a comparison, or needs to prove a point, or sees a red sunset, time and again he will find himself phrasing his comment in terms of a folk saying, proverb, or prophecy.

In an introductory note to Nebraska Folklore Pamphlet No. 9, the first of two from which the following items were selected, the editor writes that "a Nebraska *origin* is not claimed for the proverbs and sayings in this pamphlet. They are, however, *used* in Nebraska, and have been collected by field workers on the project, volunteer contributors, and grade and high school pupils over the state. They have been confirmed by numerous consultants, persons of all ages and occupations. The more familiar this material is to Nebraskans the more truly does it merit its place in Nebraska folklore, and the more its value will increase with the passing of time." One of the tests of a folklore item, in fact, is whether it has been collected in several areas and variations, for it is the essential nature of all folklore that it be traditional—diffused through time—and in wide currency—spread over geographical space.

A belief or a saying, although often containing the same kernel of wisdom as a proverb, may be expressed in a variety of ways, thus differing from a proverb, which retains a rigidly fixed form—that is, is usually expressed word for word the same way. Many of the proverbs current in pioneer Nebraska came from the pages of the Bible, which sometimes represented the entire pioneer library. Others will be recognized as of Shakespearian origin. As with all folklore, origin is not taken into account when determining the authenticity of a proverb as folklore: the principal test is its currency in tradition.

A collection of Nebraska sayings, proverbs, and beliefs with any pretensions to completeness would require a volume to itself; the intention here has been simply to offer a representative sampling. The interested reader is referred to Margaret Cannell's *Signs, Omens and Portents in Nebraska Folklore*, Louise Snapp's *Nebraska Proverbial Lore*, and Louise Pound's "Nebraska Snake Lore," in her *Nebraska Folklore* (see Bibliography, pages 386, 387, and 385).

LOVE AND MARRIAGE

The first man who walks across the threshold of the door above which the lucky part of a wishbone has been placed will be the future husband of the one who put it there.

The first man a girl meets after walking seven [railroad?] rails without falling off will be her future husband.

Name the four posts of a bed in which you are sleeping for the first time with the names of the four men you like best. The one about whom you dream will be your future husband.

By naming the buttons of a girl's gown with the following verse you may learn the occupation of the man she will marry:

> Rich man, poor man, beggar man, thief,
> Doctor, lawyer, merchant, chief.

The one who takes the next to the last piece of cake on the plate will marry a rich mate.

Peel an apple without allowing the peeling to break. Holding it in your right hand over your head, circle it around you three times and drop it over your left shoulder. The letter it forms is the initial of your future husband.

If you walk downstairs backward at midnight while looking in a mirror, your future husband will look over your shoulder.

Hold a burning match. The burned end will turn toward your sweetheart.

If you find a stem in your tea, it indicates a beau. The length indicates his height. Bite it and lay it near the thumb of your left hand. Double your right fist and strike the stem with the part of the fist next to the little finger. Each time you strike it name a day of the week, beginning with the present day. Your beau is coming to see you on the day you name when the stem sticks to your fist.

If you spill dishwater on your apron, you will have a drunken husband.

Stamp a hundred white horses and you will marry the first man with whom you shake hands. To stamp, lick your right thumb, touch your left palm with it, strike your right fist on the place where your thumb touched.

If you see the new moon over your right shoulder, say,

"New moon, true moon, pray let me see
Who my husband is to be.
The color of his hair, the clothes he is to wear,
The happy day he weds me,"

and the man you dream about that night is the man you will marry.

Sneeze on Monday, sneeze for news;
Sneeze on Tuesday, new pair of shoes;
Sneeze on Wednesday, sneeze for danger;
Sneeze on Thursday, meet a stranger;
Sneeze on Friday, sneeze for sorrow;
Sneeze on Saturday, see your sweetheart tomorrow.

The girl who catches the bride's bouquet will be married next.

If two forks, knives, or spoons are accidentally put at your place at the table, you will be married soon.

Put a ring, a penny, and a thimble in the wedding cake, and when it is cut, the one who gets the penny will receive money, the one who gets the ring will be married next, and the one who gets the thimble will sew for a living.

If you sit on the table, you will be married before you are able.

If four people cross hands in shaking hands, some one of them will be married soon.

If you break a needle when sewing a garment, you will be married before the garment wears out.

If a girl takes the last piece of bread on the plate, she will be an old maid.

If you put your shoes on the table, you will never be married.

Three times a bridesmaid, never a bride.

If someone sweeps under the chair you are sitting on, you will be an old maid.

Write your sweetheart's name below yours. Strike out the letters that are the same in both each time they occur. To find out the state and relationship of affections, first say on the uncanceled letters of each name: "Love, hate, friendship, courtship, marriage."

To find out if your sweetheart loves you, pluck the petals of a daisy, saying as you pluck one petal, "He loves me," and as you pluck the next, "He loves me not." The last petal gives the true answer.

The girl that whistles or a hen that crows always catch the nicest beaux.

For good luck the bride should wear something old and something new, something borrowed, something blue.

> Married in red, wish yourself dead;
> Married in black, wish yourself back;
> Married in blue, you'll always be true;
> Married in green, ashamed to be seen.

If the bridegroom carries the bride over the threshold of her new home, it will bring luck and happiness to the couple.

It is bad luck to take the wedding ring off.

> Happy is the bride that the sun shines on
> And woe to the bride that the rain rains on.

> Married in white, chosen all right;
> Married in gray, go far away;
> Married in brown, live out of town;
> Married in blue, your mate will be true;
> Married in white, quarrel and fight.

If your shoestring comes untied, your sweetheart is thinking of you.

If your knees are ticklish, you like the boys (or girls).

Dream of a wedding, you'll hear of a death.

It is bad luck to postpone a wedding.

Have a friend snap and name the apple you are about to eat. When you reach the core, take out one seed at a time, saying:

> "One I love, two I love, three I love, I say,
> Four I love with all my heart, five I cast away,
> Six he loves, seven she loves, eight they both love,
> Nine he comes, ten he tarries,
> Eleven he courts, twelve he marries,
> Thirteen they quarrel, fourteen they part,
> Fifteen he dies of a broken heart."

To sit on the table is a sign that you want to marry.
If your nose itches you will kiss a fool.

Absence makes the heart grow fonder.
All is fair in love and war.
All the world loves a lover.
A woman's "no" means "yes."

> Change the name and not the letter;
> Change for worse instead of better.

Cold hands, warm heart.
Distance lends enchantment.
Every Jack has his Jill.
Faint heart never won fair lady.
Love is blind.
Love will find a way.
Marriages are made in heaven.
Marry in haste and repent at leisure.
The longest way round is the sweetest way home.
There are just as good fish in the sea as ever were caught.
'Tis better to have loved and lost than never to have loved
at all.
True love never runs smoothly.
Two is company, three is a crowd.
When poverty comes in the door, love flies out the window.
Where cobwebs grow, beaux never go.

VISITORS AND TRAVEL

If a broom falls across the doorsill, a stranger is coming.
If a dish towel falls on the floor, an untidy person is coming.
If a fork falls, a man visitor is coming from the direction
toward which the prong points.
If a knife falls on the floor, a woman visitor is coming.
If a spoon falls on the floor, a child is coming.
If you dream of the dead, you will hear from the living.
If you take bread when you already have some, someone who
is hungry is coming.
If you walk in one door of a residence and out another, you
will bring company.

If your cat washes its face, you will receive visitors.
If your right hand itches, you are going to shake hands.
A scratch on the arm indicates a journey.
If the soles of your feet itch, you are going to travel.

GOOD LUCK: HOW TO DETECT IT

Blow on a ladybug and say: "Ladybug, Ladybug, fly away home; your house is on fire, your children will burn." If the bug flies away, you will have good luck.

If your left palm itches, you will receive money.

See a pin, pick it up; all the day you'll have good luck.

Seeing a spider brings good luck.

Seeing the moon over the right shoulder is a sign of good luck.

To find a four-leaf clover is a sign of good luck.

If each person at the table makes a wish before a person celebrating his birthday blows out the candles on his cake, all wishes will be granted within a year—if all the candles are blown out at one breath. Otherwise, as many years must elapse as there are candles left burning.

GOOD LUCK: HOW TO MAKE IT

To find a horseshoe is good luck. To place it above the door brings good luck, but it must be placed with the ends pointing up so that the good luck will not run out.

If you leave [on] a garment which you have accidentally donned wrong side out, it will bring you luck.

Upon seeing the first star of the evening say,

"Star light, star bright, first star I've seen tonight,

I wish I may, I wish I might, have the wish I wish tonight,"

and your wish will come true.

If you say "Money, money, money" while a star is falling, you will receive money or some other good fortune.

If you sleep on a recently extracted tooth, it will be transformed into a nickel.

If you plant potatoes on Good Friday, you will have a good crop.

Carrying a rabbit's foot brings good luck.

If two persons say the same thing simultaneously, they may have a wish granted by hooking the little fingers of their right hands together while they make the wish, after which one says, "Needles," and the other says, "Pins." Then, placing their thumbs together, both say, "Thumbs."

If you get the bubbles from your tea or coffee with your spoon before they reach the edge of the cup, you will receive money.

If you do not put your tongue in the hole from which a tooth has been pulled, a gold tooth will grow in that place.

If you stamp a hundred white horses, say "Give, give me good luck," and make a wish, your wish will come true. If you stamp a hundred Model T Fords and make a wish, your wish will come true.

BAD LUCK: HOW TO DETECT IT

If you sew on Sunday, you will have to rip it out with your nose.

If a (black) cat crosses your path, it is a sign of bad luck.

It is bad luck to walk under a ladder.

Breaking a mirror brings seven years of bad luck.

Sing before breakfast, you'll cry before night.

Starting a journey on Friday brings bad luck.

The number 13 is unlucky; Friday the thirteenth is very unlucky.

If it rains into an open grave, there will be another death in the family within a year.

A black Christmas, a full graveyard.

It is bad luck to give a person anything sharp unless he gives you a penny for it, for it may cut the friendship.

If one passes the salt and pepper without placing them on the table, bad luck will come.

Thirteen at a table brings bad luck to all present; one will die within a year.

To dream of muddy water is a sign of death.

To dream of fire is a sign of danger.

It is bad luck to take off another person's ring.

If you tell the wish you make, it will not come true.

Bad Luck: How to Change It

To say "God bless you" to one after he sneezes brings him luck or wards off bad luck.

Boasting of good luck will break the spell unless you knock on wood.

To break a spell of bad luck at cards get up and walk around your chair.

If two persons walking together pass on opposite sides of a tree or post, they must say "Bread and butter" or they will have a falling out.

If you cross your fingers, you can keep away impending trouble.

When you go back into the house for something you have forgotten, you will have bad luck unless you sit down before going out again.

If you spill salt, you will have bad luck unless you throw some over your left shoulder.

Weather

If muskrats build large, thick houses, the winter will be severe.

If animals have heavy fur coats, the winter will be severe.

If the groundhog sees his shadow on February 2, there will be six more weeks of cold weather.

If pigs gather straw, it is a sign of storm.

If a rooster crows before he goes to bed, he will get up with a wet head.

If swallows fly close together, it is a sign of storm.

A clear sunrise is a sign of fair weather for the next day.

A red sunrise is a sign of rain.

> Sunset red and morning gray
> Sends the traveler on his way;
> Sunset gray and morning red
> Keeps the traveler to his bed.

If the sunset is red, the following day will be windy.

A red sunrise foretells rain before the day is over.

A ring around the moon is a sign of storm and the number of stars within the ring indicates the number of days before the storm.

If you can hang a powder horn on the lower part of the crescent moon, the weather will be rainy.

Green in a cloud indicates hail.

> Mackerel sky, mackerel sky,
> Never long wet, never long dry.

> Rainbow at night, sailor's delight,
> Rainbow in the morning, sailors take warning.

A rainbow is a sign the rain is over.

If it rains before ten o'clock, it will rain every day for a week.

Rain before seven, quit before eleven.

If it rains on Easter Sunday, it will rain for the following seven Sundays.

Rain when the sun shines, rain all day tomorrow.

> If the first of July be rainy weather,
> 'Twill rain off and on for four weeks together.

If March comes in like a lion, it will go out like a lamb; if it comes in like a lamb, it will go out like a lion.

The first three days of spring rule the spring months.

April showers bring May flowers.

PERSONALITY TRAITS

If your eyebrows meet, you will become wealthy.

A high forehead is a sign of intelligence.

Large eyes signify intelligence.

A large mouth is a sign of generosity.

Small ears indicate stinginess.

A person with a pointed nose is meddlesome.

Red hair is the sign of a hot temper.

Eyes set close together indicate a bad temper.

A person with a pointed chin is snoopy.

A person with little eyes is shrewd and treacherous.

Monday's child is fair of face,
Tuesday's child is full of grace,
Wednesday's child is loving and giving,
Thursday's child works hard for a living,
Friday's child is full of woe,
Saturday's child has far to go,
But the child that is born on the Sabbath Day
Is blithe and bonny and good and gay.

Blue-eyed beauty, do your mother's duty;
Black-eyed pick-a-pie, turn around and tell a lie;
Green-eyed greedy-gut, turn around and eat the world up.

MISCELLANEOUS BELIEFS

If you play with a toad, you will get warts.
Lose a hairpin, lose a friend. Find a hairpin, find a friend.
If a person's ears burn, it is a sign someone is talking about him.

Sneeze on Monday for health,
Tuesday for wealth,
Wednesday the best day of all;
Thursday for losses,
Friday for crosses,
Saturday for no luck at all.

Carrying a raw potato in one's pocket cures rheumatism.

MISCELLANEOUS PROVERBS

A bad penny always returns.
A bird in the hand is worth two in the bush.
A burnt child dreads the fire.
A cat may look at a king.
A dog that will bring a bone will carry one.
A man convinced against his will is of the same opinion still.
A new broom sweeps clean.
A rolling stone gathers no moss.
A still tongue makes a wise head.
All is well that ends well.
All that glitters is not gold.

All work and no play makes Jack a dull boy.
An empty wagon makes the most noise.
An apple a day keeps the doctor away.
Anything worth doing at all is worth doing well.
Ask me no questions and I'll tell you no lies.
Beauty is as beauty does.
Beauty is only skin deep.
"Because" is a woman's excuse.
Birds of a feather flock together.
Blood is thicker than water.
Charity begins at home.
Chickens come home to roost.
Children should be seen and not heard.
Constant dripping wears away stones.
Curiosity killed a cat.
Don't bite off more than you can chew.
Don't count your chickens before they're hatched.
Don't cross the bridge before you come to it.
Don't holler before you're hurt.
Don't judge others by yourself.
Don't stick your nose into other folks' business.
Early to bed and early to rise makes a man healthy, wealthy, and wise.
Easy come, easy go.
To err is human.
Every cloud has a silver lining.
Every dog has his day.
Every man for himself and the devil.
Everything is grist for the mill.
Finders keepers, losers weepers.
Fine feathers do not make fine birds.
Fools' names, like fools' faces, always appear in public places.
Forbidden fruit is sweetest.
Give a dog a bad name and you might as well hang him.
Give him an inch and he'll take a mile.
Gone but not forgotten.
Good riddance to bad rubbish.
He can who thinks he can.
He who laughs last laughs best.

He would steal pennies from a dead man's eyes.

Hell is paved with good intentions.

His bark is worse than his bite.

Hitch your wagon to a star.

Honesty is the best policy.

If "ifs" and "ands" were crocks and pans, we wouldn't have to buy any.

If the shoe fits, wear it.

If wishes were fishes, we'd have some fried; if wishes were horses, beggars might ride.

It's a long lane that has no turning.

It is better to be an old man's darling than a poor man's slave.

It is darkest just before dawn.

It is useless to lock the barn door after the horse has gone.

It never rains but it pours.

It takes a rogue to catch a rogue.

It takes two to make a quarrel.

Leave well enough alone.

Let a sleeping dog lie.

Let the Devil take the hindmost.

Little pitchers have big ears.

Lost time is never found again.

Love me, love my dog.

Murder will out.

Never look a gift horse in the mouth.

Never put off till tomorrow what you can do today.

Never trouble trouble till trouble troubles you.

No news is good news.

No rest for the wicked.

Nothing is sure but death and taxes.

Oil and water won't mix.

Opportunity knocks but once.

Out of sight, out of mind.

Paddle your own canoe.

People who live in glass houses shouldn't throw stones.

Root, hog, or die.

Salt the cow and catch the calf.

Show me a liar and I'll show you a thief.

Something is rotten in Denmark.

Speak when you're spoken to.
Stick to your bush.
Still water runs deep.
Strain at a gnat and swallow a camel.
Strike while the iron is hot.
Take care of pennies and the dollars will take care of themselves.
The best of friends must part.
The customer is always right.
The die is cast.
The early bird catches the worm.
The good die young.
The race is run.
The world is my oyster.
The worm will turn.
There is more than one way to skin a cat.
There is no fool like an old fool.
There is nothing new under the sun.
Time and tide wait for no man.
Two heads are better than one.
Ugliness runs clear to the bone.
What is sauce for the goose is sauce for the gander.
Where there is a will, there is a way.
Where there is smoke, there is fire.
You are a long time dead.
You can lead a horse to water, but you can't make him drink.
You can't get blood from a turnip.
You can't have your cake and eat it too.
You can't judge a man by the coat he wears.
You can't make a silk purse out of a sow's ear.
You can't tell from the looks of a frog how far he can jump.
You might as well have the game as the name.
You never miss the water till the well runs dry.
You would lose your head if it weren't fastened on.

BIBLICAL PROVERBS

A good name is better to be chosen than great riches.
A house divided against itself cannot stand.
A little child shall lead them.

A little leaven leavens the whole loaf.

A soft answer turneth away wrath.

Get thee behind me Satan.

He that is without sin, let him cast the first stone.

It is easier for a camel to pass through a needle's eye than for a rich man to enter the kingdom of Heaven.

Judge not lest ye be judged.

No man can serve two masters.

Pride goeth before the fall.

Spare the rod and spoil the child.

The Lord loveth a cheeful giver.

The poor you have always with you.

The wages of sin are death.

The way of the transgressor is hard.

What shall it profit a man if he gains the whole world and lose his soul.

Whatsoever a man soweth so shall he reap.

Whom the Lord loveth he chasteneth.

Children's Games

Children are perhaps the most conservative cultural group in our society. Few new items are added to the traditional repertoire of games, and those that enter this tradition endure for centuries. The games collected here are not unique to Nebraska or to pioneer times; they are games children play all over the United States (in some cases, all over the world) and many which originated hundreds of years ago are being played today on Nebraska's playgrounds.

Nebraska Folklore Pamphlet No. 7, the second of two devoted to children's games, has this to say concerning the provenience of the material:

> Knowledge concerning the playing of games in this collection has been gained by several years of contact with groups of children through the teaching and supervision of games. Their authenticity as Nebraska folklore has been confirmed by original research in which several schools of the state have aided, and by bibliographical research.

> The State of Nebraska is young, comparatively speaking, and her folklore could be of rather recent origin. Nevertheless, these games are not only Nebraska folklore, but for the most part are traditional to all English-speaking people and to many European countries.

OUTDOOR GAMES

CROWN THE CAT

Also known as "Cat and Rat," "Chase the Squirrel," and "Follow Chase."

The players stand in a circle with their arms outstretched and their hands joined and raised high. Two players—the rat and the cat—stand outside the circle at opposite sides. The rat says, "Ready," and runs among the players, in and out and across the circle, beneath the outstretched arms. The cat must follow the exact course of the rat or he is crowned and another cat is chosen. If the rat is caught, the cat becomes the rat and chooses another cat.

The following dialogue often precedes the chase:

Cat: I am the cat.
Rat: I am the rat.
Cat: I will catch you.
Rat: You can't.

Then the chase begins.

DROP THE HANDKERCHIEF

All the players but one stand about a foot apart in a circle. One player, who is "it," passes around the outside of the circle and drops the handkerchief behind someone. The players may not look behind until the dropper has passed by them. The one behind whom the handkerchief has been dropped picks it up and chases the dropper, who tries to reach the vacant place in the circle—left by the one who now has picked up the hand-kerchief—without being touched by him. If he is touched, he must enter the center of the circle, called, by tradition, the "mush pot." The only way he can then get out is to seize the next dropped handkerchief before the receiver discovers it behind him. He then becomes the chaser, and the receiver who did not discover the handkerchief must go to the mush pot.

ITISKIT, ITASKIT

This is a variant of "Drop the handkerchief"; it is also known as "Hunt the Squirrel" and "Drop Glove."

The players stand in a circle about a foot apart, much the same as in "Drop the Handkerchief." One player skips around the outside of the circle as the group sings. He drops a handkerchief behind someone standing in the circle. Except for the music, the game proceeds as described in "Drop the Handkerchief." Sometimes the child outside the circle touches the other on the shoulder. He must then pick up the handkerchief and run in the *opposite* direction. When the two meet, they curtsy three times and then run on, each trying to outrace the other to the vacant place in the circle. The loser takes the handkerchief and the game continues. In another variant a child called the "squirrel" touches a player, who then must pursue him in and out of the ring until he is caught, following the exact path of the squirrel as in "Crown the Cat." The singing ceases when the chase begins. Sometimes the pursuer is entitled to a kiss, if he catches the fugitive before she reaches the vacant place.

I - tis - kit, I-tas - kit, A green and yel-low bas - ket. I
wrote a let - ter to my love, And by the way I dropped it,
dropped it, dropped it. A lit - tle boy came and
put it In his pock - et, pock - et, pock - et.___

Itiskit, Itaskit,
A green and yellow basket.
I wrote a letter to my love,

And by the way
I dropped it, dropped it, dropped it.
A little boy came and put it
In his pocket, pocket, pocket.

THE FARMER IN THE DELL

This game of choosing "still retains the characteristics of the game in old England, from whence it came. The Farmer in the Dell was a country dance known over the greater part of England" (15).

The players clasp hands in a circle and walk around, singing; one player stands in the middle of the circle. As the second verse is sung, the one in the middle chooses a player from the ring, who then goes and stands in the center of the ring with the first player. As each verse is sung, the last one chosen selects another from the outside ring. When the last verse is sung, those in the center form another ring and the two circles move as fast as possible in opposite directions until the ring breaks. The "cheese" then becomes the new "farmer." Sometimes the game ends in clapping hands instead of the rapid circling.

The farmer in the dell,
The farmer in the dell,
Heigh-ho! the cherry-o,
The farmer in the dell.

The farmer takes the wife,
The farmer takes the wife,
Heigh-ho! the cherry-o,
The farmer takes the wife.

The wife takes the child,
The wife takes the child,
Heigh-ho! the cherry-o,
The wife takes the child.

(*The same verse pattern is repeated
with the following changes:*)
The child takes the nurse . . . .
The nurse takes the dog . . . .
The dog takes the cat . . . .
The cat takes the rat . . . .
The rat takes the cheese . . . .
The cheese stands alone . . . .

ROUND AND ROUND THE VALLEY

*Also known as "Go In and Out the Window," this is "a very old
traditional game based upon village marriage festivals, at which it
was customary for the young men and women to go through the
houses in a long procession"* (1). *According to Eloise Linscott, "In
the figure of this game we see the dance of a particular group of
craftsmen, the weavers. As a love game, where one might openly
show his preference, it was popular in the eighteenth century"* (15).

The players join hands and form a circle while one player
dances around the circle singing the first verse. As the second
verse is sung, the players raise their arms to form "windows"
and the player outside the circle goes in and out of alternate
windows until he has completed the round. As the third verse
is sung, he stands facing some other player in the ring. During
the fourth verse he takes this player's hand and stands with
him in the ring. Then the player who was chosen goes outside
the ring and the game begins again.

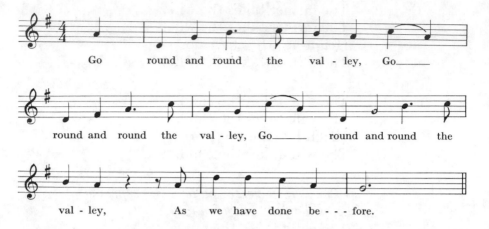

Go round and round the val - ley, Go____ round and round the val - ley, Go____ round and round the val - ley, As we have done be - - - fore.

Go round and round the valley,
Go round and round the valley,
Go round and round the valley,
As we have done before.

Go in and out the windows,
Go in and out the windows,
Go in and out the windows,
As we have done before.

Now stand before your partner,
Now stand before your partner,
Now stand before your partner,
As we have done before.

Now follow him to London,
Now follow him to London,
Now follow him to London,
As we have done before.

OATS, PEAS, BEANS, AND BARLEY GROWS

This game is about six centuries old. It is widely known in France, Sweden, Italy, Sicily, Spain, and Germany (1).

The players join hands and circle about a player in the middle while they sing the first verse of the song. Then they pause, drop hands, and go through the motions suggested by the second verse. During the third verse the players join hands and circle again. The "farmer" selects a partner and they skip around the circle in the opposite direction of the other players. During the fourth verse the couple kneels and curtsies. The one chosen now becomes the farmer and the game continues.

Melody for first, second, and fourth verses:

Oats, peas, beans, and bar - ley grows, Oats, peas, beans, and bar - ley grows,___ You, nor I, nor no-bod-y knows How

Melody for third verse:

oats, peas, beans, and bar - ley grows. Wait-ing for a part - ner, Wait-ing for a part - ner, O - pen the ring and take one in, And kiss her when you get her in.

Oats, peas, beans, and barley grows,
Oats, peas, beans, and barley grows,
You, nor I, nor nobody knows
How oats, peas, beans, and barley grows.

Thus the farmer sows his seed,
Stands upright and takes his ease,
Stamps his foot and claps his hands,
And turns about to view his lands.

Waiting for a partner,
Waiting for a partner,
Open the ring and take one in,
And kiss her when you get her in.

Now you're married, you must obey,
You must be true in all you say,
You must be kind, you must be good,
And make your husband chop the wood [*if girl is chosen*].
And keep your wife in kindling wood [*if boy is chosen*].

THE NEEDLE'S EYE

Also known as " Threading the Needle." Since, according to one authority, this game was said to be performed to make the hemp grow, it "is reminiscent of the oldest of the sacred dances, executed in the spring of the year to bring fertility to the land" (15).

Two children face each other and form an arch by raising their arms and clasping hands. Singing, the other children form a line and pass under the arch. As the last "Because I wanted you" is sung, the leaders drop their arms around the child passing under the arch. The player is then taken aside and asked, "Do you choose needles or pins?" The child makes a choice and is assigned to the team designated by the symbol he chose. When all have been caught, a tug-of-war is held between the teams. Sometimes the game is played by older children as a kissing game. The line is formed by boys and girls in alternate order. A boy and girl are caught at the same time. The pair kisses and takes its place behind the opposite leaders. This game may also end in a tug-of-war.

(The) nee-dle's eye that doth sup-ply The thread that runs so tru - ly;

(There's) man-y a lass that I've let pass Be - cause I want-ed you.   Be-

cause I want-ed you,____ be - cause I want-ed you; There's

man - y a lass that I've let pass Be - cause I want-ed you.

The needle's eye that doth supply
The thread that runs so truly;
There's many a lass that I've let pass
Because I wanted you.

Because I wanted you, because I wanted you;
There's many a lass that I've let pass
Because I wanted you.

GREEN GRAVEL

Eloise Linscott writes that this game "was once descriptive of the ceremony of washing and burying the dead, in which the whole village took part. . . . The turning back is part of a curious funeral ceremony of ancient times called ' Dish-a-loof,' in which death was followed by clapping of hands and bell ringing to ward off evil spirits and to call all good men to pray for the departing soul. The final verse that deals with the letter sustains the belief in communion with the dead. The green gravel is the grass; the letter is the communion symbol" (15).

The children form a circle and march around, singing. As the smallest child is named, he turns his back to the center of the ring. The first verse is repeated until every name has been called and all have their backs to the center. Beginning with the smallest again, the names are called and the second verse is repeated until all have their faces turned to the center once more. In a variation of this game, two players hold up their hands after all the children have faced outward and the others, still holding hands, pass through, thus turning their faces to the center again.

Green gravel, green gravel,
The grass is so green,
The fairest of maidens
That ever was seen;
O [name], O [name],
Your true love is dead,
The king sends you a letter
To turn round your head.

Green gravel, green gravel,
The grass is so green,
And all the fair maidens
Arrayed to be seen;
O [name], O [name],
Your true love's not slain,
The king sends you a letter
To turn back again.

KING ARTHUR WAS KING WILLIAM'S SON

The words of this song seem to be of English origin, but some think they may derive from a ballad concerning a romantic kidnaping in Sweden in 1287. In the process of adaptation, however, the original significance of the ballad has been almost lost (1).

The leader chooses one from a row of hats on the floor, puts it on his head, and marches around in a big circle, singing the verse. After completing the circle he places the hat on another player's head. The player chosen marches behind him and they make the circle, singing the first verse as they do so. This procedure is followed, with the first and second verses sung alternately, until all are in the marching circle. The leader then goes to the center with the first player chosen and the others march around, singing the third and fourth verses as the couple in the center kneel and salute. The leader then rejoins the circle and the second player chosen goes to the center. The game continues and the third verse is repeated until everyone has been in the center.

When the game is played by older children and adults, only one hat is used. A young man puts the hat on a girl and they march around singing. After they have completed the circle, the girl puts the hat on another boy among those in the waiting group and he follows the first couple. When the circle is again completed, he puts the hat on another girl and the game continues until all are marching. The fifth verse of the song may be substituted for the third, and the fourth verse may be omitted.

King Ar-thur was King Wil-liam's son, And when the bat-tle he had won, Up-on his breast he wore a star, And it was called the sign of war.

King Arthur was King William's son,
And when the battle he had won,
Upon his breast he wore a star,
And it was called the sign of war.

King William was King James's son,
And all the royal race he run;
Upon his breast he wore a star,
And it was called the sign of war.

Star of the East, star of the West,
Star of the one you love the best.
If she's not here, don't take her part,
But choose another with all your heart.

Down on the carpet you must kneel,
As the grass grows on the field,
And rise again upon your feet,
And give your bride a kiss so sweet.

Say, young lady, will you 'list and go?
Say, young lady, will you 'list and go?
The broad-brimmed hat you must put on,
And follow on to the fife and drum.

DARE BASE

Also known as "Prisoner's Base." This game was played as early as the thirteenth century and is mentioned in Edmund Spenser's Faerie Queene (5).

The players form two teams of equal number. A straight line divides the field into approximately equal halves and each team occupies a half. A prison is established in the extreme left-hand corner of each field. The players from each team venture into enemy territory and if tagged are placed in prison. A captive must remain in prison until one of his side comes and touches him. The prisoner and his rescuer may be tagged before reaching their own territory and returned to prison. The game ends when one side makes prisoners of all the opposing group or when a free man enters the enemy prison when it holds no captives.

Fox and Geese

A large circle from fifteen to thirty feet in diameter is traced in the snow. Five paths are made across the circle through the center. The "fox" stands in the middle of the circle and attempts to catch the "geese" whenever they venture away from an intersection, where they are safe. A goose may not turn back nor make an angle at an intersection. The goose who gets tagged becomes the fox. A more complicated variation is played with two circles, one within the other. In this version the geese may turn at any intersection, but there may be only one goose in each section of the circle.

Hide and Seek

Also known as "I Spy."

The player who is "it" stands at a goal or base, usually a door, a tree, or the side of a building, and hides his eyes. The other players scatter and hide while he counts aloud to one hundred. Then he says:

> "Bushel of wheat,
> Bushel of rye,
> All not ready holler 'I.'"

If anyone calls out "I," the goalkeeper counts again and repeats his rhyme. As a last warning he calls:

> "One, two, three,
> Look out for me,
> For I am coming,
> And I can see."

Then he starts in search of the players. When he spies one, he runs to the goal and hits it three times with the flat of his hand, saying: "One, two, three for [name of player]." The game continues until all are caught or until the goalkeeper, tired of hunting, calls: "All who are out may come in free." If "it" strays too far from the goal, a player may make a run for it, and if he reaches the goal before the goalkeeper, he hits it three times and says: "One, two, three, I'm in free." The first player caught becomes "it" in the next round.

LEAPFROG

Also known as " Leader and Footer," " Bung the Bucket," " Par," "Johnnie Ride a Pony," "Cavalry Hill," "Saddle the Nag," "Spanish Fly," and "Skin the Goat."

In the simplest form of this game a player bends over and places his hands on his knees. The jumper runs from a base or line and vaults over the back of the other player by placing his hands flat on the shoulders of his human obstacle. After running a few steps he bends over. The third player jumps over these two, runs on, and bends over. This continues until there are no more jumpers; then the boy at the back becomes jumper. The game may be converted into a race by forming two teams. When the first boy who bent over makes his run over all the backs, he races to a goal line; the first team to reach it is the winner. A player can demonstrate special skill by asking for "high back," which means that the bent-over players stand with their hands on their upper thighs, providing a higher obstacle for him to clear.

LONDON BRIDGE

No children's game has aroused more speculation over its origin than " London Bridge." Eloise Linscott has traced it to a medieval belief that at death "the soul separated from the body and, before reaching its final destination, was forced to cross a bridge," where the Devil usually was waiting. If he could be bought off, the soul crossed the bridge and was assured of eternal peace (15). William S. and Ceil Baring-Gould suggest that the game may "reflect an actual occurrence—the destruction of London Bridge by King Olaf and his Norsemen in the early part of the eleventh century, after a battle with King Ethelred of England" (2). And Henry Bett has pointed out that the game and its accompanying rhyme "preserve unmistakable traces of human sacrifice at the building of a bridge. There are many variants but they nearly all agree in these suggestive particulars—the bridge has fallen down, and attempts to build it up with different materials are all failures, whereupon there follows—with an apparent lack of connexion—the arrest of a prisoner" (3).

Two players with arms raised and hands clasped form an arch, the "bridge" under which the line of players passes, hands clasped and singing. The children in the line sing the first verse, those in the arch the second, and so forth. The game may be varied by having all of the players sing all of the verses. When the words "Here's a prisoner I have got" are sung, the bridge "falls" or, if the game is to end in a tug-of-war, the arms drop to catch the largest player. When "Off to prison he must go" is sung, the players in the arch take the captive to one side and ask him to choose between gold and silver, lemons and oranges, or other such items. The captors have previously decided which article represents each side. The captive then joins the side of the symbol that he has chosen. When all players have been captured and have chosen a side, the game ends in a tug-of-war. If there are a great number of players, more than one arch can be formed. The tug-of-war may be omitted; in this case, the first or last two captured become the new arch and the game begins again.

Lon-don Bridge is fall-ing down, Fall-ing down,— fall-ing down,
Lon-don Bridge is fall-ing down, My fair la - dy.

London Bridge is falling down,
Falling down, falling down,
London Bridge is falling down,
My fair lady.

Build it up with bricks and mortar,
Bricks and mortar, bricks and mortar,
Build it up with bricks and mortar,
My fair lady.

Bricks and mortar will not stay,
Will not stay, will not stay,
Bricks and mortar will not stay,
My fair lady.

Build it up with gold and silver,
Gold and silver, gold and silver,
Build it up with gold and silver,
My fair lady.

(*The same verse pattern is repeated with the following changes:*)
Gold and silver will be stolen . . . .
Build it up with iron bars . . . .
Iron bars will bend and break . . . .
Get a cock to crow all night . . . .
Here's a prisoner I have got . . . .
What has this poor prisoner done . . . ?
Stole my watch and lost my key . . . .
A hundred pounds will set him free . . . .
Stole my hat and lost my keys . . . .
Off to prison he must go . . . .

DRAW A BUCKET OF WATER

Two girls face each other and clasp hands at arm's length. Two more do the same, crossing the first couple's arms at right angles. The couples brace their feet and sway backward and forward as they sing. As the song ends, the children raise their arms, with their hands still clasped, and drop them behind the other couple. They then dance around as they sing the song again. Sometimes the game is played with eight children. Four stand waiting until the above performance is completed. Then, as the song is repeated over and over, one child pops into the center of the ring at each verse. The song is sung a fifth time, with great jogging and jumping, until all fall down.

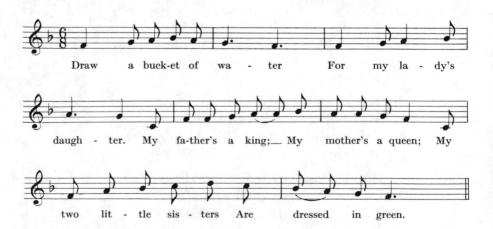

Draw a buck-et of wa - ter For my la - dy's daugh - ter. My fa-ther's a king;— My mother's a queen; My two lit - tle sis - ters Are dressed in green.

Draw a bucket of water
For my lady's daughter.
My father's a king;
My mother's a queen;
My two little sisters
Are dressed in green.

Stamping grass and parsley,
Marigold leaves and daisies.
One in a rush,
Two in a rush,
Please, little girl,
Bob under the bush.

ANTE I OVER

The players divide into two equal teams. A ball about the size of a baseball is thrown over a small building, high board fence, hedge, or curtain which hides one group from the other. Each group selects an umpire who checks on the opposite team. The ball is thrown by any member of the group, and he shouts "Ante I Over." The group on the other side makes ready to catch it. If the ball fails to clear the obstruction and falls back, the group must shout "Pig tail" or "Back ball." Then they shout "Ante I Over" and throw the ball again. If the ball is caught after being thrown over, the group that catches it must run to the other side and tag as many members of the other team as possible, touching each one with the ball. The throwing team, upon discovering that the ball has been caught, also runs to the other side. Thus the groups exchange sides each time the ball is caught. If a player is tagged, he becomes a member of the team that tags him. The game may end at any time, and the team with the most members wins. If the ball is not too hard, it may be thrown to tag players.

OLD WITCH

Here is an excellent example of the relatively rare folk drama. The tag game tacked to the end of the short play is merely a casting device and has no function within the play itself.

Five to ten children can play this game. The players are Old Witch, Mother, Eldest Daughter, and the younger children whose names are Monday, Tuesday, and the other days of the week. A place is selected to be the family's home, and the game begins with the mother and children in the home and the witch lurking near by. She peeps out occasionally, waiting for the mother to leave the home. The mother says to the eldest daughter, "I am going to the garden." To the other children she says, "Monday, take care of Tuesday; Tuesday, take care of Wednesday," and so on; and to the last child she says, "Saturday, take care of yourself." Then she says to the eldest daughter, "Make sure the old witch does not carry off any of your sisters. Get dinner and do not let the pot boil over." As soon as the mother is out of sight, the old witch approaches, stooped over and walking with a cane. She comes to the door of the home and raps with her cane.

Eldest Daughter: Come in.
Old Witch: Let me light my pipe at your fire. My fire is out.
Eldest Daughter: All right, but do not dirty the hearth.
Old Witch: Oh, no indeed. I will not dirty your hearth.

The eldest daughter turns her back to the old witch, who blows into the fire and makes a hissing sound to represent the pot boiling over into the fire. The eldest daughter runs to the door and calls, "Mother, mother, the pot boils over."

Mother: Take a spoon and skim it.
Daughter: Can't find it.
Mother: Look on the shelf.
Daughter: I can't reach it.
Mother: Stand on the stool.
Daughter: Stool's broken.
Mother: I suppose I must do it myself.

The mother comes back and immediately misses Monday.

Mother: Where is Monday?
Daughter: Look in the pantry.
Mother: Monday! Monday! (*Looks in the pantry.*) She isn't there.

The daughter suggests other places to look—upstairs, down in the cellar, and so forth. When she can think of no more places to look, she says, "Monday must have gone with the old lady who came to ask for a light for her pipe."

"That was the old witch!" exclaims the mother. She seizes the eldest daughter and pretends to beat her severely. The girl weeps and promises to watch her sisters more carefully if her mother will stop beating her. The action is then repeated until all the children, including the eldest daughter, have been taken by the old witch. The mother then goes in search of the children. She meets the old witch and asks, "Which path leads to the witch's house?"

Old Witch: Both paths.
Mother: Which is shortest.
Old Witch: This one.
Mother: I'll take it.
Old Witch: An ugly bull blocks the path.
Mother: I'll go the long way.
Old Witch: A fierce dog guards the path.
Mother: I will slip by while he sleeps.

The old witch runs ahead of her until they come to the old witch's house. The mother tries to enter.

Old Witch (blocking the way): Your shoes are too dirty.
Mother: I'll take them off.
Old Witch: Your feet are too dirty.

The mother grows tired of pacifying the old witch; she pushes the witch aside and enters the house. The children all stand with their hands over their faces.

Mother: These look like nice pies.
Old Witch: Very nice pies.
Mother (tasting pie): This needs more sugar.

After the old witch stirs in more sugar, the mother tastes again and says, "This tastes like Monday." Monday uncovers her face and the mother says, "It is Monday." She shakes her and says, "Run home, Monday." The mother then tastes each pie, adding more sugar or salt or fruit to each, after which she recognizes the taste of her children. When all have been sent home, the witch starts to run. The mother and children chase her, and the one who catches her becomes the next old witch. The second becomes the mother, who names those who are to be her children.

INDOOR GAMES

ANIMAL, VEGETABLE, MINERAL

One player is sent from the room. While he is gone the others decide upon some article in the room. He is then called back and tries to find out what has been selected by asking questions which can be answered yes or no. Beginning with "Animal? Vegetable? Mineral?" he asks each player a question in turn. His further questions may be prompted by articles he sees about him in the room. Anyone who answers other than yes or no becomes "it." If the player fails to guess the object, he is sent from the room while another article is chosen and the game is repeated.

HUNT THE THIMBLE

A variant of "Animal, Mineral, and Vegetable," also known as "Hide the Thimble" and "I Spy."

One child sends all the others from the room, after which he places a thimble in an inconspicuous place (but in plain sight). He calls the others back into the room and they search for the thimble. As each one sees the thimble, he says "I spy" and sits down. If it is rather difficult to find, the hider says "warm" when a searcher is near the thimble and "cold" when he goes away from it. After all have found it, the one who saw it first has the privilege of hiding it again. The game may be varied by sending only one child or half the children from the room while the others hide the thimble. Then the group sings a song and as the searcher or searchers get near or far from the thimble, the music gets softer or louder.

BUTTON, BUTTON

The players sit in a semicircle with palms held together. The player who is "it" holds a button between the palms of his hands and goes from one player to another, passing his clasped hands between those of the seated players. He secretly leaves the button in the hands of one of the players, but continues to play around the circle to mask the fact that he has already deposited the button. Then he says, "Button, button, who has the button?" Everyone guesses, in no particular order, and the one who guesses correctly passes the button next.

CROSS QUESTIONS AND CROOKED ANSWERS

The players, each with two slips of paper, sit in a circle. One player whispers a question to the next and receives an answer. The answering player then asks the player next to him a question and receives an answer, and so on around the circle. Each player then writes down on one slip the answer he gave and on the other the question he asked. The questions and answers are then collected in separate containers and passed back to the players in mixed order. Once more each player asks his neighbor a question, this time, however, reading the question from the slip of paper he has just received; the next player reads the answer from the slip of paper he has just received. The *non sequitur* answers furnish good entertainment.

BROTHER, I'M BOBBED

All who do not know the game leave the room. Two chairs are placed in the middle of the room. One who knows the game sits blindfolded on one chair, and one of the novice players is brought into the room, blindfolded, and seated on the other chair. There is suddenly the sound of a whack and the first player says, "Brother, I'm bobbed," and makes a great fuss. He tries to guess who did it but is unsuccessful and so receives further blows. The new player receives a whack, fails to identify the culprit, and receives further blows. The whacks grow more numerous and severe, and the new player is told that he will not be released until he guesses who is wielding the rolled newspaper. At last, in desperation, he takes off his blindfold and learns that the player in the other chair has been his tormentor, who was complaining of blows he did not receive and whose name, therefore, did not occur to the second player. The player just "bobbed" now becomes the "bobber" and a new victim is called in.

FORFEITS

One player sits on a chair in the middle of the room and acts as the judge. The leader stands behind him and holds a forfeit, some article like a knife, handkerchief, ring, necklace, or shoe— each player has surrendered one such item—over his head. He, the leader, then says, "Heavy, heavy, hangs over thy head." The judge then asks, "Fine or superfine?" If the article belongs to a boy, the leader answers, "Fine"; if a girl, "Superfine." The leader asks, "What must the owner do to redeem it?" The judge pronounces sentence and upon completion of the sentence the article is returned to the owner.

The following stunts are samples of the sentences imposed by the judge:

Ask a question that cannot be answered in the negative. (*What does y-e-s spell?*)

Pay a compliment to each person in the room.

Leave the room with two legs and come back with six. (*Walk out and bring back a chair.*)

Sit on a fire. (*Write "a fire" on a slip of paper and then sit on it.*)

Yawn until someone else yawns.

Make a speech on any subject assigned by the judge.

Hold one foot in your hand and hop around the room on the other.

Put four feet against the wall. (*Place the feet of a chair against the wall.*)

Make a pile of chairs as high as your head and then take off your shoes and jump over them. (*Jump over your shoes.*)

Kiss a book inside and outside without opening it. (*Take the book outside of the room and kiss it, then inside and kiss it again.*)

Take another boy by the arm and lead him before each lady present. Kiss the hand of each lady and after each kiss, carefully wipe the other boy's mouth with a handkerchief.

Crawl under the table and bark like a dog.

Imitate a little German band. (*Three or four forfeits are thus paid at the same time.*)

Bestow a smile on every person in the room.

Laugh in one corner of the room, sing in the second, cry in the third, and whistle or dance in the fourth.

Answer "no" to a question asked by each member of the group.

Put one hand where the other cannot touch it. (*Put the right hand on the left elbow.*)

Two players stand on an open newspaper so that they cannot touch each other. (*The newspaper is placed over the sill of a door and the door is closed between them.*)

Feed another player while blindfolded.

While blindfolded, blow out a candle.

Bray like a donkey.

Sing up the scale and down again.

Bow to the wittiest, kneel to the prettiest, and kiss the one you love best.

Eat a yard of string, rabbit fashion—nibbling it up into your mouth.

Toast your own health in a laudatory speech.

Sing a lullaby to an imaginary baby in your arms.

Say "Six mixed biscuits" six times.

Stand on one foot and count backwards from 100.

Count as far as you can with a single breath.

Say the alphabet backwards.

Spell Constantinople. (*As the victim reaches the syllable "ti," all the onlookers cry "no," which seems to indicate that a mistake has been made but "no" is in fact the next syllable.*)

Put on the hat of any person present and imitate him.

Stand on one leg and crow and flap your arms.

Make your will; bequests must be made to people present. (*The others have decided, without the forfeit payer's knowledge, what four things he must leave before his forfeit is completely paid.*)

While blindfolded, turn around three times and kiss the hand of the first person you touch.

Play an imaginary instrument.

Repeat a verse of poetry and count the number of words in it as you proceed.

Spell your own name backwards and in one breath.

BITE THE APPLE

The players' hands are tied behind their backs. Each player tries to bite an apple which is suspended from a string so that it hangs before his mouth. Sometimes a boy and a girl try to bite the same apple.

APPLE DUCK

A boy and a girl (or several players) try to capture, with their mouths, apples floating in a large pan of water. This and the game above are especially appropriate for Hallowe'en parties.

GOSSIP

The players are seated in a circle or a row. The leader hands a slip of paper with a short paragraph on it to the first player, who whispers it to his neighbor. Each player whispers what he can remember of what he has heard to his neighbor, until all have heard the gossip. The last player repeats aloud what he has heard, and this is compared with the paragraph on the paper.

GOING TO JERUSALEM

Also known as "Musical Chairs."

All the players are seated in chairs which have been placed facing alternately in opposite directions. While someone plays the piano, the leader carries a cane and walks around the room, saying, "I'm going to Jerusalem." Every few minutes he stops before some player and taps his cane on the floor. The player immediately rises and follows him, leaving a vacant chair. The leader continues to summon followers until all are marching. The music suddenly stops and all scramble for a seat, including the leader. There is, of course, one less chair than there are marchers; the one who fails to get a seat falls out of the game and one chair is taken from the row. The game continues until no chairs and only one player is left; he then becomes the new leader. The game may be played for the selection of partners. Two rows of chairs are used, one for the boys and another for the girls. The two who are left without chairs when the music stops become partners. The game continues until all have partners.

INDOOR–OUTDOOR GAMES

BLIND MAN'S BUFF

The center of the room is cleared and "Buff" (the player who is "it") is blindfolded. The other players ask, "How many horses has your father?" Buff answers, "Three." "What color are they?" "Black, white, and gray." And finally the players chorus, "Turn around three times and catch whom you may." Buff gropes about and tries to capture one of the other players. If he does catch one, he must identify him without removing his blindfold. If he guesses correctly, the captured player becomes Buff; otherwise, he must again be Buff. This can also be played as a circle game. The players join hands and circle around Buff until he claps his hands three times. Then, still blindfolded, he points to someone in the circle. This person then enters the circle and tries to evade Buff. If caught, he must submit to examination for identification, and the game proceeds as above.

JACOB AND RACHEL

Also known as "Reuben and Rachel." Basically it is a variation of "Blind Man's Buff."

The players join hands and form a circle. One player, "Jacob," stands blindfolded in the ring. The players circle around him until he calls "Stop" and points toward the ring. If he is pointing at a girl, she becomes "Rachel" and enters the ring. If he points between players or at a boy, the players circle again, until Jacob finally picks a Rachel. After she enters the ring, Jacob calls, "Rachel, where art thou?" Rachel must answer, "Jacob, here I am." At intervals Jacob calls "Rachel," attempting to locate her. After Jacob catches her, he has to guess who she is. Then Rachel is blindfolded and selects a

Jacob, whom she must catch and identify in the same way. Sometimes the ring of players assist Jacob or Rachel by making the ring smaller or larger.

FIND THE SLIPPER

All the players but one stand in a circle with hands behind their backs. The "slipper" (which can be any easily handled item) is passed around the circle behind the backs of the players and the player in the center tries to locate it. All the players make motions as if passing the slipper, so that it is difficult to find. When the player in the center finds it, the one who had it at that moment goes into the center. The players may also sit in a circle with their feet drawn up, so that the slipper can be passed under the knees. If the players sit, "it" stands outside the circle.

DO THIS, DO THAT

The players stand in a semicircle and face the leader. He acts out some activity, such as jumping, skipping, sewing, washing, dancing, and so forth, then assumes a pose and says, "Do this." The other players must follow suit. If the leader says, "Do that," the players who imitate him must drop out of the game and pay a forfeit.

Pioneer Cooking

Ever since the Divine Creator set the Universe spinning, man has depended on the good earth for his food, his raiment, and his equipment; and on our Sheridan County farm we certainly did find it the only source of things to keep soul and body together. Mother Nature, not a scientist with a test tube, originated the food we put on our table.

Charley O'Kieffe

The following account, taken from Nebraska Folklore Pamphlet No. 28, introduced the pioneer recipes collected in this volume.

Early Nebraska cooking, because of its lack of variety, often became unappetizing for even the least fastidious settlers. Sowbelly (salt pork), corn meal, and coffee were nearly always on the table for the main meals.

Corn

Corn, because it was cheaper and easier to grow than other foods, was the staple diet. Attempts were made to break the monotony by serving it in many different ways, but it still remained, as one old settler said, *corn*. Corn muffins, griddle cakes, corn cake, hominy, dry corn and milk (parched corn, ground and eaten with milk), corn on the cob, and corn gruel (for invalids) were some of the ways in which pioneer housewives attempted to disguise it on the table.

A more successful variation of the use of corn was new corn meal. This was considered a great delicacy in the '70's

307

and '80's, probably because it could be served only during the few weeks of the year when immature corn ears were available. These immature ears were first dried thoroughly in the sun, then ground off on a home-made gritter, which often consisted of a tin pan with its bottom perforated by nails. Matured corn was usually ground at a local mill, and the family sifted out the hulls with a wooden-rimmed shaker sieve.

Coffee and Substitutes

Coffee was sold green. The pioneers had to roast and grind it themselves. If they didn't own a small coffee mill, the beans were mashed in a bag. When the pioneers couldn't get to town or were short of money, a substitute coffee was used. Mrs. Nicholas Sharp, who lived in Gage County as early as 1867, tells of mixing corn meal and sorghum together until it became browned. It was pulverized before being placed in a coffee pot with water. The only resemblance this mixture had to boiled coffee was the color. When the amount of real coffee in the house was limited, a common practice was to reinforce it with a substitute. Some frontier connoisseurs even went so far as to consider two parts of dried peas to one part of coffee better than "straight" coffee. One settler tells how the Indians taught her to make "corn coffee." This was done by baking a whole ear of corn until it was burnt black, then putting it into the coffee pot. Other makeshift coffee substitutes consisted of parched barley, rye, wheat, and dried carrots.

Sorghum and Sugar

Very little canning was done in the 1870's because white sugar was both scarce and expensive. Later, as time went on, it came into more common use until virtually everything that required sweetening contained sugar in place of sorghum or honey. But sorghum, prepared at local sorghum mills, was the prevalent substitute for sugar for many years. It was used in pies, jellies, custards, bread, and coffee, although honey and maple sugar, with their more delicate flavors, often took its place when they could be obtained. On some occasions, when not even sorghum was available, a substitute of substitutes in the form of boiled-down watermelon juice was used. Mr. Swanson, who lived in Boone County during the '80's, mentioned another sugar substitute in the form of corncobs boiled down for their corn syrup. "It was good corn syrup, too," he adds. "I remember how we boys liked it."

What was known as "C" or "Orleans" sugar came into use during the late '70's and '80's. This sugar, shipped from Louisiana, was made by evaporating most of the moisture from corn syrup. This sugar was difficult to handle because when it became dry it formed into lumps that were quite hard. Frontier storekeepers constantly added water to it in order to keep it from lumping and to maintain its "selling weight."

Much of the early white sugar was sold in the form of cubes, commonly called loaves. (One loaf was usually equal to one teaspoon of granulated sugar.) This sugar was at first used only for such pioneer luxuries as pies, cakes, and jellies, and on the table. Dainty tongs, with which to pick up the sugar loaves, invariably hung on the side of the sugar bowl in well-appointed homes. But most settlers were not so formal. They picked up a cube with their fingers, and often put it in the mouth, holding it between their teeth and sipping coffee or tea through it. This rustic custom was supposed to improve the flavor of both the sugar and the coffee.

Smoked Meat

It was natural for the settlers to look forward with keen anticipation to butchering, since it meant fresh meat for the entire family and the neighbors, who, when they butchered, returned like portions of meat. A portion of pork, after being fried, was kept in large clay crocks, which were filled with lard. Some of the meat was smoked.

Nicholas Sharp, who came to the state in the 1870's, says that a makeshift smokehouse was sometimes made out of an inverted barrel placed over a small trench. Holes were bored in the side of the barrel for the insertion of sticks. The meat was hung on these sticks, under which a smoky fire was kept burning in the trench. After the smoking process, hams were wrapped in gunny sacks and covered with flour paste. This paste made an air-tight covering that helped to mellow the meat.

Preserving Fruits and Vegetables

Fruits and vegetables of many kinds were dried for off-season use. Pumpkins were sliced into thin rings and strung on cords in the sun, as were squash, apples, and even rhubarb. Pumpkin, according to Miss Estella Allen, who lived near Fillmore during the '70's, was also kept for winter use by cooking until most of the moisture had evaporated; then it was made into patties and thoroughly dried in the sun. String beans were strung and dried on cords. When cooked, both pods and beans were used.

Charles Miller, who lived in Thayer County during the '70's, says he always thinks of dried apples when pioneer fare is mentioned. A meal of water and dried apples made him feel as if he was moving through the air in a toy balloon. But the dried apples, for many, were an unsavory food. They were tough, leathery, dirty-brown in color, and nearly always fly-specked. One settler in Gage County described them in this ditty:

> Spit in my ears and tell me lies,
> But give me no dried apple pies.

Most of the frontier fruit, which grew wild, was found along the creek banks. It was the custom for the entire family to go fruit hunting in season. Plums, blackberries, gooseberries, grapes, currants, and wild strawberries were some of the most common of these fruits. In the summer and fall, attempts were always made to preserve wild fruits for winter use, though without sugar, which was scarce. Nicholas Sharp says that wild plums, always plentiful, were put in barrels after they had been scalded, and weighted down with a lid. Their own liquid, which turned into a form of vinegar, kept the fruit, although it was always sour and often unpalatable. When it was possible to obtain sorghum from the local mills, usually in the fall, the plums were sweetened with this sweet molasses, and stored in jars. Tomatoes were kept in the same way except that a strong salt brine was added. The brine had to be soaked out with cold water before the tomatoes could be eaten. Mr. Sharp, in his reminiscences, adds that prairie chickens and fish were salted down and kept in the same manner.

Mrs. Nellie Magee, who lived in Saunders County in the 1870's, has the following story to tell about corn-and-apple drying: "A young farm girl named Luella 'hired out' to a neighboring housewife during the fall season of 1872. Luella, who was a newcomer in Nebraska, did not understand all of the frontier customs, so every once in a while she made some strange mistakes. The most humorous of these occurred one afternoon when the lady of the house made preparations for drying corn and apples. The apple drying was simple, as all it required was a sharp knife with which to peel the fruit, after which the apples were sliced in round rings, threaded, and hung in the sun to dry. The housewife was called away to see a sick neighbor before Luella came to the corn. Luella, left alone, started in with the corn in the very way she had with the apples. She cut the kernels off the cobs, then began stringing them.

"Impatience could not have been one of Luella's faults, or tedious work a boredom. Because, during the course of the afternoon, she strung corn until all of the cotton thread was exhausted, after which she used spools of silk sewing thread. The housewife, upon her return near suppertime, stood speechless when she saw the bizarre effects created by the lines of gay-colored threads which carried their burdens of sweet-corn kernels. Needless to say, Luella finished her education on corn drying by using a lean-to roof and some mosquito netting."

Cookstoves

One of the early cookstoves (which was also used for heating the house) was the hay burner, used because of the scarcity of wood in a plains country. This resembled the ordinary cookstove except for the method of fuel feeding. Fuel was supplied by two iron pipes, or cylinders, about three feet long, racked full of hay and fastened to the rear of the stove. A spring forced the hay into the firebox as it was needed. A supply of a dozen pipes were kept filled and on hand for reloading the stove. Buffalo chips had been a common fuel before the years of settlement; later, when corn was raised on a large scale, corncobs were substituted for hay. The hay burner was then replaced by the common iron cookstove, still used by most of the Nebraska farm homes today [1940]. This stove was in wide use in the '70's in the eastern portion of the state, where wood could be found along the creek banks. Much of the wood, however, was green cottonwood that wouldn't burn readily. The sticks of wood had to be placed in the oven to be dried out before being used for fire.

In the summer, cooking was sometimes done out-of-doors in a *fire trench*, a small pit dug in the ground about a foot deep, two feet long, and wide enough to allow the pans to be placed over it. Mrs. Annie Ducker, who came to Custer County in 1873, tells of her father's first dugout, for which furnishings were so scanty that they had to use a blanket for a door. They had no cookstove at first; so, in order to bake bread, her brother dug a hole in the side of an earth bank and built a fire in it. This rude fireplace was used for several months. The practice was also common among ranchers on the roundup and freighters camping along the trail.

Another kind of cooking apparatus, used by the German-Russian settlers, was the brick oven built into a wall of the home. This oven was heated by lighting in it a fire of straw, hay, or other material and allowing it to burn out. The brick walls of the oven retained enough heat for cooking or baking.

A postscript to this account comes from Charley O'Kieffe's recollections. "During the summer months," he writes, "weeds contributed much to our table. As in most countries, weeds—

vegetables out of place, as some people call them—grew in profusion, creating lots of problems and entailing lots of work in their eradication or control. But in the O'Kieffe home our slogan was: 'If you can't beat 'em, eat 'em.' The names of three of these helpful little pests come to mind as I write: pigweed, lambsquarters, and pussley [purslane]. . . . Mother had a way of slipping a small hunk of salt pork in the pot with the cooking weeds and, brother, that made the difference" (18).

All the following recipes are more than seventy-five years old, and some have been in use for more than a hundred and twenty-five years. They were brought to Nebraska by settlers from the Eastern states, and by early immigrants from Czechoslovakia, Poland, Germany, Sweden, and Denmark. A few recipes, like the one for preparing wild rabbit, originated in the state. Most of the recipes were obtained by interviewing pioneers; the remainder are from the files of the *Nebraska Farmer* for 1877, the *Fremont Herald* (1878), and the *Seward Reporter* (1875).

BREADS, CEREALS, AND STUFFINGS

STARTER

Before the turn of the century, bread starter, also known as "sponge," was commonly used as a substitute for dry yeast. Often begun from a portion of a neighbor's starter, it was kept alive by sprinkling sugar over it after the portion needed for baking bread had been taken out. A cup of starter was considered equal to one cake of dry yeast or two cakes of compressed yeast.

CORN BREAD

Collected from Louise Pickrel, who won first prize with this recipe at the 1908 National Corn Exposition in Omaha and the 1909 Nebraska State Fair in Lincoln.

One cup of sponge, one cup of corn meal, two cups of flour, two teaspoons of salt, five teaspoons of sugar, and two tablespoons of melted or creamed lard. The sponge is prepared by soaking one-half cake of dry yeast in one-half cup of warm water and stirring in enough flour to make a thin batter (about one-half cup). This is allowed to stand overnight. The next morning scald the meal with one cup of boiling water; let it stand until lukewarm; stir in the sponge and add salt, lard, and two cups of flour (or enough to knead well). Let it stand until it gets light (about twice the original size). Mix it down until no air bubbles appear and let raise again. Make into small loaves and let it again stand until light. Bake one to one and one-half hours in a moderate oven.

CORN BREAD

One quart of good buttermilk, soda enough to neutralize the acid, salt to taste, three eggs, butter the size of a walnut, and corn meal to make a very thin batter. Beat well, turn into a buttered pan, and bake in a moderate oven. Do not mix the batter too stiff.

JOHNNYCAKE

One quart of corn meal, one teacup of cream. Put the cream in a quart cup and then fill it with sour milk. Add two eggs, two tablespoons of white flour, one teaspoon of saleratus [soda] and one-half cup of sugar. Sugar may be omitted. A little salt must be added. Bake in two pie tins for one-half hour.

GRAHAM BREAD

Prepare a sponge; put into a baking pan the next morning a proportionate quantity of flour, two-thirds graham and one-third white. To each quart add a large handful of Indian meal [corn meal] and a teaspoon of salt. Make a hole in the center of this mixture and add the sponge with two teaspoons of molasses for each medium-size loaf. The dough should be very soft. It will take a longer time to raise than white bread. When light, knead again, make into loaves, and set in a warm place for a second raising. Bake steadily in a moderate oven for a much longer time than you would allow for white bread.

GERMAN-RUSSIAN BREAD

Mix a regular bread dough. Add six egg yolks, one quart of warm milk, one-half pound of melted butter. Beat six egg whites, add one cup of sugar, and mix all of the ingredients together. Let raise the same as plain bread and bake in loaves.

MUFFINS WITHOUT YEAST

Three pints of flour, one quart of milk, two eggs, three teaspoons of baking powder with the flour. Beat the eggs very light and mix. Bake in muffin pans in a quick oven.

SODA BISCUITS

Take four large cups of sifted flour in which one large teaspoon of soda and two teaspoons of cream of tartar have been well mixed with one teaspoon of salt. Add one-half cup of butter and mix thoroughly. To this add a pint of sweet milk, a little at a time, and mix with as little kneading as possible. Bake in a quick oven for eight to ten minutes.

SWEDISH COFFEE BREAD

One and one-half quarts of milk, one cup of bread starter, three cups of sugar, one-half pound of butter, one teaspoon of ground cardamon seed, enough flour to make a soft dough, one teaspoon of salt. Mix the flour, warm milk, one cup of sugar, and the starter. Set to raise. When light, add rest of sugar, cardamon seed, butter, and flour. Work well. Let raise again before rolling out.

RYE BREAD

Take one quart of warm water, one teacup of yeast, and thicken with rye flour. Put in a warm place to raise overnight. In the morning scald one pint of Indian meal [corn meal] well. When cool, add sponge, salt, a little molasses, one pint of warm water, and rye flour to knead very soft. Let raise and place in pans. Again let raise; then bake. The dough should never be molded stiff for rye bread and the flour may be wholly worked in with an iron spoon instead of hands.

BROWN BREAD

Three cups of corn meal, two cups of rye flour, two-thirds of a cup of molasses, three and one-half cups of warm water, and one teaspoon of soda. Steam for four hours.

BOSTON BROWN BREAD

Collected by the Nebraska Department of Public Instruction.

One cup of rye meal, one cup of granulated corn meal, one cup of graham flour, two cups of sour milk, three-fourths of a teaspoon of soda, one teaspoon of salt, three-fourths of a cup of molasses. Mix and sift the dry ingredients; add molasses and milk. Stir until well mixed. Turn into a well-buttered mold and steam for three and one-half hours. The cover should be buttered before placing on the mold and then tied down with string; otherwise the bread in raising might force the cover off. The mold should never be filled more than two-thirds full.

BREAKFAST MUFFINS

Two eggs, well beaten with a cupful of sugar, and a lump of butter the size of an egg. To this add one pint of milk with a teaspoon of soda, one quart of flour, and two tablespoons of cream of tartar. Bake in muffin rings or in gem pans in a quick oven.

BUCKWHEAT CAKES

Collected from the Nebraska Farmer, *1877.*

Mix one-half cup of wheat flour with one quart of buckwheat flour, add one large tablespoon of salt, and then add gradually a scant quart of warm water mixed with one-fourth cup of yeast. Let it raise all night. In the morning add a quarter of a teaspoon of soda and bake immediately. Bake on a smooth, well-greased iron griddle, taking care to scrape it well after each baking; use as little grease as possible. The cakes should not be larger than a small saucer and should be served at once.

MUSH ROLLS

One quart of boiling water, well salted; stir in corn meal as for mush. One cup of lard and butter, one cup of sugar; mix into mush. When cool enough, add one pint of bread sponge. Let raise, stiffen with flour, and let raise again. Roll out, spread with butter, cut round, fold over, put in pan. Let raise again and bake.

OATMEAL MUSH WITH APPLES

Collected by the Nebraska Department of Public Instruction, in 1911.

Core the apples, leaving large cavities; pare and cook until soft in a syrup made by boiling sugar and water together. Fill the cavities with oatmeal mush; serve with sugar and cream.

INDIAN MEAL MUSH

Collected from the Seward Reporter, *August 12, 1875.*

White and yellow corn meal are made into the well-known mush called hasty pudding. It should be stirred very gradually into boiling water to avoid lumping. It should cook from one to two hours.

MEATS

WILD RABBIT

After cleaning the rabbit, wash it in cold water and hang to freeze in order to loosen the meat fibers. Soak it for a short time in salt water before cooking; this will draw out the blood. Cut into pieces and wash each piece in cold water. Put the pieces in a stew pan filled with water to which a pinch of soda has been added. Bring to a simmer. Remove from the stove and pour off the water. Put the rabbit back in the pan and stew the meat for about three hours. When the meat is loose from the bone but not shredded, add fat with a little bacon, and fry or bake for about one-half hour.

PRESSED CHICKEN

Collected from the Nebraska Farmer, *1877.*

Cut the chicken into about four parts and boil them in as little water as possible; when tender take the meat out but keep the broth boiling. Take off the skin, pick the meat from the bones, chop it, put in some butter, pepper, and salt, and use this broth to moisten the meat. Dip off the oil before adding the broth to the meat. Press.

SWEDISH MEAT BALLS

One and one-half pounds of lean ground pork, one-half pound of ground beef, one egg, one-half cup of bread crumbs soaked in milk, one cup of freshly mashed potatoes. Salt and pepper to taste and add a little allspice. Mix and roll into balls and then fry. After frying, put on a little water and cover. Place on a very slow fire for ten or fifteen minutes to simmer.

DANISH SPICED MEAT ROLL

Clean a beef flank. Cut away all bones and spread on a board. If it is too big, cut into desired sizes. Sprinkle with salt, pepper, and a layer of sliced onions. Roll the flank tightly together and sew with strong thread. Soak in a strong salt brine for three days. Before cooking, wind tightly with strong string to prevent meat from falling apart. Place in a pan with enough water to cover the meat and then cook it until tender. When it is done, put it in a heavy press for a day. Remove the string and slice in thin slices.

SWEDISH HEAD CHEESE

Three pounds of pork shank, one pound of veal shank, two pounds of beef shank, two pig's feet. Boil everything together. When cool, slice into cubes, put in a cloth, and season with pepper and salt. Pour hot juice over it and let stand in a pan with a heavy weight on it. After it is pressed, remove the cloth and place the meat in a brine in a crock.

KOLDAIMA

Collected from Mrs. John A. Anderson of Lincoln.

Take one medium head of solid cabbage and boil until half done; remove and drain until cool. Take beef or veal and grind fine. Season with salt and pepper, a little butter, cream, and a pinch of sugar. Work all together until well mixed; cut large leaves from cabbage, place spoonful of mixture in each leaf, roll, fold, and fasten with toothpicks. Brown in butter, add enough water to cover, and boil slowly for one and one-half hours. May be served with brown gravy.

BOHEMIAN PRESSED BLOOD SAUSAGE

Boil head, snout, ears, tongue, and a piece of meat from the neck. When done, cool and dice. Add rendered lard and cracklings, fresh blood, salt, pepper, ginger, and allspice fried in lard. Fill a cleaned pork stomach with this and boil an hour. When you pierce it with a toothpick and no blood runs out it is done. Place in a press in a warm place. Serve with vinegar and pepper or vinegar and onion.

POLISH BLOOD SAUSAGE

When killing pork, catch the blood and beat it so it will not clot. Boil a piece of pork from the neck and a piece of leaf lard until partly done, then cut up fine. Divide this into two parts. To one add stale white bread soaked in milk and squeezed dry, half the blood, salt, grated lemon rind, pepper, ground allspice, ginger, cloves, minced onion fried in lard, and enough melted lard to make it rather moist; mix well. Fill a thoroughly cleaned casing, fasten the ends, and boil. To the other half add barley that has been boiled, the rest of the blood, salt, pepper, and the spices listed above. Put in the casings and boil.

Varonikas

Collected from Rabbi Harry Jolt of Lincoln.

One cup of left-over mashed potatoes, two eggs, four table-spoons of Matzoth (kosher) flour, chopped left-over veal, salt, and pepper. Add beaten eggs, flour, and seasoning to the potatoes and mix thoroughly. Shape into balls. Scoop a hole in the center of each ball and fill with chopped meat. Cover the opening with the potato mixture. Roll again, dip in matzoth meal and egg, and fry in chicken fat until golden brown.

VEGETABLES

Hominy

Use white corn if available; it must be plump. Shell and boil in a weak lye until the hull is broken. Clean off the lye, fill a kettle, or turn the corn into a dishpan. Rinse well (the old way is nine times, but six will do). Clean the kettle and return to the stove; add plenty of water and boil until the corn is very tender, which usually takes an entire day. As the water boils away add more hot water.

Baked Cabbage

Boil a firm, white cabbage for fifteen minutes in salted water; change the water for more that is boiling and boil until tender. Drain, cool, and chop the cabbage fine. Place chopped cabbage in buttered baking dish.

To make the sauce: put a tablespoon of butter in a pan. When it bubbles up well, stir in one tablespoon of flour, one-half pint of stock, and one-half pint of water, both boiling. Stir until smooth, season with salt and pepper, and mix well with four tablespoons of grated cheese. Pour this over the cabbage, sprinkle with rolled crackers, dot with lumps of butter, and place in a quick oven for ten minutes.

PICKLING CABBAGE
Collected from the Nebraska Farmer, *1877.*

Remove large leaves, grate them nicely, boil until tender, and drain. Boil vinegar, pepper, allspice, sugar (one teacup to each quart of vinegar, or more if the vinegar is very strong), etc. [*sic*], for five or ten minutes and pour over the cabbage.

PUDDINGS

GREEN CORN PUDDING
Collected from the Nebraska Farmer, *1877.*

Twelve ears of green corn (grated), one quart of sweet milk, three tablespoons of sugar, and three eggs. Bake in a buttered dish until the mixture begins to thicken. Butter the top and bake brown.

POPCORN PUDDING
Collected from the Seward Reporter, *August 12, 1875.*

Soak two quarts of freshly popped corn in three pints of sweet milk overnight. When ready to bake, add three well-beaten eggs, a little salt, and sugar to taste. Bake like a custard pudding.

SWEET POTATO PUDDING
Beat to a cream one pound of butter and one pound of sugar. Boil and mash fine two pounds of sweet potatoes; beat the potatoes by degrees into the butter and sugar. Add five well-beaten eggs, a wineglass each of wine, brandy, and rose water, two teaspoons of mixed spices, and a half-pint of cream. Bake in a crust.

SOUPS

CORN SOUP

One pint each of corn, boiling water, and milk, one slice of onion, two tablespoons of butter, two tablespoons of flour, one teaspoon of salt, a few grains of pepper. Chop the corn, add the water, and simmer for twenty minutes; run the mixture through a sieve. Scald the milk with the onion and add the milk to the corn. Thicken with mixture of butter and flour. Add salt and pepper.

DANISH DUMPLING SOUP

Collected from Reverend S. S. Nielsen of Lincoln.

Put four pounds of boiling meat in a kettle with enough water to cover. When boiling, skim the soup until it has a clear appearance. Add diced carrots, minced onions, and celery and salt to taste. When the meat is about done, add diced potatoes. Before serving, add dumplings.

GERMAN-RUSSIAN FRUIT SOUP

This traditional Good Friday dish was known as Schnitzsuppe.

Two pounds of mixed dried fruit, one pound of raisins, one tablespoon of flour, one-half cup of milk, one-half cup of sugar, and one egg. Cook the mixed fruits until tender. Mix the flour and milk, and add to the soup while it boils. Mix the sugar and egg; add to the soup but do not boil.

PRINCE WILLIAM SOUP

Cook slowly, in enough water to cover, a mixture of dried fruits such as apricots, prunes, peaches, pears, raisins, and currants. Add a little soaked tapioca to thicken and cook slowly until done.

SAUCES AND PICKLES

PRESERVED GREEN TOMATOES

Boil green, stemmed tomatoes in plenty of water until tender, but do not let them break. Pour off the water. Make a syrup, allowing one pound of sugar to each pint of boiled fruit. Add bruised ginger, lemon peel which has been pared very thin, and lemon juice to taste. Boil the tomatoes until they are very clear. Just before removing from the fire, add a small quantity of brandy (about two tablespoons to six pounds of fruit).

Chow-Chow

Chop fine two quarts of green tomatoes, one quart of white onions, one dozen each of green peppers and cucumbers, and one large head of cabbage. Season with mustard and celery seed to taste and cover with the best cider vinegar. Boil slowly for two hours, stirring often. Take from stove and add two tablespoons of salad oil. Cover tightly and keep cool.

Green Tomato Pickles

Chop fine a bushel of green tomatoes and drain in a colander. Add one-quarter pound each of white mustard seed and whole allspice, six green peppers chopped fine, three tablespoons of ground cloves, and one teacup of salt. Mix well and put into a stone jar. Add one gallon of hot, scalded vinegar and set away to cool. Cover tightly when cool.

CAKE AND COOKIES

Many of the following recipes were prepared with sugar substitutes, usually sorghum molasses or wild honey. See pages 308 f.

Poverty Cake

Collected from the Seward Reporter, *August 12, 1875.*

Two cups of thin cream, two cups of chopped raisins, two cups of sugar, four cups of flour, one teaspoon of soda, salt, and spice.

Soft Gingerbread

Half-cup of sugar, half-cup of molasses, one cup of shortening, two eggs, one heaping teaspoon of soda, and flour. Do not make too stiff. Stir the soda in the molasses till it foams and beat the eggs and sugar together.

GINGERBREAD

One cup each of sugar, molasses, buttermilk, and sour cream, butter the size of an egg, one tablespoon of ginger, one teaspoon of soda, one teaspoon of any kind of spice, flour enough to roll out. This recipe will make three loaves, to be baked in long tins.

RAILROAD CAKE

Beat two eggs in a teacup and beat well. Then fill the cup with sweet cream; add to this one cup of sugar, one and one-half cups of flour, and one teaspoon of soda.

FARMER'S CAKE

Beat together one egg and the yolk of another, one cup of sugar, and a lump of butter as large as a hen's egg. Add half a nutmeg, one cup of sour cream, two-thirds of a teaspoon of soda, and one heaping cup of flour. The whites of two additional eggs and a teaspoon of essence of lemon may be added; the nutmeg may be omitted.

SWEET CORN CAKE

Collected from the Nebraska Farmer, *1877.*

Beat three eggs lightly; add one cup of sour milk or cream, one cup of flour, one and one-half cups of sugar, and one-half cup of butter or lard; then add corn meal to make a middling stiff batter, nutmeg or any kind of spice, and one teaspoon of soda. Baking powder and one cup of raisins may be added.

SPONGE CAKE

Beat together four eggs and two coffee cups of sugar. Add two coffee cups of flour, two teaspoons of cream of tartar, one teaspoon of soda, and then two-thirds of a cup of boiling water. Add lemon to flavor. Place in a well-heated oven.

COFFEE CAKE

One cup each of brown sugar, butter, strained coffee, and molasses, three well-beaten eggs, one pound of raisins, two cups of flour, and two teaspoons of baking powder.

PORK FRUIT CAKE (I)

Pour one pint of boiling water over one pound of finely chopped pork; let stand until cool. Add one cup of molasses, two cups of sugar, two eggs, one tablespoon of cinnamon, cloves and allspice, two teaspoons of cream of tartar, one teaspoon of soda, one pound of chopped raisins, and enough flour to make it the consistency of any stirred cake. Bake very slowly. The longer the cake is kept, the better it becomes.

PORK FRUIT CAKE (II)

Three-fourths of a pound of pork chopped fine, one pound of raisins, one pound of currants, one pound of sugar, three-fourths of a pound of citron, one gill of molasses, four cups of flour, one teaspoon of soda, two eggs, one teacup of water.

ROYAL FRUIT CAKE

Five cups of flour, five eggs, one and one-half cups of sugar, one cup of molasses, one and one-half cups of butter, one teaspoon of saleratus [baking soda], one-half cup of milk, two pounds of chopped raisins, three pounds of currants, two teaspoons of allspice, two tablespoons of cinnamon, and two teaspoons of cloves.

APPLE BREAD

Weigh out one pound of fresh, juicy apples; peel, core, and stew them to a pulp in a porcelain kettle or stone jar placed in a kettle of boiling water. Mix the pulp with two pounds of the best flour, the same quantity of yeast you would use for common bread, and as much water as will make it a fine, smooth dough. Place in a pan in a warm place to raise for at least twelve hours. Shape in long loaves and bake in a quick oven.

APPLE SHORTCAKE

Make a soft dough as for biscuits. Roll this out and put a layer in a jelly pan. Over this spread a layer of stewed apples; sprinkle with sugar and spices, dot with small lumps of butter, and add another layer of dough, applesauce, and spices as above. Top with a very thin layer of dough and bake in a very quick oven.

SWEDISH GINGER COOKIES
Collected from Mrs. John A. Anderson of Lincoln.

One cup of butter, one cup of brown sugar, one-half cup of molasses, two beaten eggs, one teaspoon of baking powder, one-half teaspoon of soda in the molasses, one-half teaspoon of cloves, one teaspoon of cinnamon, and one-half teaspoon of ginger.

GENUINE GINGER SNAPS

One cup of shortening (equal parts of butter and lard), one pint of molasses, one-half pint of brown sugar, one tablespoon of ginger, one teaspoon of cloves or cinnamon, flour. Mix well until it becomes a pliant dough. Roll thin and bake in a quick oven.

HONEY COOKIES

Beat together until they froth two eggs and one pint of honey. Add one-half cup of butter and one cup of sweet milk. Add one-half grated nutmeg, flour, and yeast powder.

KLEJNER COOKIES
Collected from the Reverend S. S. Nielsen of Lincoln.

Mix one pint of sweet cream, two eggs, and one tablespoon of sugar. Work in as much flour as it will take to make the mixture slip off the hands. Roll it out until it is the thickness of the back of a knife. Cut in strips five by two inches. Cut a slit in the middle of each strip and stick one end through the slit so that the cake is twisted in the middle. Cook in hot grease until light brown.

RHUBARB TARTS

Cut the stalks from the leaves and peel off the skin. Dice, wash, and put into a saucepan with no more water than that which adheres to them. Add enough sugar to make the sauce sweet. Simmer slowly until thick. When done and cool, line patty pans with good stiff paste, add filling, and bake in a quick oven.

GERMAN-RUSSIAN DOUGHNUTS (KLÖSSE)

Mix four cups of flour, three eggs, one-half cup of sugar, two cups of milk, two teaspoons of baking powder, and two teaspoons of salt. Roll flat, cut into five-inch squares, and slash the centers. Fry in hot lard. Take one-half cup of sugar and put into a large sack. Drop the cooked doughnuts into the sack and shake so that the sugar coats the doughnuts.

KOLACHES

Scald one pint of milk and let it cool until lukewarm. Dissolve one and one-half cakes of compressed yeast in one-fourth cup of lukewarm water to which has been added one teaspoon of sugar. Let raise while the milk cools. Add the dissolved yeast to the cooled milk and make a sponge. Let it raise until light and roll out to a half-inch thickness. Cut out with a biscuit cutter. Make a depression in the center and fill. Let raise and bake in a quick oven. Any of the following fillings may be used:

Fruit filling: Mash stewed prunes. Add sugar and cinnamon. Sprinkle with coconut or chopped nuts. Apricots, peaches, apples, or any canned fruit may be used.

Poppy seed filling: Grind poppy seeds and boil in just enough water to keep moist. Then add sugar, cinnamon, maple syrup, raisins, and three or four ginger snaps.

Cottage cheese filling: Combine grated lemon rind, one-half cup of sugar, one tablespoon of cream, two egg yolks, and one pint of dry cottage cheese.

JAMS AND JELLIES

CURRANT JELLY

Strip the currants off the stems and bruise them thoroughly. Put on the fire to heat and strain them when they reach the boiling point. To each pint of juice add a pound of loaf sugar. Boil for fifteen minutes.

RHUBARB JAM

To six pounds of diced rhubarb add six pounds of lump sugar and six large, seeded, finely sliced lemons. Put the fruit into a bowl and cover with crushed sugar. Let stand for twenty-four hours. Boil slowly for three-quarters of an hour; do not stir too much but do not allow the mixture to stick to the bottom of the pan. If the fruit is gathered in dry weather, it will keep any length of time.

Nebraska Folk Cures

Pauline Monette Black

[This monograph, published in 1935, is Number 15 in the University of Nebraska Studies in Language, Literature, and Criticism. It is presented here in slightly abridged form.]

Folk cures form a conspicuous part of Nebraska lore. Nebraska pioneers from many states and many countries brought with them certain remedies which they believed particularly efficacious, and which became a tradition in families or communities throughout the state. The cures in the following collection have come directly from the residents of the state and are not limited to any specific locality. They have been recorded as nearly as possible just as the informants gave them. Some alterations have been made in diction and sentence structure to clarify ambiguity. The collection is doubtless incomplete, but it lists, I believe, most of the folk cures now prevalent, or used at one time, in Nebraska. Only a few suggestions have been made concerning the origins of the remedies. In these instances the informant knew the immediate source of the cure which he reported. Obviously in a state where the population is as mixed as in Nebraska, any attempt to trace all folk cures to accurate sources would be futile.

The remarks prefacing each section reveal that some of the diseases for which there are folk cures lend themselves more readily to strange remedies than others. I do not know the explanation for their greater popularity. Nor do I know how widely the cures listed in the following pages are believed in and made use of at the present time. Many have been reported to me as currently employed here and there over the state with faith in their efficacy. Some are cited by their contributors as traditional cures of doubtful value. Others are kept alive in the mouths of persons who repeat them with unmistakable jocularity or skepticism.

CURES FOR ACHES

Headache and earache seem to be the most frequent aches for which folk cures have currency. Toothache cures, which are also common, are treated under a separate heading.

Although there seem to be no explanations in Nebraska for the origin of earache or headache, one informant from Table Rock, Nebraska, submits a curious explanation for chronic headache. She affirms that the combings of hair from the head of a person who has headache always must be burned, lest some bird find them and build its nest with them. If the latter happens, the person from whose head the combings were taken will suffer from headache until the fledglings leave the nest.

Headache

Blow smoke in the ear of a person who has headache.

Carry rattlesnake rattlers in your hat band to cure headache.

Wear earrings to cure headache.

Cure headache by rubbing a stone on your forehead. (Reported as an Indian cure.)

Tie a red bandana handkerchief around the head to cure headache.

Let your hair grow long to cure and to prevent headache.

A person born in October has power to cure a headache by rubbing the forehead and temples.

Paste a leaf of cottonwood on each temple and leave it there until it falls off and takes the skin with it. The patient will never again be bothered with headache.

Put a mustard plaster on the back of the neck and one under each foot. Let them stay on about five minutes and then remove. The headache will be gone.

If a man has headache, put a bowl on his head. Then cut his hair around the bowl, and burn all the hair. This will stop headache.

Soak the feet in hot water to cure headache.

Earache

Heat a seeded raisin very hot over a kerosene lamp or a fire. Put the raisin into the aching ear and close the entrance with cotton.

Drop one drop of very cold water into an aching ear. This is a permanent cure for earache.

Bake a potato, split it and put it over the ear to let the steam go into the ear.

Thin out a piece of cotton and fill it with black pepper. Make a small ball of it and put it into the ear.

Drink camomile tea to act as a sedative when you have earache or headache.

Melt a grubworm and use the warm oil in the ear of a person who has earache. The aching will stop.

The wax in the ear of a person who does not have earache will cure the earache in another person's ear.

Chop onions and strong tobacco together, using half as much tobacco as onions. Wrap in a wet cloth and roast in ashes. Squeeze out the juice and put three or four drops into the ear. It gives almost instant relief to earache.

Put human milk in the ear to cure earache.

Pour a teaspoonful of warm water into the ear. Let it remain awhile, then let it run out.

Put mare's milk in the ear to cure earache.

Put sweet oil or olive oil in your ear to cure earache.

Have someone blow smoke in your ear to cure earache. The smoke must be from a pipe.

Have someone spit tobacco juice in your ear to cure your earache.

COLDS AND RELATED AILMENTS

It is not surprising that more cures are available for colds than for any other ailment. There are few persons who have not at some time experienced one or more symptoms of a cold, thereupon finding themselves the center of interest to solicitous friends, each of whom volunteers the best and only home remedy which will exterminate the cold germ. Their suggestions may range from wearing a soiled, black cotton stocking around the neck with the heel always placed directly over the Adam's apple, to plasters made of mustard, lard, turpentine, or onions. There are many variations of these remedies. Some persons prefer a clean silk stocking to one of soiled, black cotton. Others advocate the healing propensities of a red, wool sock. The plasters themselves vary much in the number and proportion of each ingredient used and the exact location of the plaster to assure the best results to the patient.

Cold

For a chest cold, make a flaxseed poultice and put it on the chest.

For a cold on the lungs, put heavy brown paper over the lungs.

Wear a mustard plaster made from a mixture of mustard and white flour, then mixed with water and spread between two cotton or wool cloths.

Put three tablespoons of asafœtida into one quart of whiskey. Shake well. For children the dose is one tablespoonful. Adults should use their own judgment as to the amount.

Make a tea from the leaves of the mullein plant. Gather the leaves when the plant is in bloom.

A mixture of turpentine and lard rubbed on the neck and the chest will cure a cold.

Gargle a solution of salt and vinegar for a cold.

Rub on goose grease. It must be goose grease rather than any other kind to cure the cold.

Drink whiskey with rock candy dissolved in it to cure a cold.

Wear a clean, silk stocking around your neck to cure a cold.

Grease the chest and neck with hot skunk oil to cure a cold.

Drink a tea made of sage and catnip to cure a cold.

Eat asafœtida as well as wear it around your neck.

Gather the red seeds of the sumac bush. Make a tea of them and sweeten well with honey or sugar. Drink to cure a cold.

Eat fried onions to cure a cold. Put fried onions around your neck also.

Put some honey on a sheet of heavy paper. Hold it over a kerosene lamp until the honey boils, then eat the honey. This will cure a cold.

Spread a woolen cloth with butter. Sprinkle it with pepper and put it on the chest to cure a cold.

Drink horehound tea for colds.

Wrap a cold wet cloth around the neck, then a dry cloth over the wet cloth before going to bed.

Rub a mixture of camphor and lard on the neck and chest.

Drink hot ginger tea to cure colds.

Slice a lemon, rind, seeds, and all, and boil it in a cup of water until there is about a cup of pulp left. Let it set all night and eat it in the morning before breakfast. Repeat this for three days.

Soak the feet in hot water in which mustard or ginger has been added.

Wear an onion plaster on your chest to cure a cold.

Rub goat tallow on the neck and chest.

Skin a skunk. Then cut the ribs and legs from the rest of the body. Put the body in a pan over the fire in the open. Cook until no more grease will come out. Then take out the meat which is left, and give the grease by teaspoonfuls to the sick person.

To cure colds, rub the chest, the palms of the hands, and the soles of the feet with goose grease.

Cold Sores

Rub earwax on cold sores to cure them.

Rub the head of a match over them.

When you think you are getting a cold sore, rub behind your ear and then rub your lip. Do this three times in succession. Cold sores will not come then.

Cough

Gather the blossoms from elderberry bushes and dry them. Make them into tea to give as a cure for a cough.

For a tickling cough caused by getting the feet wet, take one-half of a teaspoon of plain coal oil straight down. It gives instant relief.

Make a syrup of kerosene, sugar, and onion juice, and take as often as necessary to cure a cough.

Make a syrup of flaxseed for cough medicine.

Make a syrup of vinegar, butter, and molasses.

Make a syrup of slippery elm bark steeped in water and mixed with honey and licorice.

To cure a tickling cough, cut all the fuzz off a feather, leaving only a brush-like surface. Tickle your throat with it to counteract the original tickle.

Mix sulphur, molasses, cream of tartar, flaxseed syrup, and slippery elm bark to make a cough syrup.

Croup

Apply a flannel cloth saturated with lard, kerosene, and turpentine to the chest to cure croup.

For croup, drink a mixture of alum and sugar. Boil the leaves of the horehound plant. Take the liquid and make a syrup of it by adding sugar or home-made syrup or rock candy.

Pour hot water over mullein leaves. Let it steep a few minutes, then draw the water off and sweeten it a little. This cures croup.

Eat a teaspoonful of kerosene to cure croup.

Render lard from a skunk and apply it to the throat and chest of a child who has croup.

Sore Throat

Touch the tongue with a drop of oil of wintergreen for an instant cure for sore throat.

Boil the inner bark from an oak tree until you obtain a dark brown fluid. Cool, and gargle three times a day.

Cut bacon in strips and dip it in vinegar. Then tie it around the throat to cure sore throat.

Eat raisins to cure a sore throat.

Wear a slice of fat pork under a flannel cloth around your neck.

Wear a necklace of amber beads to cure or to ward off sore throat.

Make sliced tomatoes into a bandage and tie them around the throat.

Wear a red woolen sock bound around your throat. The sock must have been removed recently from the foot so that it is still warm.

Wear a soiled, black, cotton or wool stocking around the neck to cure sore throat.

Wear a rubber band around your arm to cure sore throat.

Wear some red wool yarn around your neck to cure sore throat.

Put a slice of fat salt pork on your throat. Be sure to cover it with your own dirty stocking, and put a piece of flannel on the outside. Some persons sprinkle pepper on the pork.

Influenza

To cure influenza, the Indians in Nebraska placed the sick person in a little tent and packed hot rocks around him. Friends outside the tent kept heating rocks and packing them around the sick Indian. As soon as he was wet with perspiration he leaped out into the ice-cold water to chase the evil spirit away. Many of the Indians died from this "cure."

Pneumonia

Fry sliced onions with rye flour and make a poultice of it. Apply this to the chest and lungs to cure pneumonia.

Cut a live chicken in two and place it over the lungs of a sick person to cure pneumonia.

Rub the chest and the neck with kerosene and lard.

Cook onions thickened with cornmeal, and place the mixture while it is warm over the lungs.

Wilt large cabbage leaves over a fire to make them soft, then put them over the sick person's chest, sides, and back. Wrap a thin cloth around them to hold them on and pour on hot vinegar. It will make the person sweat and break up the pneumonia.

Whooping Cough

Drink warm mare's milk to cure whooping cough.

One drop of belladonna taken on sugar three times a day will cure whooping cough.

Make a drug from the buttercup to cure whooping cough.

Chestnut leaves made into syrup will cure whooping cough.

Colic

Take a teaspoonful of soot in a cloth. Pour over it three table-spoonfuls of hot water. Let it steep awhile, then give the baby a teaspoonful every half hour.

Have the baby's mother chew caraway seed and blow her breath in the face of the child who has colic.

Feed a baby a few drops of peppermint on a teaspoonful of sugar, or a lump of sugar, to cure colic. Sweetened water fed to the child will also cure colic.

Blow tobacco smoke in a spoonful of milk and give it to the child.

Hiccoughs

Let someone scare the person who has hiccoughs and the fright will cure him.

Drink nine swallows of water, holding the breath. Then think of the person with whom you are in love and take the tenth swallow. The hiccoughs will be gone.

When you have hiccoughs think of a member of the opposite sex. If that person loves you, the hiccoughs will go away.

Fill a dessert spoon half full of sugar and fill the rest with vinegar. Swallow this to cure hiccoughs.

If you have hiccoughs, think of someone. If that person is thinking of you, the hiccoughs will leave.

Hold the breath and count to ten and the hiccoughs will be gone.

Drink ten swallows of water without drawing a breath.

Eat a teaspoonful of sugar and follow it immediately with a drink of water.

Have someone pull your tongue hard until your mouth bleeds a little. This is a sure cure for hiccoughs.

Other Cures

Smoke mullein leaves in a pipe to cure catarrh.

To cure chills, wear nutmeg on a string around your neck.

Drink warm animal blood to cure consumption. (This cure is used widely along the Dismal River in Thomas county.)

Eat quantities of watercress as a salad to cure lung trouble.

To cure quinsy, gargle gunpowder and glycerin mixed.

EYE TROUBLE

Eyes lend themselves readily to superstitious cures based upon charms and incantations. The most widely circulated eye cure is for sties. Despite the fact that sties are now much less common than they once were, one can find many suggestions for curing them or transferring them from one person to another.

The most popular cure is to rub the sty with a gold wedding ring. The ring has long been the symbol of eternity, possessing extraordinary remedial powers. "But the real merit of the wedding ring is not because it is of gold, but because it is something which, once given, cannot be reclaimed. In the West Indies if you give a thing away and take it back, you are sure to have a stye, you will be told" (W. G. Black, *Folk-Medicine*, London, 1883, p. 173). Thus, the wedding ring, which can never be taken back, has in that region, special powers to cure sties. Although Nebraskans cling to this use of the wedding ring to cure their sties, they offer no explanation for its curative powers. It may be that the Nebraska cure is an outgrowth of the superstition prevalent in the West Indies and widely accepted in the Old World.

There are two current explanations in Nebraska for the coming of sties. One is that if a person urinates in the road he will get a sty. The other is that sties are caused by a chair which is so held above the eyes that the legs point toward the eyes. Persons believing this are careful when carrying a chair never to lift it so high that the legs point toward them. This belief is common in Swedish communities and is of Swedish origin. The word "sty" in Swedish is *stolsteg* which literally means "stool step." In other words, if the stool or chair "steps" on you, you will get a sty. It was suggested in Oakland, a Swedish community in Burt county, that perhaps fear of the chair's hitting the eye may cause eye strain eventually leading to a sty.

A wedding ring rubbed on a sty in the eye will cure it. The ring may be either gold or brass.

To cure a sty, rub it with a cat's tail.

Rub turpentine on a sty that has just started.

Spit on a sty to cure it by rubbing a moistened finger over it.

Startle the person who thinks a sty is forming on the lid of his eye, and the sty will never come.

Walk to the first corner and repeat:

> Sty, sty go off my eye
> And take the first that passes by.

Be careful that you are not the first to go by that corner yourself or you will get the sty back.

Rub scraped potato on your eye.

Go for a ride early in the morning. Stop at the first crossroads and say:

> Sty, sty, come off my eye
> And go to the next passer-by.

Do not look at this spot again until you are sure that someone has gone by.

Bathe sore eyes with tea made from mashed mulberry leaves to heal them.

For inflamed eyes, make an eye wash from the root of wild roses. (This cure was reported as of Pawnee Indian origin.)

Rub the eyes with saliva every morning before breakfast.

For sore eyes, bathe the eyes and the head with cold water night and morning, and bathe the feet at night in cold water.

For sore eyes, do not use any water about the eyes or the face.

For swollen eyelids and sore eyes, apply a poultice of flaxseed.

Piercing the ears strengthens the eyes.

To remove a foreign object from the eyes, slip a wet flaxseed under the eyelid. It will catch the object on its sticky surface and carry it out.

Put cow's milk in a baby's eyes to cure sore eyes.

Avoid wearing rubbers in the house because to do so causes one to develop weak eyes.

Peel potatoes and put the peelings over the eye to cure inflammation.

Bathe sore eyes in rain water and sugar to cure them.

Apply raw beefsteak to black eyes to draw out soreness.

Wearing gold rings in pierced ears will cure weak eyes. (A cure practiced daily by a person living in Lincoln.)

To cure cataract in the eyes, grind up egg shells into a fine powder and sprinkle them into the eye.

Rub a black eye with a silver knife to draw soreness out.

To remove an object from the eye, make a loop from a long horse hair. Put it into the eye and close the lid. When the hair is pulled out, it will bring the object with it.

To cure cross-eyes, pierce the child's ears and insert gold hoops.

A baby's first tear will cure a blind man of blindness.

INFLAMMATION AND INFECTION

Folk cures for inflammation and infection are homemade poultices which have power to draw out the poison or the soreness. No charms are connected with these cures. If a superstitious element enters in, it lies in the strict adherence of some persons to one specific poultice and their firm belief in the efficacy of that particular concoction above any other. An informant from Custer county relates the following incident:

> A woman of seventy, our next-door neighbor, was cutting sunflowers in her front yard with a sharp knife. The knife slipped in her hand, cutting her thumb nearly off. Refusing to see a doctor, the woman gathered some weeds from her yard, mashed the leaves to make a poultice, and bound them on the wound. Not only did she ward off blood poison, but she healed the thumb entirely by her continued applications of mashed weeds.

Cures for burns are more numerous than those for other ailments in this group. Remedies for inflammation and infection are drawn from such sources as one would expect of Nebraska pioneers, namely, animals and plants common to Nebraska.

Inflammation

Make a poultice of bread and milk to draw out inflammation.

Make a poultice of boiled onions for swollen joints or inflammation of all kinds.

Make a poultice of tumblebugs. Mash the bugs up and put them on raw.

Mix turpentine, vinegar, and eggs and apply to a swelling.

Put raw beefsteak on a bruise to draw out inflammation.

Tie a piece of salt pork upon an inflamed or infected surface.

Mix brandy, soft soap, and salt and rub the part affected thoroughly once or twice a day.

Burns

Spit on a burn to cure it.

Burns can be cured by persons who have the miraculous power of "blowing the fire out of the wound." A woman can teach a man the trick and a man can teach a woman.

Rub grease on burns to cure them.

If you burn your finger, stick it in your ear and the soreness will go away.

Put soda on a burn to cure it.

Boil about fifty strong red pepper pods. Strain the solution through cheese cloth. Reduce this to a small quantity by heating it, then pour it into a pint of melted buffalo tallow. Lard is nearly as good as buffalo tallow. The pain will leave five minutes after the application of this remedy.

If you rub the white of an egg over a burn, the burn will heal and not leave a scar.

Put salt on a burn to cure it.

Put pepper on a burn to draw soreness out.

Put ice on a burn.

Suck a burn to draw out the fire.

If you have a burn, the best thing you can do to cure it is to burn the same place over again immediately.

Apply the lining of an egg shell.

Make a paste of lard and baking soda and apply freely.

Slices of new potato applied to a burn heal it.

Cover a surface which has been burned with a lather of soft soap.

Men working with stock frequently "burn" their hands on a rope. The best remedy for this is to wash the hands in strong salt water at body temperature.

Pulverize the root of the cat-tail plant and spread it on burns as a salve. (Reported as of Pawnee Indian origin.)

Apply wet tea leaves to burns to cure them.

Applications of turpentine and gunpowder cure a felon.

Strong lye soap and tobacco boiled together and thickened with cornmeal make an excellent poultice for felons.

Use common rock salt that is used for salting pork or beef. Dry it in the oven and pound it very fine. Mix it with equal parts of turpentine and put it in a rag. Wrap around the affected parts and as fast as it gets dry put on more. This cures a felon in twenty-four hours.

Infection

Put a piece of fat bacon over the infected part.

Apply a poultice of slippery elm bark to draw out infection.

Make a poultice by putting bacon grease and salt on a rag and wrapping the rag around the infected part.

Make a poultice from the cactus plant and apply it while hot. It will draw out thorns, sandburrs, boils, or splinters. (Reported to be of Mexican origin.)

Other Cures

To cure erysipelas, apply a poultice made of beets mixed with fresh-cut chewing tobacco.

KIDNEY AND BOWEL TROUBLES

Like the cures in the preceding section, the remedies for kidney and bowel troubles seldom involve charms. For the most part these cures are various liquids or teas carefully prepared from herbs or weeds, or they are mixtures of many home ingredients. It is possible that these remedies do alleviate the pain somewhat, and benefit the patient in this way. Even though there may be no actual medicinal value in the tea, the warmth may have a propitious result.

For bladder trouble, drink much tea made from watermelon seeds.

To cure bladder trouble, boil a quart of cockleburrs and drink the tea. (This advice was given by a trained nurse to a man in the Sand Hills.)

To cure dysentery, cook the pink bark of a live oak tree for half an hour. Take a tablespoonful of this liquid every half hour as long as it is necessary.

Apply the white of an egg externally to the abdomen to cure dysentery.

For dysentery drink water in which white writing paper has been soaked.

To cure dysentery, brown a teaspoonful of flour, add milk, and boil until the mixture is smooth. Drink this.

Feed a baby the white of an egg to cure dysentery.

Drink tea made from mullein leaves to cure dysentery.

To cure bed wetting, feed the patient the hind legs of a rat fried crisp. (This cure was brought to Nebraska by a Mexican.)

Eat radishes with rock candy to cure kidney trouble.

Eat asparagus to cure kidney trouble.

Eat raisins to cure kidney trouble.

To check diarrhea, make a concoction from the leaves of horehound. (Reported as an Indian remedy.)

Drink tea made from red-root or the inside bark of a live oak to cure diarrhea.

To cure diarrhea, put one tablespoonful of flour into a glass. Add water until it is a thin solution. Add a lot of cinnamon and cloves. Pour it back and forth until the mixture foams, then drink.

Put one beef gall in a quart of whiskey and shake well. Drink a swallow three times a day, half an hour before eating. This will cure dropsy.

Carry a buckeye in the pocket at all times to cure piles.

To cure piles, apply buffalo tallow mixed with salt.

RHEUMATISM

Rheumatism cures abound in Nebraska. Many of the oldest residents in the state, ordinarily non-superstitious, still cling tenaciously to charms to ward off or to cure rheumatism.

The cures most frequently practiced in this state are those involving the wearing of copper or brass rings or the carrying of an amulet in the pocket. It is believed that persons who carry a rabbit's foot in the left pocket are never troubled with rheumatism; but if they lose the talisman or neglect to carry it in the proper pocket, they are immediately seized with excruciating pain.

One Nebraska farmer living in the Sand Hills tells his experience with rheumatism as follows:

> For years I've been wearing a copper wire around my finger and I've never suffered from rheumatism. One afternoon I was working with a team in the field too far from the house to go in for repairs. Suddenly a harness strap broke and without thinking I wired it together with the copper wire from around my finger. In just a little while I was seized with rheumatism, and it didn't quit till I put that wire back on.

The use of the ring to cure disease has been cited in connection with eye trouble. Its remedial powers are accepted so widely by folk of all countries, that it is difficult to trace its origin in Nebraska where the population is so mixed.

Cats and snakes both play an important part in folk remedies for rheumatism. Belief in their efficacy is doubtless a legacy of the old, almost universal belief in the use of cats and snakes for mysterious healing by witches.

Bare your back or arm and let someone shake a drove of bees on it to sting you. This will cure your rheumatism.

Wear a brass belt to cure rheumatism.

Sleep with a cat on the foot of your bed. When the cat gets your rheumatism, you will not be bothered with it any longer.

To cure rheumatism, put a raw, skinned herring under your left foot. (Reported as brought from Sweden.)

Rub snake oil on the patient's joints.

Take a teaspoonful of common soda three times a day in half a glass of water.

Wear a paper sack around the neck to cure rheumatism.

Rub rattlesnake oil on the affected parts. The oil must be from a rattler.

Wear the rattles of a rattlesnake or carry them in your pocket to cure rheumatism.

Boil two gallons of cockleburrs and mix the juice with lard. Rub this mixture on the affected parts. (Used much by a woman in Shubert, Nebraska.)

Rub on skunk oil, well tried, and heat it in with hot packs. This oil will cure immediately when all other oils fail.

Get some dirt from a graveyard and walk over it for ten nights and your rheumatism will be cured.

To cure rheumatism, allow a bee to sting the affected joint.

Sleep with a dog to cure rheumatism. When the dog catches rheumatism from you, yours will be gone.

Wear red flannel to cure rheumatism. No other color will work.

Carry a lucky bean in your pocket to cure rheumatism.

Use tincture of cat to cure rheumatism. (In Omaha, a Negro sold a preparation called tincture of cat to cure rheumatism and other ailments. To advertise his wares, he used a cat's skeleton mounted in a glass case.)

Put a piece of snake skin in your hip pocket.

An Irish potato carried in the pocket will cure rheumatism.

Carry a rabbit's foot in your pocket.

Bind a small potato upon the painful surface. After a while the potato will become hard as wood. Then put on a fresh potato.

Boil potatoes and then soak the feet in hot water to cure rheumatism.

If you carry a buckeye in your pocket, it will cure rheumatism. It must be carried in the left pocket, according to some persons.

Put copper plates in your shoes to cure rheumatism.

Procure the fat from an entirely black cat and use it as a liniment.

If you wear a ring made of silver, brass, or copper on your little finger, it will cure rheumatism.

Boil cactus roots to make juice. Mix juice with red clay and pack it on the affected parts.

Carry a horse chestnut in your pocket.

Make a ring from a horseshoe nail, wear on finger.

TOOTHACHE

Cures for toothache are much less extensive in Nebraska than one would expect in view of the fact that the tooth has been the subject of much curious lore from the earliest records of ancient history. Folklore of the teeth has developed prolifically in all countries. W. G. Black cites many instances of its use in the British Isles. The Nebraska remedies include the use of magic and charms and home "medicines." Although the cures for toothache are not abundant in this state, those which are in use or have been used point to many superstitious beliefs concerning the teeth.

Cures for teething as well as for toothache are included in this collection. Most of them are of a superstitious nature.

Toothache

Hold bruised horseradish leaves on the face with a heavy hot flannel cloth over them to cure toothache.

Stick a red hot needle in the center of the cavity in an aching tooth and the tooth will stop aching.

Slice a little piece off the frog of a horse's front hoof and put it between the aching tooth and the one next to it.

If you have a toothache, put a horseradish poultice on the wrist opposite the side the tooth is on, and the ache will go.

Chew tobacco to cure a bad toothache. (This cure is prevalent in the Sand Hills.)

Put gunpowder on an aching tooth to ease it.

Wear a piece of string around your neck.

Stick a toothpick into the aching tooth or the gum until the gum bleeds. Remove the toothpick and put it into the bark of a tree. No one must see you do this or the tooth will not stop aching.

Cut the first skin off the frog of a horse's front hoof and put the skin over a fire until it chars. Crumble it and put it on the aching tooth.

Put a drop or two of clove oil in the tooth cavity.

Hold whiskey in the mouth to deaden the pain. (The informant said that it was difficult to get the patient to hold the whiskey in his mouth.)

Teething

Put a string of beads (Job's tears) around the child's neck and the teeth will come through without pain. "Job's tears" are large, gray seeds.

Put a rattlesnake rattle in a tobacco bag and hang the bag around the child's neck during teething.

When a baby is fretful while teething, string three large snake rattles on a red cord and put it around the child's neck. Do not remove until child is through teething.

Give the baby cartridges from a six-shooter to chew while it is teething. They must be from a six-shooter.

Let the baby chew rattlesnake rattles to help his teeth through.

Give the child Job's tears to cut teeth on.

Rub the baby's gums with an ivory ring or a celluloid ring.

Rub the baby's gums with a silver thimble to bring teeth through.

In order to cut teeth without pain, a baby must wear a red, flannel vest.

Rub the swollen gums of a teething child with the brains of a freshly killed rabbit to bring the teeth through.

WARTS

Cures for warts are more numerous than are those for any other ailment with the exception of colds and other diseases grouped under that heading on page 331. Considering the fact that warts are seldom found now, this seems strange. The oldest living settlers of Nebraska tell of early days when warts were common, and there was much debate as to the cause of this affliction and the best means of getting rid of it.

It was a commonly accepted belief that handling toads was responsible for the appearance of warts on one's hands. Some persons went so far as to say that the number of warts which appeared would correspond definitely to the number of protuberances on the toad. This belief concerning the origin of warts is upheld now mainly by children, who are responsible for the perpetuation of many superstitious cures. Children are fascinated by charms, and warts seem to yield themselves readily to charm cures. By charm is meant "a treatment whose action is not apparent even to the people who use it. It is taken as a cure on faith, and the possibility of curative action never questioned." (Walter R. Smith, "Animals and Plants in Oklahoma Folk-Cures," *Folk-Say*, Norman: University of Oklahoma Press, 1929, pp. 72–73.) The latter part of this statement is essential. One must have absolute faith in the cure before any healing will result. Thus, it is possible to dismiss the person who has no luck with a specific cure as one who shows a positive lack of faith.

It is possible to classify the cures for warts under eleven headings, namely: bean-, bone-, corn-, meat-, pebble and stone-, pin and needle-, potato-, rag-, string or thread-cures, cures for transference, and miscellaneous cures. Under the first nine headings the cures are chiefly variations of the same cure; for instance some persons maintain that meat which has been rubbed on a wart to cure it should be buried; others assert that unless the meat is thrown over the left shoulder, no cure will take place. Still others insist that only when the meat is fed to a dog will the warts disappear.

Associated with warts is a belief in the transference of disease which is seldom found with regard to other ailments. Warts may be "sold" to a person who becomes afflicted immediately and in turn must sell them to another to rid himself of them. Warts also may be transferred to someone by putting pebbles in a sack and leaving the sack for some unwitting person to pick up. Anyone unfortunate enough to pick up a stick which has been rubbed on another's warts may find himself the immediate recipient of these annoying little tumors.

It is probable that this idea of transference of warts came from the British Isles. W. G. Black in his chapter on "Transference of Disease" says, "In Cheshire the absolute transference of warts is worth noting." Black also cites similar examples found in Lancashire and Scotland.

Bean

Face the front door at home. Bite a bean in two and rub it on each wart. Then throw the bean over the left shoulder and never look for it. The warts will disappear.

Cross a wart with a bean and feed the bean to a rooster. The wart will soon leave.

Select a large, dry bean either navy, Boston, or lima bean. Rub it gently over the afflicted area and plant the bean. If it sprouts and grows, the warts are guaranteed to be removed. If it fails to sprout, repeat the treatment.

Split a bean. Cut the wart and put a drop of blood in the bean. Then bury the bean at midnight. Turn around three times and walk home without speaking to anyone on the way. The wart will disappear. The blood on the bean draws the wart toward it.

Toss a bean over your left shoulder into a well. Your warts will soon leave.

Take a leaf from a string bean vine and rub it on the wart. When the wart is green, hide the leaf. The wart will disappear.

Split a bean in two and rub one half on the wart, then bury it. Throw the other half of the bean as far as possible. When the buried half decays, the wart will disappear.

Steal some white beans from your neighbor and bury them. When they rot, your warts will be gone.

Bone

Walk in the woods until you find the bone of an animal. Rub the bone carefully over the wart with the side which was next to the ground. Then dig a hole in the ground and bury the bone. When it decays the warts will disappear.

Rub the wart with a bone which you find under a tree. You must hunt until you find the bone under a tree, then after rubbing the wart with it, put the bone back in its identical position.

Pick up a bone from the ground and rub the warts with it. Then throw the bone backwards as far as you can. Do not look back at the bone, and your warts will come off.

Corn

Steal a grain of corn and destroy it so that its owner will never have it again, and your warts will leave.

Rub the warts with a kernel of corn and feed the corn to a rooster. Be sure the rooster gets it and your warts will disappear.

Touch seventeen different kernels of corn to each wart, then feed the corn to the chickens. If they eat the corn, the warts will disappear.

Bury a small bag of corn. When the corn decays, the warts will leave.

Throw away a grain of corn for each wart, and the warts will soon disappear.

Cut a corn cob crosswise and take out the white pulp center. Put this on the wart. Then fill the inside of the cob with soda and add a drop of vinegar to boil the soda way. Hold this over the warts. Repeat two or three times a day until cured.

Pick the wart open and rub it with the pulp inside of a kernel of corn. Then feed the corn to a chicken.

Throw a handful of corn in a well to cure warts. When the corn decays, the warts will disappear.

Meat

Rub the wart with a piece of raw meat. Bury the meat under a stone upon which water drips. When the meat decays, the wart is gone.

Put a slice of fat pork between two boards and put the boards under the eaves. Eventually your warts will be cured.

Rub a piece of meat over the warts, then feed the meat to a dog. Warts will soon leave.

Throw a piece of fat meat over your left shoulder and never go back to hunt for it.

Tie beefsteak on warts.

Rub a piece of bacon on a wart and then bury the bacon in the ground. By the time the bacon has decayed the wart will have disappeared.

Steal a slice of bacon from your mother and fry it. Put it between two bricks and bury it. When the bacon rots, the warts will fall off.

Pebble and Stone

Touch every wart with a pebble. Put the pebble in a bag and bury the bag at night.

Rub the wart with a smooth stone, then hurl the stone without looking at it, over the left shoulder. The warts will be gone before long.

If you make a little bag, drop a white pebble in it for every wart you have, and bring it at midnight to the cross-roads without letting anyone see or know of it, your warts will disappear.

Pin and Needle

Prick the wart with a needle. Run the needle into a grain of corn and bury the grain of corn.

Stick a pin through the wart and burn the end of the pin.

Pick a wart with a new pin and then throw the pin away. The warts will soon leave.

Potato

Carry an Irish potato in your pocket to cure warts.

Cut a slit in a potato. Pinch it over the wart, so that the wart is in the slit. Then bury the potato. When it decays, the wart will disappear. (Reported as brought to Nebraska from Germany.)

Cut a potato in half. Rub each piece on the wart and fit the pieces together again. Then throw the potato over your shoulder. Do not watch where it goes. When the potato rots, your warts will disappear.

Cut a potato. Rub it on the wart and then bury the potato. When the potato decays the warts will be gone.

Rag

Rub a dish rag on the wart, and bury the rag under a rock.

Rub an old, much-used rag on the wart and then bury the rag in the ground secretly. The wart will soon disappear.

Rub a stolen dish rag over the wart and bury the rag behind the barn. When the rag decays, the wart will be gone.

If you have a wart, have someone else hide your dish cloth. You must not know where it is hidden. When it decays your wart is gone.

Steal your neighbor's dish rag. It must be your neighbor's or the cure will not work. Bury the rag, and when it rots the warts will be gone.

Steal a dish cloth, preferably from your mother. Dampen it and pass it over the warts. Take the cloth in a paper sack and bury it by the light of the moon. The warts will disappear within the week.

Rub a dish rag on the wart and bury the rag anywhere in the ground. When it decays, the warts disappear.

Steal your mother's dish rag, and bury it in the damp ground on the north side of a building before the sun rises and before you eat breakfast. When the rag has decayed your warts will disappear.

String or Thread Cures

To cure a wart, let someone tie a thread around it three times and then bury the string in the ground where human foot cannot tread, as under a stone wall or a building. No word must be spoken during the ceremony. As the string decays, the wart will disappear.

Tie a silk thread around a wart. Burn up the rest of the thread and the wart will go away.

Tie one end of a string around the wart and the other around a door knob. Shut the door hard in order to yank the wart off.

Tie a knot in a string for each wart and bury the string under a hog trough. Let no one see you do it or know of it.

Tie a silk thread around the wart and keep pulling it tighter and tighter until the wart comes off.

Tie knots in a string for each wart. Bury the string under the eaves where the rain can drip on it. When it rains, the warts will go.

Rub the wart with twine and bury the twine under the eaves.

Tie as many knots in a string as there are warts on the hands. Bury the string in the ground. When it decays the warts will disappear from the hands.

Tie a knot in a string for every wart. Walk backward to a stone and lay the string under the stone. When the string rots the warts will be gone.

At night bury a short, white string in the ground. When you awaken in the morning, the warts will be gone.

Transference of Warts

Rub the wart with a penny and give the penny away. The wart will go with it.

You may sell a wart for any amount and the purchaser will get the wart.

Count off the number of warts you have on another's hands, touching the person's skin for each wart. Your warts will soon disappear and the other person will have them.

Put one pebble in a box for each wart. Wrap the box in paper and place it in some conspicuous place where someone is sure to pick it up. The person who picks it up will have the warts and yours will disappear.

Pick the wart until it bleeds, then rub the blood on a smooth rock. Tie the rock up in a package and drop the package in the road. The person who picks it up will get the wart.

Count your warts with the point of a pin. Hide the pin. If anyone finds it and uses it, he will get the warts. If you bury the pin, the warts will disappear later.

Stick a pin in the wart, wrap the pin in a corn shuck, and put the shuck in the road. The first person who steps on the shuck will get the wart.

Miscellaneous Cures

Rub your wart with a wedding ring to cure it.

Rub the wart with a penny and throw the penny as far as possible.

Sell the wart for a penny and hide the penny in a clock.

Tie a horsehair into as many knots as you have warts. Insert it into a bottle of water and secrete it in some damp, dark place for nine days. The warts will leave.

Tie a horsehair around the warts. They will soon leave.

When the moon is full, pull up a green weed, any kind of weed that is green, rub the wart with it, and throw the weed away without looking at it.

The first Friday of every new moon for three nights, look at the moon and repeat the following three times: "What I see increase and what I feel decrease." Rub the wart and it will disappear.

Burn the wart with a match and it will disappear.

Let someone rub a match over the wart until the match smokes. When this happens, hide the match. If the person who has the wart ever finds out where the match is, his wart will return.

Rub two sticks over the warts. Take the sticks to the forks of the road and put them down in the form of a cross. Do not look back at the sticks and the warts will go.

Cut notches in a stick corresponding in number with the number of warts. Throw the stick away and the warts will disappear.

Steal a fish head, rub it over your warts and then bury it, so deeply that no animal can dig it up. Warts will disappear in a week.

Pick open a wart until it bleeds, then let a hen pick it. It must be a hen and not a rooster or the wart will not leave.

With a sharp knife, preferably clean, carefully cut off the top of the wart. Wash this dissected part, tie it in a cotton bag and throw it away. If someone picks up the bag, the wart will leave, otherwise it will remain. (Used by a woman in Lincoln who says the cure worked.)

Rub the warts over a dead body and they will soon disappear.

Cut a raw egg in two and then throw a dishpan over your left shoulder. This will cure warts.

Rub your warts with butter to cure them.

Apply olive-oil externally to the warts to cure them.

This is called the wishing, wart-removing treatment. After a rigid period of concentration, wish that the wart be removed to some other living animal, such as a dog's ears or the back of a cat.

Bathe warts with vinegar to cure them.

Take a broom straw and break it at the joint. Then rub it on the wart to cure the wart.

Milkweed applied to a wart as often as you think necessary will get rid of the wart.

Throw your gum in the cistern and your warts will disappear.

Go to the cemetery at midnight with a dead cat. Go to the grave of a friend, stand on it, and rub the cat across the wart. The wart will leave.

Take as many peas as there are warts, toss them into a well and run under a roof before the peas hit the water. (Someone else may throw the peas for you.) When the peas decompose, the warts will come off.

To cure warts, cut a patch in them.

Cut a hole in the top of a turnip and put salt in the hole. Then put the sap on the wart.

Pick the wart so the skin is broken. Put on a grain of concentrated lye the size of a pin head. When the lye eats the wart, pull off and put on pure vinegar to keep the lye from eating on through the hand. (A woman in Kearney says that she removed seven warts in this way.)

Rub a wart on the bottom of a shoe sole. When the sole wears out the wart will be gone.

Wash your hands in water found in a hollow stump to cure warts.

If you spit on a wart every morning just after you wake up, the wart will disappear in time.

Wet your hand, cover it with salt, and let a horse lick it. The warts on the hand will disappear. (A citizen of Lincoln says that his warts disappeared after this treatment.)

Count your warts as you touch them with your finger. Do it several times every day and they will soon leave. (A woman in Buffalo County says her warts left in one month after this treatment.)

WOUNDS

Included in this section are remedies to stop the flow of blood from cuts and sores, from a nail in the foot, and from nosebleed. In the first two instances these cures are not of a superstitious nature, but for the most part they consist of adaptations of various home products, such as poultices of weeds or animal fat, sugar, and flour. In the case of nosebleed, however, nearly all of the remedies are superstitious with little in them to effect a cure except the user's faith in their potency.

Stop bleeding by applying spiderwebs to the wound.

If an artery is cut, sear it with a hot iron. If it is a vein, apply a mixture of charred feathers and cobwebs and bind it on the cut.

If anyone bleeding from a cut will hang a bunch of keys around his neck, the blood will stop flowing instantly.

Put soda on a cut to stop its bleeding.

Mix brown sugar and whiskey, and put the solution on the bleeding surface to stop bleeding.

Put sugar on a cut to stop bleeding and heal the wound.

To stop bleeding, apply a handful of cobwebs to the wound.

Apply flour to a cut to cure bleeding.

Use milkweed lotion (the sweet juice of milkweed) on cuts and sores to heal them.

Put the cut in kerosene to stop its bleeding.

Put the cut in mud to heal it.

To stop a wound from bleeding, apply the lining of an egg shell.

Apply sheep tallow to heal sores and cuts.

Soak arnica leaves in alcohol and apply to cuts.

Tie a chew of tobacco on the wound. This was used on a citizen of Lincoln when he cut his foot badly with a garden hoe. The wound healed in a short time.

The root of the hop vine (crooked root) is used to heal wounds.

Apply puff balls to the wound to stop bleeding. (Puff balls are similar to toadstools.)

Nose Bleed

If a woman has nose bleed, have a man read a chapter in a book to her to cure it. If a man is afflicted, have a woman read to him. The charm will not work if the two are of the same sex.

Hang a butcher knife down your back to cure nose bleed.

Stand with your back to a mulberry tree. Measure your height on the tree, and then bore a hole in the tree there. Cut a lock of your hair, put it in the hole, and drive a rusty nail in it. Your nose will never bleed again.

Put a nickel in the roof of your mouth and hold it up with your tongue. At the same time hold both hands high up in the air.

Wear a wool thread around your big toe to cure nose bleed.

Wear a red necklace around your neck to cure nose bleed.

Put a folded piece of cardboard under your upper lip.

Put a small piece of brown paper under your upper lip to stop nose bleed.

Put a penny under the upper lip and a cold key down your back to cure nose bleed.

Wear a blue bead on a single thread around the neck to cure nose bleed.

Apply cold wet cloths to the back of the neck.

Mash a lead bullet flat around a string and put the string around the neck.

Let the blood fall on an axe or knife and stick the weapon in the ground. The nose will soon stop bleeding.

Wear a red string around the neck to cure nose bleed.

Put a cold coin on the back of the neck.

Put a key on a red flannel string and hang it around the neck.

Put a wet cloth to the nostrils to clot the blood.

Put a half dollar under the upper lip.

Put ice on the back of the head or on the forehead.

Put a dime on the back of the tongue.

Put a nickel under the upper lip.

Put a brown cigarette paper in the roof of the mouth to cure nose bleed.

Put a penny in the mouth.

Hang the head over the back of a chair.

Nail in the Foot

Pull the nail out, grease it, and throw it in the fire. This will keep the foot from ever getting sore.

Put a slice of fat salt meat over the wound.

Make a poultice by scraping raw beets and apply it to the wound.

Soak the foot in kerosene.

Soak the foot in hot water into which has been dissolved a lot of Epsom salts.

Hold the foot in hot ashes.

Let a pup lick a sore that will not heal. It stops the bleeding and cures the sore.

When medical aid was not available, Nebraska settlers used to keep a wet rag on a gunshot wound until the wound healed.

Indians split cactus leaves, burned the thorns off, heated the leaves thoroughly, and bound them on the wound.

BITES AND STINGS

When the early settler homesteaded in Nebraska one of the cures which he needed most to know was a remedy for the deadly bite of a rattlesnake. Because most available to him, his most frequent cures were poultices made from such plants as the cactus or the soapweed, or grease or lard from animals, or their warm intestines applied to a wound to draw out poison. Tobacco afforded the most popular poultice. Captain Lute North of Columbus, Nebraska, a resident of the state since 1856, told of a man whom he once saw cured of a rattlesnake bite by application of tobacco. Another man chewed quantities of it and kept the hand well poulticed. According to Captain North, the man who was bitten recovered from the bite without getting sick, but the man who chewed tobacco for the poultices became very ill.

The rattlesnake, which corresponds to the viper of other folklore, has been used much in Nebraska as a cure for such diseases as goiter or headache. Strangely enough, however, only in one case was it reported to have been used as a cure for its own bite. In this instance, a man from Thomas County who was bitten immediately cut off the snake's head, and then split open its body, cutting it into three-inch pieces. These he applied immediately to the wound, discarding each piece as it became saturated with the poison. In this instance the snake was not used because of any charm which the man associated with the snake, but as a poultice in an emergency.

Snake Bite

Cut a snake bite criss-cross, then spit tobacco juice on it or empty a pipe on it.

If there are any chickens available, cut one open either after it has been killed or while it is still alive, and put it over the snake bite. Before long the chicken will be all green from the poison which it has drawn out. It takes nearly a dozen chickens to draw all the poison from the wound.

For rattlesnake bite in an emergency, beat cockleburrs to a pulp and apply the pulp as a poultice to the wound.

Kill an animal, preferably a cow, and slit a hole in its abdomen. Bury the snake bitten area into the middle of the animal. Leave it there until the carcass becomes cold and then remove. The poison from the bite will be drawn out.

Suck a snake bite to heal it.

Apply the warm flesh of an animal to draw out poison.

Drink all the whiskey you can hold to cure a snake bite.

Pack mud on a rattlesnake bite to cure it. (This cure was used by a citizen of Logan County when he was fourteen years old. He was alone in a cornfield when a snake bit him. He sat down immediately and began to pack mud on the bite until the pain was gone. Then after packing fresh mud on it, he went home. The process took him half a day.)

Soak the bite in coal oil for a long time.

Puncture the skin around the bite with the sharp points of the soapweed to let the poison run out.

Keep jabbing the swollen places with sharp knives until the black blood and water come out. This will be the poison.

Cut the outside prickles off the cactus found in the Sand Hills. Mash the inside of the plant and apply it to the bite as a poultice. Keep it moist with water and change as often as it becomes warm.

Apply hog lard to the wound. Heat the lard and have the patient drink all he can.

Scarify the flesh as deeply as the fangs went and make at least two incisions. Then apply table salt.

Apply a mixture of turpentine and gunpowder to a rattle-snake bite to cure it.

Bury that part of the body bitten by the snake in the ground and soak the earth with sweet milk.

Mash the roots of the milkweed and apply it to a rattlesnake bite. Also give the patient half of the milk internally. (Reported as an Indian cure.)

Dog Bite

Rub axle grease on a dog bite to cure it.

When it was thought that the dog was mad, a stone called a "mad stone" was rubbed over the bite to cure it. This stone was found inside a deer.

Sting

Pack mud on the part which has been stung by a bee or a wasp.

For the sting of a bee or a wasp, wrap the leaf of a tomato vine over it.

Hold a sting in turpentine to cure it.

For stings, pull the stem from a pipe and put the excess nicotine collected there on the sting.

Apply common soda, moistened, to cure a sting.

Mash the leaves of any kind of vegetation and apply them to insect bites or stings. Apply soda and vinegar mixed to stings.

Put tobacco juice on a hornet sting to cure it.

Poison Ivy

Mix nightshade berries with cream and apply to parts affected by poison ivy.

Wash the affected parts with strong salt water.

Wear an ordinary fishing sinker around your neck on a string to cure or to prevent poison ivy.

Pack mud on poison ivy sting to cure it.

Carry a pocketful of cartridges in your pocket to prevent or to cure poison ivy. The lead in the cartridges effects the cure.

Rub the poisoned parts with pure apple vinegar.

Nettles

Take the slime off a fish that you have just caught and put the slime on the stinging surface.

Pack mud on nettle sting to cure it.

Put tobacco juice on nettle sting to cure it.

MISCELLANEOUS

There are numerous cures which cannot be classified conveniently in the foregoing sections, nor are there enough for any one disease to justify their segregation into a separate division. It seems expedient, then, to treat them collectively here. Many of the cures for the complexion, and for asthma, goiter, and ringworm, are decidedly superstitious. Boils and corns are treated with home remedies, some of which may have healing propensities. The unclassifiables, listed under Other Cures, are especially representative of Nebraska folk cures as a whole, and range from cures for tears caused by peeling onions to cures for muddy drinking water, insanity, vermin, stammering, cracks between the toes, and seven-year itch.

Asthma

Drink tea made from jimson weed to cure asthma.

Blindfold the asthma sufferer, lead him into the woods, and bore a hole at his exact height in a tree. Put a lock of hair in the hole and plug it up. When the child grows taller than the plug, his asthma is supposed to leave. (Practiced by a Nebraska attorney upon his grandmother's request. The asthma left him but returned in twenty years.)

If you have asthma, keep cats around you. When nine cats have caught asthma from you, you will be cured. (Practiced by a doctor in Thomas County.)

Go down to a river and catch a frog. Pry its mouth open and blow your breath into it. This must be done before daylight. The frog will die before sundown with asthma, but the person will never have it again.

Make a drug from the buttercup to cure asthma.

Make a tea from the leaves of sumac and drink it.

Mix bee's honey with sulphur and take a teaspoonful every hour until relieved.

Stand the child up to a tree which is as tall as he is. Pound some of the child's hair into the tree. If the tree outgrows the child, he won't have any more asthma. If the child outgrows the tree, he will always have asthma.

Boils

Make a bread and milk poultice with saffron fried and flour mixed in it.

Put a strip of bacon on the boil. It will soon bring the boil to a head.

Apply a poultice made of soft soap and strained honey.

Apply a poultice made of plantain leaves.

Apply a poultice of sugar and soap.

Swallow nine shots from a shot gun shell to cure boils.

Apply a poultice of flaxweed meal. Keep it moist and as hot as can be stood.

Apply bread and milk.

Make a poultice from the cactus plant. Bake the plant and then split it and apply to the boil while hot.

Complexion and Skin Troubles

Wash the skin in buttermilk every day to cure freckles.

To remove tan, soak wild tansy in buttermilk for several days. Wet a cloth in the solution and apply it to the tan several hours a day.

Put some oatmeal in a little bag of cloth and soak in half a cup of milk. When the milk gets syrupy, rub it on the tan or freckles. Repeat until freckles and tan disappear.

Apply beef tallow or mutton suet, rubbed well into the skin, to heal chapped hands. Do not wash until healed.

Rub buffalo tallow on chapped hands to heal them.

Wash the hands in strong, hot, salt water, then in soap and water, and then dry them.

For chapped hands, rub vaseline on them and then coat them thoroughly with dry oatmeal and put on cotton gloves.

To remove freckles, slice raw cucumbers and rub them on the face.

To remove freckles, tie a horsehair into as many knots as you have freckles. Insert the hair into a bottle of water and put the bottle in a damp, cool place. After nine days the freckles will disappear.

Arise at dawn, bathe the face in dew, and say while doing this:
"Beauty come. Freckles go.
Dewdrops make me
White as snow."
The freckles will all disappear.

To cure freckles, go through the following ceremony: Arise early on the first day of May and without saying anything to anyone, bathe the face at dawn in the dew. Then rub the hands on another part of the body, repeating at the same time, "In the name of the Father, Son, and Holy Ghost." The freckles will leave. (Brought to Nebraska from Germany by the informant's grandfather.)

Brown egg shells in a pan in the oven. Take them out and roll them into a fine powder. Eat the powder and it will immediately clean your system and clear your complexion.

Wash the hands in the first snow and it will prevent them from becoming chapped.

Corns

Put onion skins on a corn to heal it.

Put raw pork on a corn to cure it.

Tie a piece of fat salt pork on a bunion. Put a fresh piece on every night for a week.

Put wood ashes in hot water and use the solution as a foot bath to heal corns and bunions.

Cut cranberries in two and put the halves on a corn to cure it.

Rub kerosene on a corn to cure it.

Put a slice of salted lemon on your corn for ten nights, then your corn will disappear.

Spit on corns every morning just after you awaken, and they will disappear.

Goiter

A string of any kind of heavy beads worn around the neck will cure goiter.

Wrap a snake around the neck and allow it to creep off, and the goiter will disappear.

Wear a piece of velvet ribbon around your neck to cure goiter. (Practiced regularly by a woman in Kearney.)

If a person who has goiter will go into a room where a corpse is lying and take the hand of the dead person and rub it over the goiter, the goiter will disappear.

To blow in fire gives one goiter, but to inhale smoke will cure it.

Wear a gold chain around the neck to cure goiter.

A string of amber beads worn around the neck will cure goiter.

Ringworm

Rub a cigar stub on the ringworm and it will disappear.

Press the open end of a thimble around ringworm to cure it.

To cure ringworm, take a copper one-cent piece and place it in enough butter to cover it. Let it stand twelve or fourteen hours. When the butter is green around the copper, take this green stuff and place it on the ringworm. It eats in and kills the germ.

Use an egg shell for a measuring cup. Take one measure of these ingredients: beaten egg yolk, turpentine, coal oil, vinegar, and salt. Rub the solution on the ringworm.

Apply wet gunpowder three times daily for four or five days to kill ringworm.

Rub a green walnut skin on ringworm to cure it.

Other Cures

Let a cow lick straight hair to make it curly.

To make straight hair curl, eat charcoal from burned food.

To make a cowlick part the other way, put raw egg white on it.

To cure measles, eat a roasted mouse, well done.

To cure measles, drink lots of cold water and lemonade.

For indigestion, eat the dried lining of a chicken gizzard. (Old settlers used to save old chicken gizzards in a bottle so that the linings would be available for indigestion.)

For stomach trouble or poisoning, chew tobacco well. Then swallow tobacco, juice and all. (Reported as an Indian cure which was supposed to drive out devils.)

To prevent crying while you are peeling onions, cut the onions under water.

To prevent tears while peeling onions, peel them over a flame.

To prevent tears while you are peeling onions, hold a darning needle dipped in kerosene in the mouth while peeling.

For cramps in the legs and feet at night, turn your shoes upside down under the bed when you go to bed. (The informant said he had proved the truth of this cure at least seventy-five times.)

For cramps in the feet, put the feet in hot ashes.

Soak frozen feet in kerosene to cure them.

For frost-bitten feet, fingers, or ears, apply scraped Irish potato.

Chew slippery elm bark to cure or to ease menstruation pain.

Drink a tea made from tansy as a relief for menstruation pain.

To regulate menstruation, eat beet juice which has been thickened with corn starch and seasoned with sugar and vinegar.

To cure a fever, make mustard plasters and put one on the bottom of each foot and one on the back of the neck.

Rub pepper on a patient when his temperature is below normal. (Practiced by a practical nurse.)

For labor pains, boil a gold ring and drink the tea from it after it has cooled by having the early morning dew settle on it.

If during pregnancy, the mother will concentrate on any quality or talent which she wishes her child to have, the child will be blessed with this trait.

Have the patient blow through a turkey quill as hard as she can to ease her labor pains. (This was called "quilling" and was used by some of the oldest settlers of the state.)

Hold the edge of a sharp axe against the abdomen of a woman suffering from labor pains. This will take her mind off her trouble and ease the pain.

Spit on a birthmark every day to cure it.

If someone will get up out of bed early in the morning and lick the baby's birthmark three times for nine successive mornings without saying a word to anyone, the mark will disappear.

Rub the birthmark with a piece of raw meat and then bury the meat. When the meat decays the birthmark will be gone.

To cause the wind to blow so that the windmill will pump water for cattle, get up on the windmill tower and whistle. The wind will soon begin to blow.

To alleviate suffering from lack of water, put a bullet in your mouth. A dime or a piece of copper will also do. The cactus plant is also especially effective.

To cure a person who has ague, dig a ditch in the ground big enough for him to sleep in. Have the person strip off all his clothes and lie down in the ditch. Cover him all up with dirt, leaving only his head uncovered, and in the morning he will be perfectly well.

To cure backache, fold a big piece of red cotton flannel six feet by two feet wide, and cut a hole in the fold and fasten the side with safety pins. Backache will soon leave and never return if you leave the flannel on.

To cure a person or an animal who has eaten strychnine, give him a large dose of salt swallowed with grease, or if grease is not available, a little water. If the person lives five minutes after the salt reaches his stomach, he won't die from the poison.

Drink tea made from the fruit of the cactus plant to cure gall-stones.

Hold an onion to the nose of a person about to faint, or to one who has fainted to revive him.

To cure lockjaw, make a tea from cockroaches and drink it.

For tape worm, feed the patient ground glass to cut the tape worm up.

To cure stammering, get a child near an animal that is being butchered and as soon as the lungs are out of the animal, rub them vigorously into the child's face, especially around the mouth.

If you get a pain in your side any time you are outdoors, pick up a rock, spit on the side of it that lay next to the ground, and put the rock back as it was when you first found it. The pain will disappear.

If the bark of the elderberry bush is scraped in one direction, it acts as a laxative. If it is scraped in the other direction, it acts as an emetic. (Reported as an Indian remedy.)

For pain, apply a hop bag wrung out in hot water.

Feed a sick baby on cow's milk with sage tea mixed in it. (Mrs. H. O. Skiles of Lincoln said that her grandmother fed her six weeks old granddaughter on this prescription. She asserted that it cured her after doctors had said she could not live.)

Apply kerosene to the head to kill vermin, such as lice.

A dead hand touched to a cancer will cure it.

To purify muddy drinking water, peel off the skin and stickers of the cactus plant. Slice them and scatter the pieces over the top of the water. They will soon sink to the bottom carrying all sediment with them.

To keep the feet from getting cold, put pepper in the bottom of the shoes. Red pepper is hotter than black.

For cracks between the toes, tie a string through the middle of the cracks and leave it there until the crack heals.

For appendicitis, apply hot pans over the region of the appendix.

For enlarged joints, wrist bones, or knuckles, go to the prairie or pasture. Then seek a well-bleached animal carcass. Take one of the bones from the carcass and rub it against the affected parts. Walk slowly away, throwing the bone over the left shoulder. Do not look back at the bone ever. (Reported to be of German origin.)

For neuritis, empty whole mustard seeds into sweet cider and drink a lot of the solution.

For night sweats, put a pan of water under the bed before you go to bed and you will not be troubled with the ailment.

For summer complaint, string allspice around your neck.

Put salt on the tongue of a person who is dying of apoplexy and he will get well.

If a person is in bed with a fever, burn black feathers in a pan under the bed to cure him.

To avoid giving a child a hairlip, a pregnant woman should not see an axe in a chopping block. If she does see this, her child will be born with a hairlip.

To cure seven-year itch, mix gunpowder and lard and rub it on at bedtime.

If a person is insane, stick his head in a furnace and he will be normal.

To cure mumps, take the tonsils from a squirrel and bind one tonsil under each jaw where the mumps are. (This cure was used by a citizen of Nebraska City.)

To cure hay fever, smoke coffee grounds in a pipe.

For dandruff, rub kerosene on your head.

For perspiring feet, put powdered alum in the shoes two or three times a week.

Apply fish oil to cure stiff joints.

DUNG AND RELATED CURES

Many folk cures involve the use of dung. In fact traditional cures of this sort are so numerous that they need a special section, although the groupings of other sections are based on the type of diseases rather than on methods of curing them. The testimony of residents of long standing from different counties in the state seems to indicate that dung was probably the most widely used cure in the earliest days of the settlement of Nebraska. That it is still used in some localities is certain.

There is no better way to illustrate the acceptance of dung as a cure than by citing instances in which it was used. The following incidents were told to the present writer's father by Dick Rutledge, a pioneer who fought Indians on the Platte with Buffalo Bill. He was also with Kit Carson two years.

When he was a boy, Rutledge was hitching a horse to a post when suddenly he caught his finger between the rope and the post with the result that his finger was severed completely from his hand. His sister immediately picked up the severed member, applied fresh, warm cow dung to it, and bound it back on the hand. The pieces grew together again, although the finger remained a little crooked.

At another time Rutledge was a sheriff. He and his posse were chasing train robbers with whom they had a fight. A deputy's leg was shot off just above the foot, leaving only a little skin on it. The nearest doctor was three days distant by horseback, a fact which necessitated instant treatment with materials at hand. Rutledge picked up a blanket, took a man with him, and walked until he found some sleeping cattle. Gathering up their fresh dung in the blanket, the men took it back to the wounded man and bound up the stump of his leg with it. Then after putting him on a horse, they rode three days to a doctor, who marvelled at the perfect condition of the wound. Six months later the man was well and able to go out with the next posse. There are any number of similar stories which old settlers can tell.

For inflammation, pack fresh, warm cow dung on the inflamed surface.

To cure wounds, apply a mixture of lime and pulverized cow chips.

For snake bite, apply fresh, warm cow manure.

To cure milk leg, apply cow dung over the inflamed part.

For inflammation of the breast in nursing mothers, called "caked breast", put on warm cow dung. Change the applications frequently enough to keep warm dung on. (Used by a woman in Omaha.)

Pack fresh cow dung on sunburn to cure it.

Children who run barefooted and stub their toes, tearing the skin, immediately put their feet in warm cow dung to cure the sore.

Pulverize dry cow chips and apply to a bleeding wound to stop the bleeding.

Spit under a cow chip and walk around it three times to cure hiccoughs.

For ant bites, apply mud or fresh cow dung.

To cure measles, make a tea from sheep dung. This is called "nanny tea".

To cure earache, make a tea from sheep pellets and pour while warm into the ear.

To cure hives, make a tea of sheep manure and drink a lot of it while it is warm.

To cure chilblains, cook chicken manure and pour off the liquid. Make a poultice of the residue and apply.

For rattlesnake bite, apply buffalo manure to the wound.

To cure earache, pour warm urine into the ear.

To cure bladder trouble, follow a coyote or a badger until you see him urinate on the brush or the grass on a prairie. Gather only the wet brush. Boil it and drink the tea. The cure is almost instantaneous.

Application of human excrement as a poultice on a felon is a never-failing cure.

To cure freckles and tan, wash your face in human urine every night. (Practiced in Thomas County.)

Wash rope-burned hands with cowboy urine to heal them.

To cure saddle-sores on horses, wash them with cowboy urine.

Wash the sore eyes of animals with human or animal urine to heal them.

PREVENTIVES AND CURE-ALLS

Somewhat different in nature from the cures for specific diseases is the collection in this section which comprises means of preventing disease. In most cases the preventive is very inclusive, and is for any and all disease. In some instances it is supposed to ward off some special trouble, such as smallpox, rheumatism, or keeping a child from growing a dog's tooth. In most cases, however, it is for general contagious diseases.

It was the belief of many families until a few years ago that every spring the blood becomes sluggish and unclean, thereby making a person highly susceptible to disease. Such families, therefore, had their own spring tonics which were taken regularly by each member to insure his resistance to disease. In most cases these remedies were a concoction of herbs and weeds, mixed according to the prescription handed down in a particular family.

Two cure-alls guaranteed by their advocates to cure anything, are mentioned at the beginning of the list.

Cure-Alls

One or two medicine peddlers appear in Omaha every year selling snake oil supposedly from Indian formulas. This Indian snake oil cures everything, but is especially good for rheumatism and rejuvenation.

As a general cure-all, many people used to "let the blood," which meant cutting the patient's skin to let the blood run freely.

Preventives

Carry a rabbit's foot around the neck to prevent contagion.

Until a baby is six months old his clothes must be put on over his feet rather than over his head to prevent stunting his growth. His nails, until he is a year old, must be bitten off instead of cut or he will steal when he is grown.

Wear a bag of garlic around your neck on a string and it will keep away all infectious diseases.

Wear a bag of asafœtida around the neck to ward off infectious diseases. (Some persons say the asafœtida must be on a blue yarn string; others that it must be on a red string; and others that the bag must be of red flannel.)

Nebraska people used to keep a billy goat in the yard always as a preventive or cure-all.

Sleep with the windows tightly closed at night to prevent the bad night air from bringing in illness.

Do not eat fruit at night or it may make you ill. "Fruit is gold in the morning, silver at noon, but lead at night."

Put a few drops of camphor on a handkerchief when you are going to a public gathering to keep contagious diseases away.

To prevent still-birth, get all children in the neighborhood to beat tin pans in the sick room to drive the devil away. (Used in Kearney.)

Plant sunflowers around the house as a preventive for all disease.

For a general antiseptic to prevent disease, use very strong soap suds of yellow or home-made soft soap. (The informant gave the following testimony with regard to preparing this soap: "Everyone had an ash hopper built in the back yard. Wood ashes from a stove were poured in. Then water on this until the ashes were saturated and began to leak out the bottom into a pail placed there to receive it. Then all old grease scraps or cracklings were put in and boiled together until a smooth soft soap was formed.")

Do not eat chokecherries and then drink milk within three hours. It will cause horrible swellings and probably death.

Punch a hole in a dime and run a string through it. Wear the dime around your ankle always to prevent all sickness.

Wear a bag of camphor around your neck to protect you against all ills.

Wrap a spider in silk and seal it in a nutshell. Then suspend it around the neck on a string. This will prevent or cure disease.

Burn orange peelings on the stove to cure or to prevent influenza.

Hang a bag of sulphur around your neck as a general cure-all and preventive. This is especially good to prevent a cold.

If there is contagion or influenza in the neighborhood, slice onions in a dish and place them in some part of the room. The onions will absorb any germs there may be in the room.

Burn sulphur right on top of the cook stove to ward off influenza.

A string of greased yarn worn around the neck will prevent colds, croup, and other infectious diseases.

Wear a string with three knots tied in it around the neck to prevent croup.

To prevent influenza or colds, put a few drops of eucalyptus oil on the handkerchief.

Drink sassafras tea to prevent spring fever.

To prevent summer complaint, drink tea made from horsetail leaves. (Horsetail weed is found in the Sand Hills.)

To prevent spring fever, drink red clover tea.

To prevent spring fever and to purify the blood, drink tea made from dock roots.

Drink molasses and sulphur to purify the blood and prevent spring fever. Take it three evenings in succession, then skip three evenings.

To prevent crooked teeth, put a tooth in a crack as soon as it is pulled.

When a child's tooth was pulled, the tooth was kept so that a dog or cat wouldn't get hold of it until another tooth came in. If a dog or a cat did get the tooth then the child would grow a dog or a cat tooth in place of his own, depending upon which animal found the tooth.

Do not throw a tooth away after it is pulled, for if you do and a dog should step on it, a dog's tooth will come in where that one has been pulled.

Wear a lump of asafœtida around the neck to ward off smallpox.

Wear a string of rattlesnake rattlers around your neck to prevent smallpox.

Carry a buckeye in your pocket and you will never have rheumatism.

To prevent insanity caused by a bite from a mad dog, kill the dog immediately.

To prevent sneezing, look at the sun when you feel inclined to sneeze.

Put asafœtida in a sock around one's neck to ward off disease.

CURES FOR ANIMAL DISEASES

No collection of Nebraska folk cures could be complete without a section dealing with the diseases of animals. Nebraska is an agricultural state given over, since the beginning of its settlement, to farming and to stock raising. Farmers and ranchmen representing many nationalities and many states in the Union have drifted into Nebraska, bringing with them their diverse methods of taking care of their livestock. With a few exceptions the following list of animal cures was contributed by the writer's father, F. J. Black. He has ranched in Nebraska most of his life, and many of the cures were used by men working on his ranch on the Dismal River in Thomas County, or suggested to him by other ranchmen. The Mexican cures cited were brought to Nebraska by three Mexicans who worked on the Black ranch from 1878 to 1900. Many of the cures are originally from Texas, and were recommended to Mr. Black by Colonel Charlie Goodnight of that state.

Although many of these cures are distinctly superstitious, the greatest number of them are applications of simple home remedies which may or may not actually help an animal. Originally they were used when there were no trained veterinaries, and now they are well established on most farms and ranches.

Bellyache

For bellyache in a horse, rub turpentine in the small of his back and then grease it with bear's grease.

Bathe a horse's belly with strong red pepper tea, and then make him drink half a pint of it. He will probably stampede, but it will cure his ache.

To cure bellyache in a horse, set fire to a gunnysack. Place the sack in a bucket and hold it under the horse's nose so that he breathes the smoke.

Black Leg

Run the animal around until he gets very warm to cure black leg.

For black leg in cattle, lift up the tail and on the under side cut the loose skin which makes a little pocket. Into this pocket put a small section of garlic. (Before vaccination was known, one of the first state veterinaries told this cure to Mr. F. J. Black and showed him an animal which was still stiff, but cured after he had nearly died from the deadly disease.)

Cut a hole in the brisket and tie a piece of rope or cord through the hole.

Bladder Trouble

Saturate cloths with turpentine and hold them across the animal's loins to cure bladder trouble.

Break off a match head and insert it into the horse's penis. Relief will be sudden.

Bloat

For bloat in cattle, stick the animal with a pocket-knife between the second and the third rib and insert a quill to let the gas escape.

Drench the animal with a pint of raw linseed oil. If relief does not come in half an hour, repeat.

Botts

Drench the horse with tea made from tobacco.

If a horse has botts, bleed him under his right eye at the cord of the eye.

Drench the horse with a cup of strong coffee.

Jab a pocket-knife into the third bar of the roof of the horse's mouth.

Make a strong tea out of tobacco and mix it with sorghum molasses. Drench the horse with about a pint. The tobacco makes the botts sick.

To cure an animal of botts, cut off part of his tail.

For botts, put a rider on the horse and run him around the corral or pasture.

If a horse has botts, drench him with one-half an ounce of chloroform and one-half an ounce of spirits of niter.

Drench the horse with a pint of kerosene.

Dip a corncob in turpentine and roll up the animal's upper lip. Rub the cob vigorously on the lip and relief will come soon.

Choke

Hold the flat part of an axe against the lump in the animal's throat. Hit the axe with a hammer and break the lump.

When the choke is caused by eating dry oats, tie the horse's head up in a tree, pour six raw eggs down his throat, then close his mouth.

Pour water into a horse's ear so he will shake his head and stop choking.

Jump the horse off a high place to make him stop choking.

Make the horse jump over the wagon tongue to cure choking.

Drench the animal's nose with a quart of linseed oil to stop his choking.

Colic

Mix a pint of vinegar and a package of soda. Bridle the horse and pull his head over a limb of a tree, and pour the mixture into his nose. If there is no relief, repeat, and in ten minutes do the same thing with a pint of linseed oil and a quart of molasses.

To cure a horse of colic, put one or two tablespoons full of turpentine in a shallow saucer and hold the dish to the horse's navel. The turpentine disappears instantly and cures the colic.

Keep the animal moving continually.

Drench with soda water and half a pint of kerosene oil.

Tie the horse down and whip his belly with a wet rope.

Distemper

Make a good smoke, preferably of pine tar and feathers, and let the horse inhale it.

Burn feathers and tar in a tin can and hold it under the horse's nose. This is also used to cure distemper in cattle.

Cut the end off a large cow horn to make a funnel of it. Make a smoke of rags and chip off horn and let it go through the funnel into the horse's nostrils.

For distemper in dogs, mix gunpowder and corn bread and feed the dog as much as he will eat.

Put a teaspoonful of coal oil in each ear and then ride or drive the animal.

Eye Trouble

For pink eye, wash the eyes of the animal with salt or sugar solution.

For film over the eye, pulverize dry salt or sugar and blow it into the animal's eye with a paper quill.

For film over the eye, put salt in the eye, and lard on the outside in the hole above the animal's eye.

For cancer-eye, when it first starts cut off the upper or the lower eyelid, whichever is affected, and burn the eye well with a hot iron.

Blow powdered calomel in the animal's eye to cure film over the eye.

Fistula

Heat a sharp, pointed iron red hot, and run it through the infected or swollen part. Begin low down and burn clear through to the mane.

Rub turpentine on the affected parts. Cover with a thick wool rag or blanket and iron it with a hot iron.

Run a circle around the spot with a hot iron.

Cut the fistula out and let the horse run in the pasture for a year.

When the fistula has come to a head, tie the horse down. Then take a small lump of concentrated lye and push it into the wound. Leave it until fresh blood starts to run. Then pour melted lard into the wound to stop the lye from eating any more.

Founder

To cure a horse of founder, cut his hoofs down short in front and file them until they bleed. Then soak each foot well in hot tallow heated to about 110 degrees.

Do not give him any grain.

Clean the foot out thoroughly and fill it full of turpentine. Light a match to the turpentine until the turpentine burns out.

Cord the horse's leg until the vein puffs out, then cut the vein. Use hair from the horse's tail to cut off the flow of blood.

Stand the horse in water two or three feet deep for several hours a day for a few days.

Lampers

Cut the lampers in three places.

Cut them out and sear with a hot iron.

Grease the horse's tail and croup with old bacon rind and grease.

Lump Jaw

Tie the animal down and burn a cross on the lump with a red hot iron.

Pull the teeth of cattle to cure lump jaw.

Cut the lump open, insert salt and lime. Next allow screw worms to eat awhile. Don't let them eat too much for worms can kill an animal.

Saddle Sores

Apply axle grease to a saddle sore to cure it.

Spread strong bacon grease over the sore.

Wash saddle sores with strong salt water at body temperature.

Snake Bite

Drench the animal with warm lard out of a bottle to cure snake bite.

Make a fire right away and hold a chunk of it up close to the wound, not touching it. The heat will draw out the poison.

When a horse is bitten by a rattler, take a sharp knife and scarify the wound until it bleeds freely. Cut the tips from five or six blades of soapweed, stick them all around the wound under the skin and leave them for twenty-four hours. (Used by Escapula Gyagus, a Mexican, on the Black Ranch.)

Splint

Rub the splint with tallow and a hot mutton or calf bone.

Rub the splint with a hard twisted rope every two or three days for thirty days.

Split the skin and remove the splint with a chisel.

Sprain

Sprain or bruise on a horse may be healed by applications of bacon.

For bad sprained ankles that cannot be cured in other ways, bathe with turpentine, then light with a match and fan the flame out with your hat after a little while.

Make a pouch out of cloth. Fill with salt and tie it up. Then wet the salt and tie the pouch around the horse's ankle. This will cure a sprain.

Apply tallow and rub with a hot mutton bone.

Stifle Joint

Burn a circle around the stifle joint about four or five inches in diameter and burn a dot in the middle. Apply kerosene to the wound afterward.

Bleed the horse all around the top of his hoofs.

When all other methods fail, try this one: Tie one end of a rope sixty feet long to the sore leg and the other end to a gate post. Open the gate and let the horse run out as fast as he can. It will snap the stifle back into place.

Let the horse stand in a creek for twenty-four hours.

Tie a strong, buckskin string between the ankle and the knee of the leg that is not affected. In a while this will make the horse throw his weight on the other leg and slip the stifle back into place.

Swim the animal in the river or lake.

Sweeny

Fill a shingle full of rather long tacks. Spank the affected shoulder with this sharp surface. Then apply liniment made by beating eggs in vinegar.

Slit a place on the shoulder and insert a piece of leather.

Puncture two holes through the hide on the shoulder. Pass string through the holes and leave long ends so that you can pull the string back and forth every day.

Mix a dozen raw eggs with coarse salt until very thick. Then add bacon grease and rub the mixture over the shoulders. Leave for twelve hours.

Pull the horse's hide loose from the shoulder and knead the shoulder each day.

Bathe the affected parts with caustic balsam every other day for three days. Don't use the animal for at least a month.

Slit the horse's skin and tie mane or tail hair through the slits.

Split a small hole at the top of the shoulder and put a dime in it. Take a quill and blow the hole full of air. Then sew it up with thread to hold the air in.

Rub the shoulder regularly with a corncob.

Rub with a hot iron after rubbing the animal with a solution of five parts of castor oil to one part of croton oil.

Miscellaneous

To cure any illness in cattle, hang bittersweet around the animal's neck. (Reported to have come to Nebraska from England. Now used in Lancaster County.)

As a cure-all for the flu epidemic, hang a bag of asafœtida around the cow's neck.

After a horse has been castrated, pull the horse's tail three times and the horse will never die.

For wire cuts on stock, throw lime or puff balls in the cut.

If a dog gets poisoned, feed him washing soap suds diluted with water by forcing it into his throat through a bottle or powder horn. Vomiting occurs.

When poll-evil first starts, rub a solution of one part of castor oil to one part of croton oil on the wound. If the wound has broken, insert bulk lime into it.

For scours, bind the horse's tail about six inches from the root. Use a stout cord or hair from the horse's tail and let it stay bound not longer than four hours.

For hoof-splits, bore a little hole in the hoof at the upper end of the split with a knife. This keeps the split from running on up.

For horse blemish, apply tallow with a hot bone.

Bacon applied to a horse will make hair grow where it has quit growing.

If a dog is sick, even though you do not know just what has made him sick, feed him a tablespoonful of gunpowder, charcoal, sulphur, and saltpetre.

For chicken cholera, feed the chickens dry clabber and soda, half and half, to cure it.

If an animal is bleeding to death, apply mashed mushrooms, puff balls, snuff, cobwebs, or soot.

If a dog has running fits, feed him four doses of gunpowder.

Feed a dog four doses of chewing tobacco to cure its fits.

Appendix: Motif Analyses

These motif analyses of the tales refer to parallel situations or events as listed in Stith Thompson, *Motif-Index of Folk Literature.*

The Stump Sucker
X1241 Lies about horses.
J1516 Rogues cheat each other.

Trading by Moonlight
J1516 Rogues cheat each other.

A Threshing Hoax
X1785 Lies about stretching or shrinking.
X1810 Tall tales about miscellaneous objects.

Skunk Oil's Punkin
X1401.1 Lie: animals live inside great vegetable, usually feeding from it.
X1411.2 Lies about large pumpkins.
X1411.3 Lies about large vines.

Lining the Hymn
X410 Jokes on parsons.
X120 Humor of bad eyesight.

Grasshopper Tales
X1280.2.1 Insects eat team of horses or mules, pitch horseshoes to see who gets what is left.
X1288 Lies about grasshoppers.

Tornado Tales
X1611.1 Lies about big wind.
X1210 Lies about cows.

The Cloudburst
X1654 Lies about rain.

The Buckskin Harness
X1654 Lies about rain.
X1785.1 Lie: the stretching and shrinking harness.

The Big Cyclone
X1611.1 Lies about big wind (cyclone, tornado).

Prairie Chickens
X1110 The wonderful hunt.
N620 Accidental success in hunting or fishing.

Prairie Mirage
K1886.1 Mirage: illusory water and land.

Jud Smith's Granddad
X932 Lie: remarkable drinker.
X939 Lie: other motifs pertaining to extraordinary senses or bodily powers.
X943 Lie: remarkable thrower.
X945 Lie: remarkable hitter or striker (X982 Lie: remarkable smith).
X947 Lie: remarkable bender.

Liars' Tales
X1611.1 Lies about big wind (cyclone, tornado)

Tales of Michael Barada
X943 Lie: remarkable thrower.
X945 Lie: remarkable hitter or striker.
X953 Lie: strong puller.
X966 Lie: remarkable jumper.
X973 Lie: remarkable wrestler.

Sandhills Version
X958 Lie: hero responsible for topographical features.
  (cf. X943, X945, and X966 above.)

Amos Two-Trees and Morning Star
N343.4 Commits suicide on finding beloved dead.
T80 Tragic Love.
Q422.0.1 Beating to death as punishment.

The Cry on Blackbird Hill
N391 Lover away too long, returns, finds fiancée married.
T80 Tragic love.

The Magic of Big Bear Hollow
B601.1.1 Bear abducts girl, makes her his wife.
B16.2.5 Devastating bear killed.
B182.2 Magic bear.

Weeping Water
A911 Bodies of water from tears.
K1371.4 Abduction punished.

Lover's Leap
T80 Tragic Love.
N343.4 Commits suicide on finding beloved dead.
T81.6 Girl kills herself after lover's death.

The Spider and the Ducks
J1117 Animal as trickster.
K710 Victim enticed into voluntary captivity or helplessness.

K826 Hoodwinked dancers.
A2332.5.7 Why duck has red eyes.
K2131 Trickster makes two friends each suspicious of the other's intentions.
K1084 Liar brings about fight between dupes.

The Fox
D411 Transformation: mammal (wild) to another animal.

The Beaver
X0 Humor of discomfiture.
J1117 Animal as trickster.

The Unvisited Island
K2111 Potiphar's wife (parallel).
T71 Woman scorned in love.
T331 Man unsuccessfully tempted by woman.
K525 Escape by use of substituted object.
F912.2 Victim kills swallower from within by cutting.
S183 Frightful meal (also G60, human flesh eaten unwittingly).
S113.2 Murder by suffocation.
B551 Fish (?) carries man across water.
K211 Devil cheated by imposing an impossible task.
D380 Transformation: insect to man (?).
E32.0.1 Eaten person resuscitated.
E52 Resuscitation by magic charm.

The Two Hunters
D1402.13.3 Charm used to kill.
F522 Person with wings.
S163 Mutilation: cutting out tongue.
6303.9.6.1.1 Devil is overcome by man in fight (?).
G60 Human flesh eaten unwittingly.

The Rabbit
D985.4 Magic acorn.
B620.1 Daughter promised to animal suitor.
D315.5 Transformation: hare (rabbit) to person.
H1236.3 Quest over path guarded by hags.
H1235 Succession of helpers on quest.
N681 Husband (lover) arrives home just as wife (mistress) is to marry (?).

The Orphan Boy
S146.1 Abandonment in well.
J2175.3 Child put down well instead of bucket.
F718 Extraordinary well.
R13.3 Person carried off by bird.
N517.1 Treasure hidden in secret room in house.
C611 Forbidden chamber.
B41.1 Pegasus—winged horse.
B41.2 Flying horse.

Canktewin—the Ill-Fated Woman
N251 Person pursued by misfortune.
K2212 Treacherous Sister.
F403.2 Spirits help mortal.
S162 Mutilation: cutting off legs.
F402.1.10 Spirit (?) pursues person.
D1524.3.1 Stone (?) canoe.
D1711.13 Reptile man.
G11 Kinds of cannibals.
K512 Compassionate executioner.
D1840 Magic invulnerability.
D1847 Loss of invulnerability.
K1930 Treacherous impostor.
K629 Escape by deceiving guard (?).
H1591 Shooting contest.
E761.5.5 Life token: stone breaks (?).
G303.8.11 Devil in stone.
T92 Rivals in love.
T80. Tragic love.

The Flint Chief
G371 Stone giant.
A1414.5 Origin of flint.
F1041.1.9 Death from jealousy.
N337 Accidental death through misdirected weapon.

Neeshu
G671 Wild man (?) released from captivity aids hero.
D1318 Magic object reveals guilt.
D1841.4.3 Walking on water without getting wet.
A511.4.1 Miraculous growth of culture hero.
F717 Extraordinary pool.
B392 Animal divides spoil for animals.
B431.2 Helpful lion.
B435.4 Helpful bear.
B455.5 Helpful hawk.
B481.1 Helpful ant.
H328 Suitor test: endurance.
H970 Help in performing tasks.
H1010 Impossible tasks.

The Great Fish Who Is Called a Sand Bar
D179.2 Transformation: man to pike.
J1322 The great thirst.

The Legend of Porcupine Butte
B437 Helpful beasts—rodentia.

How Gold Came to the Black Hills
A1432.2 Acquisition of gold.
C611 Forbidden chamber.
F717 Extraordinary pool.
D2165.3 Magic used to prevent pursuit.

A Dog's Revenge
K300 Thieves and cheats.
K301 Master thief (?)

Bibliography

WORKS CITED

The number at the left corresponds to the number given in parentheses in the text to identify a source.

1. FEDERAL WRITERS' PROJECT NEBRASKA FOLKLORE PAMPHLETS. See below.
2. WILLIAM S. AND CEIL BARING-GOULD. *The Annotated Mother Goose*. New York: Clarkson N. Potter, 1962.
3. HENRY BETT. *Nursery Rhymes and Tales*. New York: Holt, Rinehart & Winston, 1924.
4. CARL W. BREIHAN. *The Complete and Authentic Life of Jesse James*. New York: Frederick Fell, 1953.
5. PAUL BREWSTER. *American Nonsinging Games*. Norman: University of Oklahoma Press, 1953.
6. S. FOSTER DAMON. "The History of Square-Dancing," *Proceedings of the American Antiquarian Society*, LXII (1952), 63–98.
7. EVERETT DICK. *The Sod House Frontier, 1854–1890*. Lincoln: Johnson Publishing Company, 1954.
8. ———. *Tales of the Frontier: From Lewis and Clark to the Last Roundup*. Lincoln: University of Nebraska Press, 1963.
9. J. FRANK DOBIE. "Ballads and Songs of the Frontier Folk," *Publications of the Texas Folklore Society*, VI. Austin: University of Texas Press, 1927.
10. RICHARD DORSON. *American Folklore*. Chicago: University of Chicago Press, 1959.
11. ALICE FLETCHER AND FRANCIS LA FLESCHE. "The Omaha Tribe," *Twenty-Seventh Annual Report of the Bureau of American Ethnology*. Washington: Government Printing Office, 1911.
12. FOSTER-HARRIS. *The Look of the Old West*. New York: Bonanza Books, 1960.
13. JOHN GREENWAY. *American Folksongs of Protest*. New York: A. S. Barnes, 1960.
14. DUANE LEACH. "History of the Santee Sioux." Unpublished M. A. thesis. University of South Dakota, 1957.
15. ELOISE LINSCOTT. *Folk Songs of Old New England*. New York: Macmillan, 1939.
16. ALAN LOMAX. *Folk Songs of North America*. New York: Doubleday, 1960.

17. JOHN A. AND ALAN LOMAX. *American Ballads and Folk Songs*. New York: Macmillan, 1934.
18. CHARLEY O'KIEFFE. *Western Story: The Recollections of Charley O'Kieffe, 1884–1898*. Lincoln: University of Nebraska Press, 1960.
19. LOUISE POUND. *Folk-Song of Nebraska and the Central West: A Syllabus*. Nebraska Ethnology and Folk Lore Series. Nebraska Academy of Sciences Publication, Vol. IX, No. 3, 1915.
20. ———. *Nebraska Folklore*. Lincoln: University of Nebraska Press, 1959.
21. PAUL RADIN. *The Trickster*. New York: Philosophical Library, 1956.
22. DOANE ROBINSON. "A Complete History of the Dakota or Sioux Indians," *South Dakota Historical Collections*, II (1957).
23. CARL SANDBURG. *The American Songbag*. New York: Harcourt, Brace, 1957.
24. STITH THOMPSON. *The Folktale*. New York: Holt, Rinehart and Winston, 1946.
25. ———. *Motif-Index of Folk-Literature*. Revised edition. 6 vols. Bloomington: Indiana University Press, 1955–1958.
26. D. K. WILGUS. *Anglo-American Folksong Scholarship Since 1898*. New Brunswick: Rutgers University Press, 1959.

FEDERAL WRITERS' PROJECT NEBRASKA FOLKLORE PAMPHLETS

The authority responsible for the original publication of the Nebraska Folklore Pamphlets included John M. Carmody, Administrator, Federal Works Agency; F. C. Harrington, Commissioner (December, 1940, Howard Hunter, Acting Commissioner); Florence Kerr, Assistant Commissioner; and D. F. Felton, State Administrator, Works Project Administration. The pamphlets were produced under the state-wide sponsorship of the College of Arts and Sciences of the University of Nebraska and under the direct sponsorship of Charles W. Taylor, State Superintendent of Public Instruction. They were compiled by workers of the WPA Writers' Program of the Works Administration in the State of Nebraska, J. Harris Gable, State Supervisor, and Robert E. Carlsen, Editor.

Following is a list of the pamphlets by number, title, and date of publication.

No. 1	Cowboy Songs	May 15, 1937
No. 2	Indian Place Legends	May 29, 1937
No. 3	Children's Singing Games	June 1, 1937
No. 4	Historical Legends	June 15, 1937
No. 5	Legends of Febold Feboldson	July 1, 1937
No. 6	Animal Legends	August 1, 1937
No. 7	Children's Games	September 1, 1937
No. 8	Legends of Feboldson and Antoine Barada	September 15, 1937
No. 9	Proverbs, Prophesies, Signs and Sayings	October 1, 1937

Selections from the pamphlets were reprinted in three 32-page brochures, as follows:

[No editor given]. *Nebraska Folklore*. Lincoln: Woodruff Printing Co., 1939.
ROBERT E. CARLSEN, ED. *Nebraska Folklore* (*Book Two*). Lincoln: Woodruff Printing Co., 1940.
ZERNE P. HANING AND ROBERT E. CARLSEN, EDD. *Nebraska Folklore* (*Book Three*). Lincoln: Woodruff Printing Co., 1941.

Other Sources

B. A. BOTKIN. The American Play-Party Song. New York: Frederick Ungar Publishing Co., Inc., 1961. Originally printed as a Ph.D. dissertation, University of Nebraska, 1937 (the edition consulted).
MARGARET CANNELL. *Signs, Omens, and Portents in Nebraska Folklore.* University of Nebraska Studies in Language, Literature, and Criticism, No. 13. 1933.
LEVERETT J. DAVIDSON. *A Guide to American Folklore.* Denver: Sage Books, 1951. Includes helpful definitions as well as a reading list.
LILIAN L. FITZPATRICK. *Nebraska Place-Names.* University of Nebraska Studies in Language, Literature, and Criticism, No. 6. 1925. New edition including selections from J. T. Link's *Origin of the Place-Names of Nebraska.* G. Thomas Fairclough, ed. Lincoln: University of Nebraska Press, 1960.
FLORENCE MARYOTT. "Nebraska Counting-Out Rhymes," *Southern Folklore Quarterly*, December, 1937.

MAMIE MEREDITH. "Charivaria," *American Speech*, 7 (April, 1933).

JAMES C. OLSON. *History of Nebraska*. Lincoln: University of Nebraska Press, 1954; rev. ed., 1966.

EDWIN FORD PIPER. "Quadrille Calls," *American Speech*, 1 (1926).

S. J. SACKETT AND WILLIAM E. KOCH, EDD. *Kansas Folklore*. Lincoln: University of Nebraska Press, 1961.

LOUISE SNAPP. *Proverbial Lore in Nebraska*. University of Nebraska Studies in Language, Literature, and Criticism, No. 13, 1933.

L. C. WIMBERLY. "Hard Times Singing," June, 1934.

Acknowledgments

Thanks are due the Nebraska State Historical Society for the use of their set of the Nebraska Folklore Pamphlets; to the reference staff of the Bennett Martin Public Library, Lincoln, Nebraska, for help in tracing obscure references; to Professor D. Jerome Tweton of Dana College, Blair, Nebraska, for help with historical contexts; to Joseph Hickerson and Mrs. Rae Korson, the Library of Congress, for tracing references and supplying unpublished materials from the Nebraska WPA files; to Mr. Paul R. Beath for permission to include three Febold Feboldson tales; to Floyd A. Miller, Commissioner of Education, State of Nebraska, for permission to reedit for republication W.P.A. Federal Writers' Project folklore materials; and to Nebraska Wesleyan University for funds for manuscript preparation.

R. L. W.

Title Index of Songs and Tales

SONGS

TALES